# Someday Street

*A Memoir*

## Barbara French

PublishAmerica
Baltimore

ISBN: 1-60703-637-1
PUBLISHED BY PUBLISHAMERICA, LLLP
www.publishamerica.com
Baltimore

Printed in the United States of America

*For Doug and Paul*

Terry F. Breidenbach
16 May 2022

# Acknowledgments

Heartfelt thanks and great appreciation go to the following people who have been invaluable, not only for insightful manuscript critiques, but for being dear friends who always offered interest, support and encouragement.

Maralys Wills, my teacher, mentor, and friend, along with her Wednesday night Novel Writing Class, gave me invaluable input.

My critique group of Maralys, Walt Golden, Pam Tallman, Allene Symons, P.J. Penman, and Ervin Tibbs was simply top notch. Each person offered his own innovative gifts that enhanced the story. Special appreciation goes to Pam for her magic touches, especially on the book synopsis and biography, and to Erv who is a great cliché catcher, has encyclopedic knowledge, and a great sense of drama. This group provided not only great writing suggestions but fascinating, informative conversations and lots of fun.

My daughter-in-law Susan French is especially treasured for being constantly interested, not only in this book, but in all books, and in my teaching. She also helped with proofreading, as did my niece Martha Peters.

Eugene Corman took his time to critique the manuscript and give me sage counsel. Michele Lack critiqued and cast an eagle eye on repeated words and unclear passages. Additionally, she sharpened episodes. Hats off to a true pro!

Additional thanks goes to the members of my two Creative Writing classes who have expressed interest, encouragement and proffered occasional critiques.

# Table of Contents

In all human experience we encounter turning points—some of our own making, some beyond our control—that inevitably change us.

Such a life-altering blow struck our family when I was very young. I can't help wondering what our lives would have been like—what I might have been like—without that catastrophe and the following chain of events.

For years I feared looking back, feared the pain, but when I finally did, I was surprised by what I found: laughter, warmth and comfort. I discovered zany antics, shining moments, and great courage. Best of all, I was enveloped with such feelings of sweet nostalgia and deep love.

As I struggled to relate my family's history, it took life as a story told in third person, expressing many viewpoints. For privacy, the characters bore different names.

At first a mystery, The Great Disaster was not what you might think, and took time to be revealed. The story starts long ago with a few silly words—words that also changed my life.

Barbara French

# Someday Street

*A Memoir*

# 1. What's the Matter with Mother?

**January 1929**

On that first day of kindergarten, Jenny Pate realized something was the matter with her mother.

Bursting with excitement, blond hair flying out from under her cap, blue eyes sparkling, she raced home all the way from the red brick schoolhouse on the hill. Behind her trailed her older brother Dale. Jenny couldn't wait to tell her mother about her teacher.

She dashed past modest bungalows in Ferguson, Missouri, a suburb of St. Louis, past brown lawns with snowy patches, up the walk to the big white colonial house that was home. Speeding through the front door, she called, "Momma! Momma! I love Mrs. McCarthy!"

Her mother's voice wafted down the hallway. "I can't hear you, Jenny. I'm in the kitchen."

Bursting into the room, Jenny skidded to a stop before the white, enamel-topped table. Her mother sat on a stool, rolling out a small piece of dough. When she pressed down the star cookie cutter, a puff of white floated up into the air and dissolved. Jenny inhaled deeply, savoring the scents of butter and cinnamon.

Nora carefully placed the last cookie on the baking sheet.

Watching her, Jenny frowned, puzzled. When she played at Audrey's house, her mother stood up while she worked, but Mother always sat down, saying she had to save her energy.

With the back of a floury hand, Nora pushed a lock of chestnut hair off her forehead, hair as limp as the woman herself. With dull blue eyes and a tired smile, she looked across at her daughter.

"Oh, Momma—" Jenny cried eagerly.

"Not now, Jenny. I have to get this cookie sheet in the oven."

"But, Momma—"

"Please wait, Jenny." Slowly Nora rose from her stool, walked with faltering steps to the black iron stove, and shoved in the cookie sheet. But then she turned, pale-faced, and murmured, "Jenny, help me."

Alarmed, Jenny raced to her side.

"Get me back to my stool. I have to sit down."

After getting her mother seated, Jenny asked, "What's wrong, Momma?"

Her mother put her elbows on the table and rested her head in her hands. "I don't know. I feel so weak."

Just then Dale walked into the kitchen.

Jenny turned to him. "Something's the matter with Mother."

"What is it?" Dale hurried to her side, peering anxiously through his glasses.

"I don't know." She inhaled. "Jenny, help me into the living room. I want to lie down. Would you watch the cookies, Dale? I just put them in."

The children quickly did as they were told.

Nora lay back on the couch with Jenny hovering nearby. In a few minutes Nora seemed better, looked up and asked, "Now, Jenny, what was it you wanted to tell me?"

Twirling, arms thrown out in joy, thrilled to have her mother's attention, Jenny crowed, "Oh, Momma, I love my kindergarten teacher!" She paused dramatically. "She has long fingernails and a rumble seat!"

Nora's sad eyes suddenly glowed, her mouth pulled up into a wide smile, and then—she laughed.

Jenny watched the transformation in awe, not sure why it was funny, but her words had moved her mother, changed her usually somber face, and made her happy. *I made Mother laugh!*

Ambling into the room, Jenny's nine-year-old brother, Dale said, "The cookies are done, Mom. I took them out." He turned to Jenny. "And Mrs. McCarthy doesn't have a rumble seat, silly. It's her car that has one."

Nora smiled. "You don't say."

"Someday I want a rumble seat!" Jenny exclaimed.

When her mother laughed again, Jenny glowed.

Later, when Mother had recovered from her spell, their neighbor, Mrs. Dunn, came over to borrow an onion. Jenny, playing jacks on the hallway floor, heard her mother in the kitchen say "...long fingernails and a rumble seat." Both women burst into laughter. Happiness surged through Jenny. She could hardly wait for her father to get home from work.

At 9:30 when Clyde finally arrived from teaching sports at the St. Louis YMCA, Jenny jumped into his arms and whispered, "Daddy, do you know what?"

Holding her in a bear hug, he whispered, "No, what?"

Jenny shouted, "I love my kindergarten teacher. She has long fingernails and a rumble seat!"

Entranced, she watched his gray blue eyes dance, his ruddy face light up, saw him throw back his head, heard his belly laugh roll through the kitchen.

She hugged him hard, thrilled she had done it again! Immensely satisfied, Jenny yearned to continue to affect people. This desire would drive her all her life—the longing to make them laugh, transform sadness into smiles, to move people.

That night after her mother and father had tucked her in, listened to her prayers, and turned out the light, she muttered a secret prayer of her own.

"Dear God, please fix whatever's the matter with Mother." She drew a breath. "Oh, please give me curly hair. And when I grow up, long fingernails, and don't forget a rumble seat!"

With a smile, she looked upward, "I hope You laughed!"

# 2. The Secret Wish

At five years old, Jenny didn't realize that her family was living on Happiness Heights, but would soon plunge down toward Poverty Place, come perilously close to Cemetery Circle, but finally manage to make a detour and end up living on Someday Street.

Someday—the enticing promise that lured them from their beds each morning. Someday—the hope that comforted them each night. Someday—the time when each one would have what he craved. Without someday, what was there for any of them?

Someday Daddy would put them on Easy Street, Mother would be all right, Dale would be a writer, and Jenny would finally be somebody.

Even though Jenny had an intense longing to make people laugh, she somehow knew she wasn't ready, that first she must learn about the world, about people, perhaps even about herself.

For a long time she had realized that adults sometimes regarded children as non-existent, talking above their heads as if they weren't even there. With an inquisitive mind and acute hearing, Jenny learned to listen and accumulated a store of family gossip—even a number of secrets she didn't yet understand.

Often at night she crawled out of bed and crept half-way down the stairs to huddle and eavesdrop on the fascinating adult conversations below. She learned that in Indianapolis, Mother's brother, Silas, was mysteriously wicked, and her parents feared something terrible was bound to happen. Jenny straightened in interest.

They said Uncle Silas smoked, drank and gambled, and his wife had been a camp follower during the war. Not sure what that meant, Jenny recognized that the hushed voices indicated it was something shameful.

But then the talk drifted to other topics. Jenny strained to hear. She made out her mother's anxious voice, "Oh, Clyde, the doctors keep saying there's nothing wrong, but I'm so tired all the time."

Just then Clyde spotted Jenny on the stairs. "Scoot, young lady. Up to bed with you!"

She ran to her room, silently worried about her mother.

Gradually, Jenny began to understand a lot about other people—and even more about herself. Though her father greeted her with "Hi, beautiful," Even at five, she knew she wasn't. She had a mirror.

To other girls, adults would say, "How pretty you look." But to Jenny, "What a nice big girl you're getting to be." She didn't need reminding that she loomed a head taller than her classmates, even the boys. Those unflattering words made Jenny grit her teeth.

Her mother said, "You take after your grandpa's side. The men are all over six feet two."

Jenny's hair was the color of drab winter weeds and straight as a ruler. It was cut butcher boy style, chin length and with bangs. How she longed for curls like other girls had, but Mother felt too worn out to wrap Jenny's hair in rags.

One day a large brown envelope arrived in the mail for Nora. "Jenny, it's from my sister in Michigan, your Aunt Madge." Pulling a gray folder from the envelope, she opened it.

A frown pinched her forehead. "It's a photograph of your cousin Tina, Madge's little girl." She sighed. "Madge was always the pretty one and, since she was older, I had to wear her hand-me-downs." She sat lost in thought. "Then, when I was to be married, Madge suddenly decided she'd get married, too, and insisted on a double wedding."

"A double wedding?" exclaimed Jenny. "What's that?"

"It's when two couples get married at the same time. We had to be married at home instead of at church because of a terrible influenza epidemic raging in 1918. Large gatherings of people were forbidden for fear of spreading the flu." Her eyes turned wistful. "I really wanted it to be just my wedding." Then she brightened. "But I got the best husband." She looked at the folder. "This picture is Madge's little girl. Tina's two years younger than you."

"Let me see," Jenny said. She looked into a heart-shaped face, lash-fringed dark eyes, and a tousle of shiny dark curls. "Tina's pretty.*"*

"Yes, she is."

Pressing against her mother's arm, Jenny said, "But Momma, I can make people laugh."

Nora hugged her. "Of course you can, dear, and you're smart. You're very mature for your age."

Later at her best friend Audrey's house, Jenny eagerly devoured the newspaper photograph of actress Janet Gaynor who'd won an Academy Award for the movie *Wings*.

With a toss of her head Audrey pronounced, "I'm going to write movies when I grow up." Then I'll get to meet all the movie stars. What are you going to be?"

Jenny fingered her hair. "I haven't decided." But she had decided, and she'd never tell. She passionately wanted more than curly hair—she wanted to wear billowy ruffled dresses, to sing beautiful songs and dance on clouds with handsome men.

She wanted to be a movie star, to be somebody someday.

# 3. Who Wants to Be Different?

Jenny performed on stage sooner than she had dreamed. In March, Mrs. McCarthy announced to her kindergarteners, "Children, we will be putting on a play for spring assembly."

"A play?" cried Jenny. "What about?"

"Next time, raise your hand, Jenny. Since we've been singing about rain and sunshine and flowers, I have a play about that. We'll perform in the auditorium and not only will your classmates attend, your families can come too."

Leaning across the aisle, Jenny whispered to Audrey, "Isn't that wonderful? I want to be in it. Do you?"

Mrs. McCarthy shot Jenny a stern look. "Jenny, please, no more talking. Everybody will be in it and you'll have to sing loudly."

Turning to Audrey again, Jenny said, "Oh dear, Mrs. McCarthy is so thin, if we sing too loud we might blow her right out the door."

Audrey giggled.

"All right, girls, heads down on the desk. Why must you talk so much, Jenny?"

*I like to talk*, Jenny thought. *At home there's nobody to talk to. Dale's always reading, Mother's always lying down, and Daddy's always working.*

Every day the class practiced their songs and, one day as Jenny was leaving, Mrs. McCarthy handed her an envelope. "Take this note and pattern to your mother. I need her to buy the material and make your costume."

Jenny gave a little skip. "You mean I get to be in the play, even if I do talk too much?"

Mrs. McCarthy smiled. "I know it's especially hard for you to be quiet, young lady. Of course you're in the play. You're one of my best singers."

At home, after reading the note and looking at the costume pattern, Jenny's mother didn't smile. "Oh, dear," she sighed.

"What's wrong, Momma?"

"Nothing, sweetheart. I wish I felt better but, don't worry, I'll get your outfit made."

Later, when Jenny saw the black material, she thought it was ugly, but her mother said it was just right for the costume.

At school, practice continued, and finally one day Mrs. McCarty said, "Now, Jenny, you sing the umbrella song."

"By myself?"

"Yes. That's called a solo," Mrs. McCarthy said from the piano. "Come face the class and when I nod, start singing."

When Jenny stood alone in front of everyone, she didn't feel at all scared. She liked doing it. In fact, Jenny liked everything until the day of dress rehearsal. In her costume of pleated black chintz and holding a black cane so that she looked like an umbrella, she turned around and saw all the other girls in fluffy dresses like ballet dancers in yellow, pink, green, and blue. *Oh, they're so pretty!*

The boys in navy blue suits and straw hats crowded around her teasing, "Jenny you look like a big old fatty in that black costume. You're ugly."

Jenny stared them down. "I'm the black umbrella and I'm supposed to look this way. And besides, I get to sing a solo!"

When the class presented the play, Jenny's family was in the audience. From the wings, Jenny watched as the boys strolled and the parasols pirouetted. Finally, after the lilting songs about spring and pretty flowers blooming after the rain, Mrs. McCarthy motioned her to move center stage. Solo or not, Jenny wasn't sure about this part. Her dreams of being a star meant wearing lovely dresses and looking beautiful.

All the other girls were colorful parasols and she was an ugly black lump. Drawing a breath, she decided she must let the audience know how sad the umbrella felt.

The spotlight blinded her, so she could see only a blur of faces. Inhaling deeply, she tried to still her trembling. The piano began, Mrs. McCarthy nodded and gave her a wink. Jenny opened her mouth and, to her surprise, her little voice came out clearly: *"Not everyone is happy when the sun comes out to shine. I have a secret wish and this is simply mine. Rain, rain, come back today. Sprinkle and thunder and pour. I can't bear to be useless, I want to be so much more. I'm the old black umbrella left out on the porch mat to dry. I'm so lonely, lost and forgotten, it makes me want to cry and cry and cry."*

Tears rolled down her cheeks. Then Audrey appeared, took Jenny's hand and led her off stage exclaiming, "Whatever would I do without my trusty umbrella!"

The audience erupted into laughter and applause and someone yelled, "Don't cry, umbrella. We love you."

The curtain fell. Then Mrs. McCarthy motioned the cast forward to take their bows when the curtain rose again.

Heart skipping happily, Jenny bowed, smiled and waved.

Afterward, parents surged backstage. Many shook Jenny's hand and she was elated at their comments: "You were very good." "Such a pretty voice." "I cried with you."

Exhilarated by her first role, Jenny's infatuation with acting grew. So what if the star was just an old black umbrella?

But as they all left the school to go home, Jenny's happiness faded as she noticed Mother's faltering steps and how heavily she leaned on Daddy.

# 4. Delightful Daddy

Before the Pates' life path plunged downward toward Poverty Place, Jenny had memories like droplets of morning dew glinting in the sun, full of rainbows.

She loved the quiet days when the aroma of baking cakes or pies filled the kitchen, accompanied by the steady thump of her mother's iron on the ironing board.

Other days, while rain spattered softly on the roof, she read Arabian night stories from the Green Books with their intricate pen and ink illustrations as she leaned back against her mother's soft warm body.

The family enjoyed sweet companionship and laughter as they played games together: Authors, Anagrams or Touring.

Sometimes Dale pumped the player piano and the lively melodies sent Jenny dancing.

Home meant calm and comfort, but Jenny yearned for something more, something provided by her father: the outside world's stimulation and excitement.

Jenny thought of her father as sunshine—radiating energy, glowing and bright. Her mother seemed like the moon—cool, quiet, and remote. Soon The Great Depression formed the shadow that threatened to eclipse them all.

Sandy-haired, ruddy-complexioned, laughing, Clyde Pate was an athlete of skill and grace, a hearty, optimistic man who perpetually sought adventure.

At times Nora's fatigue reminded him of words his stepmother had said long ago. In 1918 when he had bounded up the porch steps and announced that he and Nora were getting married, the porch swing stopped and Elizabeth Pate fell silent.

Concerned, he said, "You don't like her."

Elizabeth hesitated a moment. "I like her fine."

"Then what's wrong? I can tell something is."

She sighed. "I have a feeling that Nora's not well, Clyde. If you marry her, I'm afraid you'll have a very hard life."

"Nonsense! We've hiked, canoed and ice-skated together. I know we'll be happy!"

And their lives had been happy. Through the 1920s Clyde advanced teaching sports at the YMCAs from Ashtabula, Ohio; to Fort Wayne, Indiana; to St. Louis, Missouri. Outside the Y, Clyde lived life to the fullest, trying whatever new thrills came along.

The family photo album contained two snapshots of Clyde in an aviator's helmet and teddy-bear flying suit. Inspired by Lindbergh's 1927 flight to Paris, Clyde had gone out to Lambert Airfield and taken flying lessons.

But as he returned one afternoon, Nora met him, pale and distraught. "Jenny fell and punctured her knee on a rusty nail. I ran next door to the Dunn's and called the doctor who came to the house and gave her a tetanus shot." Nora started to cry. "But then Jenny turned red, then white, then blue. I clutched her on my lap terrified that she was dying."

"Oh, no! Is she all right now?"

"Yes, I carried her next door and called the doctor again. I was frantic. He said she'd had a reaction to the horse serum in the shot and she'd be all right. After a while she was, thank God. But Clyde, we have to have our own telephone."

So the flying lessons gave way to a phone.

Jenny's father liked to take the family on special excursions. He drove them to the St. Louis waterfront where he pointed out the posts where slaves had been chained while their families were broken up and sold. He told the children how terrible slavery was.

Another time they visited Forest Park enjoying the zoo, even though

Jenny was frightened by the enormous boa constrictors in the snake house.

Jenny far preferred attending the operettas in the outdoor amphitheatre where the family sat high up looking down at the stage. After Mother tucked away the remnants of the fried chicken and potato salad picnic, dusk fell. Soon the orchestra took its place and a breeze ruffled Jenny's hair. When *The Desert Song* began, Jenny's heart nearly burst at the beauty of the soaring melodies, the exotic sets and beautiful costumes.

At the end, engulfed in the swell of applause, Jenny clapped furiously along with all the others, longing to be one of those actresses on the stage below.

Her parents loved music. At home Nora occasionally played the piano and Clyde sang. He'd been in Glee Club at college. On Saturday afternoons, they listened to the Metropolitan Opera on the radio. Jenny even fantasized that someday she might be an opera singer.

One day while they all drove to Clyde's work, he told them about the YMCA where he was a Physical Director. "George Williams started the Y in London in 1844, as the Industrial Revolution began. Young men had flocked from their farms to the city but couldn't find jobs."

Nora said, "Those fellows were lonely and roaming streets that were mighty dangerous."

"Wanting to build their character," Clyde went on, "Williams started Bible classes."

"Sounds like he wanted to make everybody good," Dale said.

"More than that. To help those farm boys get better jobs, he started educational classes like the one in speech that Dale Carnegie conducted at a New York Y."

"But where does exercising come in?" Dale asked. "That's what you teach."

"I teach calisthenics and all sports, because Mr. Williams thought body building was important. He even figured those boys needed inexpensive places to live, so he developed dormitories in Y buildings."

Nora said, "Your father is so proud to work for the Y. He began teaching swimming at their summer camps when he was still in high school."

"He did?" exclaimed Jenny.

"Did you know Mr. Williams was knighted by Queen Victoria, because he'd done so much good?" Clyde went on. "Imagine that."

Jenny thought she'd like to meet a queen.

"We've seen pictures," Nora added, "of the stained glass window in Westminster Abbey that shows the Y emblem—the triangle that stands for Body, Mind and Spirit."

Jenny asked, "Is that the same triangle embroidered on Daddy's navy shirts?"

"Yep," Clyde replied. "I wear those shirts when I teach my classes."

When they drew up before the Y building Clyde said, "Come on, "We're going to the swimming pool. I have a surprise for you."

The family followed him to seats on the bleachers that faced the Olympic-size pool. The water shimmered and the room smelled of chlorine. The stands were crowded.

In a few minutes a muscular young man appeared. "There!" Clyde exclaimed. "The man who just dove in and is swimming down the pool is giving an exhibition for us. That's the famous Johnny Weissmuller. He's won every free style race he's ever entered, plus five Olympic Medals. You're watching a champ."

Jenny felt thrilled. Daddy always brought a stimulating world into her life. She wondered what exciting thing he'd do next.

# 5. Uncle Harry's Adventures

The spring of 1929 the Pates seemed to be living on Happiness Heights, and Clyde soon added more happiness.

When Grandma wrote in distress about Nora's youngest brother Harry, Nora said, "Clyde, I worry about Mama. Harry's eighteen and has been such a handful with Papa gone these past four years, she doesn't know what to do with him. He could end up drinking and gambling like Silas."

"Why not have Harry come live with us for a while? I know a lot of businessmen at work. Maybe I could help him get a job. Meanwhile, Harry can help around the house."

Soon Harry arrived from Indianapolis. He slept on an army cot in Dale's room, helped with household chores, and went to the Y almost every day with Clyde.

Jenny was intrigued by her Uncle Harry. One Saturday she and Dale sat with him on the screened-in porch. "Mother said you ran away and joined the circus." How Jenny longed to do something breathtaking like that. "Did you?"

Harry leaned back, and his black eyes danced. "Yeah, I sure did. But don't you or Dale get any such ideas."

"But why'd you go?" Dale asked pushing his glasses up.

Harry's chin lifted. "I got tired of all the school teachers comparing me with my five older brothers and sisters. Besides, I wanted excitement—to see the world."

*Oh, so do I*, Jenny thought.

"Then what happened?" Dale asked.

"This circus came to Indianapolis, so I wandered down and asked for a job." He grinned. "Don't forget, I'd been doing odd jobs and earning money since I was twelve years old. I'm not afraid of hard work."

"What did they say?" Jenny asked.

"They needed a mechanic. I'm tall and look lots older than I am." He laughed. "So they hired me."

"But you're not a mechanic, are you?" Dale observed.

Harry chuckled. "Not exactly. Well, not at all. But they'd have some contraption that wasn't working, so I'd pour on some oil, kick it a few times, give it a good cussing—and it would start right up. Surprised me too. For a while the circus folks thought I was pretty good. But then my luck ran out. Some machines wouldn't cooperate, and the boss said I was lousy, so I acted insulted and quit." He howled with laughter. "Anyway, I missed Mama's cooking."

Jenny and Dale couldn't help laughing. Jenny finally paused for breath. "Uncle Harry, how did you get to be so funny?"

Tilting his head, Harry thought a minute. "You know, my Uncle Jake came to paint our house when I was about four years old. He was so comical that he made me roll on the floor laughing. I think I decided right then that I wanted to be like Uncle Jake."

*I want to be like you*, Jenny thought. "Please tell us another story."

"Let's see. One cold December when I was fourteen, my friend Dick and I decided to go to Florida where it's warm. I told Mama I was going. I always told her when I left, so technically it wasn't running away.

"Both Dick and I had a little money, but we needed to make it last so we hopped a freight train and rode free. When we got to Tallahassee, it was really warm so I mailed my heavy corduroy coat home."

"What did you do in Tallahassee?" Dale asked.

"Messed around. At first we stayed in hotels and ate well, but our money went fast so we ended up bumming for food."

Jenny perked up. "Bumming? What's that?"

"You knock on somebody's door and look real sad and say," he made his voice plaintive, "we're awful hungry, can you please spare us something to eat?"

"Did they?" Jenny eyes were wide.

Harry rearranged his long legs and chuckled. "They sure did. Folks weren't afraid. They treated us mighty friendly and always gave us something."

Dale said, "I should run away and try that some time."

"Listen, Dale, absolutely not! Your folks would kick me out. Besides, sometimes it's not so much fun."

"Why not?" Jenny leaned forward eagerly.

"When our money was nearly gone, we bedded down on the roof of the YMCA. They held exercise classes up there, so we'd sleep on one exercise mat and pull another over us to stay warm. It may have been Florida, but the nights were chilly. Well, you can't believe what happened next."

"What?" both children cried.

"It snowed!"

"Snowed! In Florida?" Dale exclaimed.

"Yes, indeed. Boy, I was cold and miserable. Then Dick left and went home. So I wired my folks to send money from my account, because I wanted to go back home in the worst way."

"So they sent you the money," said Dale.

"Nope. I got a letter back General Delivery. Papa wrote, 'Since you're already down there in Florida, Mama and I think you should proceed on down to Miami. You want to see the world, so go down to Miami and have a good time.'"

"Did you?"

"No. I wired back, 'I don't want to go to Miami. I want to come home. Please wire money.' Well, they did, and I took the train home, this time riding in a coach car.

"It was Christmas Eve when we pulled into Indianapolis. Papa was waiting for me, all dressed up and looking mighty spiffy. I felt awful. My hair was dirty and needed cutting, my clothes were grimy, and I smelled. Papa looked me over, but he didn't say a word. He just bundled me into my corduroy coat. Snowflakes fell through the dark night. Down the snowy streets, Christmas lights sparkled. Our footsteps made crunchy sounds as we walked through the drifts to the streetcar line. I wished Papa would say something.

"But he didn't. We just trudged along in silence. I thought I would have a great adventure and come back home with lots of money, but I barely had enough for my streetcar fare. Papa waved me to climb up first and I dropped my coins tinkling into the box. Riding home, I didn't say anything either. I just looked at all the pretty lighted trees in everyone's windows.

"When we got to our house, I opened the door and I saw our tree ablaze with colored lights. Then all my brothers and sisters yelled, 'Merry Christmas, Harry!' As I passed, each one handed me a present. My face smarted and I hung my head. They loved me, even if I was often a trouble-maker. I didn't have a single gift for anybody—even Mama. I felt so ashamed. It was the worst Christmas Eve of my life!"

"Oh, no!" Jenny cried. The holidays were months away, but she vowed to buy or make presents for everyone in her family.

Jenny loved Uncle Harry almost as much as she loved her mother and father. But the happy times with him soon ended when he was hired by the Chevrolet factory in Kansas City. They all hated to see him go.

The night Harry left, Jenny lay between the smooth sheets staring up at the dark ceiling. How she'd miss Uncle Harry. Outside dogs barked, and a breeze blew in the window, gently billowing the lace curtains.

From the distance a lonely train whistle called out to her, "You-oo-oo-oo-oo. You-oo-oo-oo-oo." Like a liquid finger, the sound reached out across the miles, hooked itself around her heart and tugged. She felt the pull, the longing, the yearning to let it draw her from her bed, out of her room, from the house, over fields, above trees, across roadways, surmounting towns, luring her far away to some enchanted land.

Beautifully unbearable, this deep new yearning stayed locked in her heart, and never went away. She *had* to see the world. But how could she go off on her own adventures if Mother would need her?

# 6. Daddy's Not Perfect?

That summer of 1929 Clyde took the family to see a new part of the country. Jenny's father was not only an athlete, but an outdoorsman. He often went hunting, proudly bringing home quail Mother roasted, or rabbits which she turned into spicy stew.

On this vacation Clyde wanted to go fishing, so the family piled into the black Ford and drove north to Leech Lake, Minnesota.

There they rented a furnished cabin perched on a rise above the lake. Everyone helped unpack and put away the groceries, and then Mother went out on the front porch and sat in the swing. "I love these vacations," she said. "I get such a rest with nothing to do but cook and read and soak up the scenery."

Inhaling deeply, she smiled. "The air up here is fresh as—as a cool glass of water."

Jenny stood entranced before the cabin, thinking the gentle sounds of the lake lapping the shore sounded like a thirsty dog, that the pine trees waved their branches at her in greeting, that the wind hummed tunes just for her.

Later while Clyde and Dale trudged along the shore to the boat rental shack, Nora worked her magic in the kitchen whipping up potato salad, browning a ham slice and baking golden biscuits.

That night at supper when Jenny tore open her biscuit, steam wafted up. She spread butter on the feathery center and watched it melt into a yellow pool. She rolled her eyes in delight as she tasted the succulent inside and crunched the crispy crust.

Almost every night they ate bass the men had caught. Nora pan-fried the fish, serving it with fresh sweet corn, along with applesauce and brownies.

Clyde taught the children how to de-bone a fish, how to pull off the gills, slice it down the back just below the head, and carefully pull the flesh away on both sides, leaving all the bones attached to the spine.

Happily holding her skeleton, Jenny thought her father knew everything. She was convinced he was perfect.

By day, the children chased butterflies, ran shrieking from bees, fed breadcrumbs to chipmunks, and hunted rocks at the edge of the lake. By night, they chased fireflies that winked through the warm dusk. Laughing and breathless, they rocked in the porch swing listening to the frogs croak and the crickets chirp.

One night Clyde called the entire family out onto the beach to look up and watch widths of soft reds, and yellows and greens undulating like sheer scarves across the sky. "Those are the Northern Lights," he explained in hushed tones.

After dinner the next evening, Nora stood over the stove making fudge.

Gear in hand, Clyde said, "Dale and I are going fishing again."

"But it's dark, Clyde."

"We didn't catch a thing today. After dark, the fish really bite."

It seemed only a short time had passed when the men returned. "What's wrong?" Nora asked. "Fish not cooperating?"

Clyde plunked down their rods and creels in the corner, "I don't care to discuss it." He peered down at the fudge cooling in the pan. "Just dish me up some of that candy!"

Jenny noticed Dale grin and then turn away so his father wouldn't see his smile. That puzzled her.

The next morning, as Jenny looked for tadpoles in the lake, Dale joined her. "Hey," he said in a low voice, "want to know what happened last night?"

His words piqued Jenny's curiosity. "Sure."

Dale skipped a rock across the surface of the water. "Well, Dad and I got into the boat and stowed our gear. Then he went to the stern and yanked the cord that starts up the motor, only it wouldn't start.

"Dad pulled that cord again and again. He started huffing and puffing and got all red in the face, but that cranky motor just wouldn't turn over, wouldn't even cough. Then Dad got mad." He paused, eyes twinkling. "He got so mad he gave it lot of swear words!"

Open-mouthed, Jenny stared at him. Daddy never lost his temper and she'd never heard him say one bad word—ever. Mother abhorred cursing. "Daddy swore?"

"He sure did. I'd never heard him talk like that. I was absolutely shocked! He tried to start the motor again—then gave it plenty of other swear words I'd never heard before."

Jenny leaned closer. "Like what?"

"I can't tell you. Gentlemen never swear in front of ladies."

"But I want to know!"

"You can't. You're a girl."

Jenny gave up. "But then what happened?"

Dale laughed. "Nothing. All those swear words didn't start the motor either!"

Jenny felt a trifle pleased that her father could be a bit wicked after all.

# 7. Jenny's Question

The Pates found the first half of 1929 filled with notable evens. Wyatt Earp died at eighty, 150 poems Emily Dickinson's sister had hidden for forty years were discovered, and the Graf Zeppelin circled the globe in twenty-one days.

Vacation was a pleasant memory when Jenny and Dale started back to school, Jenny in the last half of kindergarten, and Dale in fourth grade where he soon won a spelling bee. "The winning word was "t-e-n-a-n-t," he proclaimed proudly.

Then on October 29, 1929, the world changed. Newspapers carried great black headlines: "Stock Market Crash!" followed by stories of panic and men jumping to their deaths from office windows.

But Clyde planted a hearty kiss on Nora's cheek and said cheerfully. "Since we don't own any stock, we don't have to worry. I'm sure it'll all work out. We're so lucky. I've got my job, we live in a spacious home, and we have our health."

Nora sank down heavily on a kitchen chair. "I don't know, Clyde. Disaster can strike anybody."

The rest of the year passed quickly with The Crash affecting the Pates almost imperceptibly at first. But then the Y cut Clyde's salary, conditions in the country grew worse, and Nora had to find ways to economize.

But in October 1930, exciting, good news arrived. Uncle Harry had been keeping company with a special girl in Kansas City and they wanted to be married at the Pate's house in Ferguson.

Mother slaved like a dozen women, washing, cooking and cleaning. But she had to stop frequently to lie down.

Grandma arrived to attend the wedding. All her children came but Silas, the drinker and gambler, who couldn't leave his work at the drugstore. The oldest was Madge, dark-eyed, dark-haired and bossy. Her husband had to stay in Michigan working. Emeline, blond and blue eyed, appeared along with her new husband, Nolan. Jenny had loved their wedding pictures, with Emeline in a shimmering white gown and a full-length wispy veil.

Uncle William, three years older than Harry, was another jolly man, blond and blue-eyed like Nora and Emeline.

They all surged into the house, laughing and chattering. The men set up chairs in the living room, while the women turned their talents to the kitchen, helping Nora prepare the wedding feast.

Jenny was thrilled with the bustle, the excited conversations, the eruptions of laughter. Best of all, she couldn't wait to see her new aunt in her bridal gown.

Finally, Uncle Harry and his bride-to-be arrived. Rose was tiny, with curly brown hair, a cute turned-up nose and blue eyes. Harry explained she had grown up on a farm in Kansas with five sisters, but none could attend. While working in Kansas City as a telephone operator, she had met Harry through a friend.

Everyone surged back into the living room and Aunt Emeline led Rose upstairs to rest and then dress for the big event.

The wedding was scheduled for one in the afternoon to be followed by the wedding feast. Soon after, the guests would all depart for their homes.

Earlier, Nora was upset when Clyde insisted they couldn't afford to buy flowers for the occasion. Since it was October, their yard was bare of blossoms.

Finally, Nora had an inspiration. The day before the wedding, Clyde had driven Nora, Dale and Jenny out into the countryside where they gathered armloads of brilliant red sumac branches. When they got home, Nora banked the leaves in front of the fireplace. "There!" She smiled. "We look festive after all—and it didn't cost a penny."

Now the Westminster clock on the mantel chimed one. The pastor took his position before the fireplace. Uncle William stood beside the groom who looked handsome in his brown suit.

At the piano, Aunt Madge began the wedding march. The guests looked up toward the stairs. Aunt Emeline, the matron of honor wearing a soft green dress, descended slowly. The music swelled. The waiting congregation fell silent. Jenny peered up eagerly. Her heart thundered in excitement. Then Rose's small figure appeared.

Jenny's heart plummeted. Her mouth dropped. She stifled a gasp and her eyes welled with tears. She couldn't believe it! Where was the long white dress and veil? The bride wasn't wearing white, but instead, a short, dark brown, street dress! She didn't look at all like a bride!

When the ceremony was over, Jenny hurried to her mother's side. "Mother, are they really married?"

Her mother looked puzzled.

Jenny went on, "How can she be married when she isn't wearing white? They aren't really married are they?"

"Of course they're married." She gave Jenny a hug. "Aunt Rose chose a nice practical dress she can wear to church and many other places. You can wear a wedding gown only once. She did exactly the right thing in these troubled times. We'll talk about it later. We need to start serving dinner."

Thoughtfully, Jenny decided that someday she would marry someone wonderful like Daddy or Uncle Harry. But she would wear a fluffy, long white dress and a full length veil. She would look like a real bride.

By nightfall the happy couple and all the wedding guests waved goodbye.

That night Jenny lay in bed, too keyed up to sleep. She heard the trolley rumble down the tracks. In the distance a dog howled and soon other dogs took up the racket. Still awake when the mantel clock chimed eleven, Jenny heard her mother's voice coming from their bedroom.

"Clyde, I'm so exhausted I can hardly drag one foot after the other."

"Now, Nora, you've put on a wonderful wedding. No wonder you're tired."

Nora sighed. "Other people don't get so worn out."

"You better go see the doctor again. Don't say we can't afford it. You go!"

But when she did, the doctor said, "Everything looks fine. You've just put on a wedding, and any woman running a big house and raising children gets tired. Just try to get more rest."

Despite his words, Nora was sure something was wrong—but what?

# 8. Worsening Woes

By 1931 the country's condition had deteriorated. Clyde's salary was cut again. Drought plagued the plains. Women in baggy sweaters with drawn faces huddled against the wind on street corners trying to sell knick knacks from their homes. Men in shiny-seated trousers lined up for free bread, heads hanging in despair. First they'd lost their jobs, then their pride, and finally their hope.

One evening Clyde bounded into the house from work, beaming. "I know how to get extra money. I've found part time work."

Nora kept darning his socks. "Honey, you put in long hours already."

His chest was out and he absolutely strutted. "I'm going to referee football games on Saturdays. Look at this." From a bag he pulled out his uniform: a black and white striped shirt, white pants and black shoes.

The following Saturday Clyde trotted off in his referee uniform— grinning.

Jenny felt immensely proud of her father, yet underneath she felt a twinge of something she couldn't identify or explain.

As Mother cleaned, Dale turned on the radio. A song filled the room with mournful tones. Mother froze, the dust cloth clutched tightly in mid air.

*"The sun shines bright—"*

"Dale!" Mother snapped, "Turn off the radio!"

Glancing up, Jenny saw tears in her Mother's eyes. Songs about home often upset her. She was sure Mother was homesick for Indianapolis and Grandma.

That song stirred an emotion in Jenny too. But how could she feel homesick when she was already at home? Then she realized she was lonely for Daddy. He was gone so much. Mother's sad face must mean she missed him too.

But in a few months, football season ended and so did the refereeing. Clyde was home more.

One morning as they got up Nora said to Clyde, "Goodness, how I perspired last night. My gown is all wet."

Clyde frowned. "Were you that hot?"

"I don't know. Why should I sweat so much?"

Eternally optimistic, Clyde said, "Don't worry, honey, everything will be all right."

But he had no inkling that everything would not be all right.

# 9. The Guilty Favorite

One Saturday afternoon, Clyde and Dale returned from swimming at the Y. Clyde ran into the backyard with natural athletic grace. Dale trailed after him. "We're going to play catch," Clyde called to Jenny. "Watch out, honey. Ready, Dale? Here's a high one."

From behind his thick glasses, Dale squinted upward and thrust his hands skyward. The ball fell right through his fingers and rolled away.

"Cup your hands, Dale, and then pull them tight against your body. That helps you hang onto the ball. Toss it back and we'll try it again."

Jenny cried, "I want to play too, Daddy. Throw it to me, throw it to me."

Dale's toss to his father was short. Clyde picked up the ball and threw it toward Jenny. "Okay, here it comes. Well, look at you. Good catch!"

All three played then, with Dale missing more than he caught, and Jenny catching more than she missed.

Dale's thin shoulders sagged. "Dad, I don't want to play any more. I'm reading a really good book. I want to go in."

"Okay, son." A flicker of disappointment passed across Clyde's face. Dale's coordination was poor, and his eyes were bad. It had been his second grade teacher who had told them Dale couldn't see the writing on the blackboard. Until then, no one had ever realized Dale had poor vision.

The night after Dale got his glasses, heading into the house after dark, Dale stopped, looked up at the sky and exclaimed, "So that's what they look like! Gosh, they're beautiful! I can see the stars!"

Today, after Dale went in, Clyde and Jenny continued to play catch until Dale came to the back door and called, "Supper's ready."

As they headed for the house, Clyde patted Jenny's shoulder. "You're lucky, honey. You were born with better eyes and athletic ability than Dale. He's like your mother. You're like me."

A thrill went through her. Daddy really loved her—loved her especially. Mother and Dale were both quiet and loved reading, but Jenny liked to run and jump and play ball, just like Daddy.

*I'm his favorite.* But after a moment, that bothered her. Maybe Daddy didn't love Dale very much. All through dinner she was quiet, feeling a mixture of joy and guilt.

She had always thought her father was perfect. Sometimes Mother said he was made of iron. Jenny felt safe knowing her father was big, strong and unafraid. Still, right now she felt a little troubled.

A few days later, the family's downward spiral began. Dale got sick.

"Scarlet fever," the doctor announced as he came down the steps from Dale's room. "Keep the little girl away."

With each trip up the stairs to care for Dale, Nora moved slower, her face paler, her breathing heavier. When Clyde got home from work, he took over. An ominous quiet settled over the house. Jenny listened to her parents' hushed worry about Dale's rising temperature, heard the clang of basins as they carried sponges and cooling water to his bedside.

Each new house call the doctor made sent Nora and Clyde into deeper despair. Jenny wandered around, lonely and afraid.

A letter arrived from Michigan that shocked them all. Tina, Madge's little girl, had suddenly died of meningitis—Tina—the cousin Jenny had envied for being so beautiful. At first she was stabbed by guilt, then terror stricken that life could suddenly turn so cruel. Dale had to get well. He had to!

Then one Sunday afternoon the doctor slowly descended the stairs. "Bad news," he said grimly. "Your son's in a coma. He has encephalitis— a complication of his scarlet fever. Even if we save him, there might be brain damage."

Whirling, Clyde turned on Jenny. "Get out of the house right now. Go out in the back yard. We can't have you catching this. Stay there until I call you."

Outside, after repeatedly pouring sand in and out of a pail in the sandbox, Jenny stopped. How could she play when Dale was so sick? She kept climbing the porch steps and trying to see through the back screen door. Dale couldn't die like Tina. He just couldn't!

The shadows lengthened. Huddling under the weeping willow in the back yard, Jenny heard the screen door squeak. Her father came out, stood on the stoop, head bent, his body sagging. Then she heard a horrible noise—a wail from deep within him, and saw his shoulders shake.

Struggling to her feet, she ran to him and threw her arms around his legs. "Don't cry, Daddy. Please don't cry."

He stiffened, drew out a handkerchief and blew his nose. "Little girls aren't supposed to see their fathers cry." He wiped his face. "Don't tell your mother."

"I won't."

He shook his head. "Dale's so sick. I couldn't bear it if we lost him." He broke down again, but for only a moment.

Jenny stood quietly, understanding that her father wasn't an iron man, knowing he loved her brother just as much as he loved her. If Dale would only get well, she'd feel better about everything.

When at last Dale recovered, she stood at his bedside and stared at him.

Finally he said, "Hey, Jenny, what's the matter with you?"

She hesitated. "I was just wondering how your brain was."

On the other side of the bed, her mother laughed. "Nothing happened to his brain, thank God."

"I'm glad," Jenny said.

Dale brightened. "Me too."

Mother said, "Dale's perfectly all right."

But all the doctor bills were definitely not all right.

# 10. Daddy Has
# Another New Scheme?

Experts began calling the failing economy The Great Depression. A heavy fog of gloom engulfed the country. Clyde's salary was cut again. Always exhausted, and more frequently negative, Nora predicted impending disaster. Yet Clyde Pate was a man who seemed able to turn the sandiest irritations of life into pearls.

One day after pouring over the bills for Dale's illness, Clyde looked up and grinned. "I have a great idea. Contributions to the Y are down, and so are everybody's spirits. The thing to do when you're feeling blue is to exercise. Everybody listens to the radio, so I'm going to sell the bosses on letting me broadcast exercise sessions on Saturday mornings. It'll serve the community, Y memberships should skyrocket, and they'll have to pay me. Then we can clean up all our bills."

"Jenny's eyes grew big. "You'll be on the radio?"

"I'm sure going to try."

Two weeks later, Clyde marched into the studio at KMOX in St. Louis. "Sorry I'm late. A traffic accident blocked the road."

Lou Barrington, the show's director, approached him. "You can't be late for radio, Pate. Now listen, just watch MacMillan, the engineer there in the control room, or me, for signals. Lord, we don't have time for a rehearsal."

Clyde chuckled. "No problem. For the past thirteen years I've led hundreds of calisthenics classes at the Y. I'll just pretend I'm conducting one here."

Barrington shook his head doubtfully. "Okay, stand at the microphone about three inches away, and say a few words so we can get a sound level."

Clyde moved to the standing microphone, eyed it suspiciously and said, "This is Clyde Pate. We'll start this morning with exercises—"

Breaking in, the director said, "See the circle MacMillan is making with his fingers. That's the okay sign. If I swirl my finger, that means to speed up. If I pull my hands apart, slow down. When the red light above the window over there goes on, we're on the air. I'm doing the announcing this morning and then I'll slip out and direct you from the control booth. We've got about two minutes until air time. Good luck."

Silence engulfed the room. Clyde swallowed, watched the second hand jerk its way around the clock, saw the light above the control room window blossom into red.

Across from him at the other side of the microphone, Barrington said, "Ladies and gentleman, for the first time in the history of radio we bring you, 'Get Fit—Stay Fit,' exercises you can do right along with us, sponsored by KMOX and the Northside St. Louis YMCA. You will be led by a Physical Director from the Y who will get you into shape and keep you there. Now, we proudly present—Clyde Pate!"

Smiling at the microphone, Clyde said, "Morning, ladies and gentlemen, and all you little kids. Push those chairs and tables out of the way. Exercise will make you well and keep you well, so let's go! We'll start with stretches to warm you up. Now, reach over your head with your right hand—and push, two, three, four, five, six. Left hand—push, two, three, four, five, six. Now, twist to the side. Reach across your waist there! Right, two, three, four, five, six. Left, two, three, four, five, six. Now, lean way over, stretch that back out, and touch your toes."

Inside the control room, MacMillan twirled the dials that regulated volume. "Oh, no," he moaned. "He's leaning over touching his own toes. He's way off mike. Whoops, now he's coming up, he's back on. No, too loud. My God, there he goes down again."

"Son-of-a-gun," Barrington slapped his forehead. "The fellow is bobbing all over the place, acting out his routine." He gestured wildly at Clyde who didn't see him and continued, barking out instructions to his invisible audience.

In exasperation MacMillan said, "He's all over the place. I can't keep him on the mike." Both he and Barrington motioned furiously, but couldn't get Clyde's attention.

Finally Barrington said, "I can't believe it. He's down on the floor doing sit-ups! Cripe! What a disaster!"

Chuckling, MacMillan said, "Thank God it's only a fifteen minute show. Wait, don't go in the studio, Barrington, you'll just rattle him more. Let him go."

Three minutes before the show's end, Barrington slipped into the studio and delivered the commercial declaring all the good reasons for joining the Y. Then he signed off the program. The red light blinked out. He turned to the perspiring, grinning Clyde.

"How was I?" Clyde asked eagerly.

"Look, Pate, we've got a big problem here. You simply can't jump all around like that. We couldn't keep your voice on the mike. You kept fading in and out. You've got to stand still, for Pete's sake."

Clyde's face fell. "I do the movements so my classes can see and follow along."

"See? This is radio. They can't see you on the radio."

"But that's the way I've always done it." He frowned. "Without doing the actions to go with my words, I'll be lost."

Barrington said sternly, "You'll have to figure out something. We can't repeat today's fiasco. Fix it by next Saturday or you're gone."

When Clyde got home, Nora greeted him at the door. "Clyde that was so exciting. You have a wonderful, deep voice. Oh, it was thrilling." Then she paused and frowned. "But, honey, something's wrong with our radio. Sometimes we couldn't hear you. You kept fading in and out."

Clyde slumped down into a chair. "It isn't the radio, Nora, it's me. I can't act out the exercises like I do at my classes. They tell me I have to stand in one spot at the microphone. I don't think I can do that." He turned to her. "Nora, what am I going to do?"

44

She looked at him fondly and smiled. "I'll tell you what, honey. Do your exercises in front of me, and I'll write down exactly what you say. That way you'll have a script, so you can stand still at the mike, and you won't have to move a muscle."

He jumped up, grabbed her into his arms. "You're the best, honey. The program should go on forever, because people really need exercise. It's a great service to everybody. Now I know it'll be a success."

But the show brought only a few new memberships, far below what was expected. People simply didn't have the money. Despite a few fan letters Clyde received, after thirteen weeks, the show was cancelled.

"It was still a good idea," Clyde said. "The money helped us, and the program helped other people, too."

"You certainly do love your work," Nora said. "I can't imagine what you'd ever do without it."

When the Pate's lives soon plunged down toward Cemetery Circle, she found out.

# 11. Losing More than Teeth

Jenny usually liked school, but not lately. She trudged down the hill toward home, her blue eyes troubled. Now in second grade, she looked homelier than ever having lost a front tooth—and today the other one was loose.

When the white colonial house came into view, she noticed her mother sitting hunched over on the concrete porch steps with her head buried in her hands. Beside her stood a galvanized bucket and a scrub brush. Something was wrong! Fearful, Jenny began to run. Reaching the steps, she cried, "Momma, Momma, what's the matter?"

Nora lifted her head and stared at her daughter with lifeless eyes. "I don't know, Jenny. I just couldn't finish scrubbing the porch. Help me into the house and I'll fix you a snack."

But inside, she sank onto the couch, lay back and closed her eyes. The brown hair framing her face was dark with perspiration, and blue veins and pale freckles stood out on her white skin. "I'm sorry, dear," she said weakly, "you'll have to get your own snack. Have an apple and some cookies and milk. Milk is good for you."

Jenny studied her mother. "Do you drink milk?"

Nora smiled wanly. "Yes, why?"

"If it's good for you, maybe you should drink more." As she went into the kitchen, a feeling of loneliness swept over her. No children her age lived on the block. Dale always had his nose in a book, and he didn't want to play girl things anyway. She had hoped Mother would work a puzzle, or listen to her read, but now Jenny wouldn't even ask. Her mother was often too tired to play.

By six o'clock, Nora managed to prepare dinner and she and the children ate in the kitchen. Dale and Jenny did the dishes. Clyde got home from the Y about 9:30.

When Jenny went to bed, he sat beside her and, as usual, made up a silly story, his ruddy face glowing with laughter.

"Look, Daddy." She tongued her loose tooth.

His blue eyes twinkled. "Maybe the tooth fairy will come, and before long you'll grow new teeth."

"But I look funny without my front teeth."

"Sweetheart, you don't look funny to me. You're my beautiful little girl."

Later, Jenny couldn't go to sleep and lay listening to the trolley car rumble down the track. After tossing and turning, she heard the downstairs clock chime a tune she loved. Then she counted the bongs—eleven.

Her mother's desperate voice floated from her parents' bedroom. "Clyde, I feel terrible, worse than ever. I'm not just tired, I'm totally exhausted. I can barely drag through my work."

"You try to do too much, honey. Let things go."

Jenny listened, feeling uneasy.

"The last time I remember feeling good was after Jenny was born and we had that nurse for eighteen months, taking care of her and the house."

"That's it then, Nora, you just need more rest."

"I wish—"

"I know. I wish we could hire help too." Clyde paused and finally blurted, "They cut my salary again."

"When?"

"A month ago. Donations are way down. I didn't want to worry you."

"Will we be able to make the mortgage payments?"

"Sure. We'll just cut back elsewhere."

"But, Clyde, we've already cut back."

He sighed. "We have lots to be thankful for. We've got a house, Nora. And I'm still employed. Millions of men are out of work."

For a full minute she didn't speak. "I feel guilty going to the doctor. We can't afford it."

"Don't worry about that. You have to go back."

"No. I know what they think. I know what the neighbors think. Maybe it's even what *you* think."

"What?"

"That there's really nothing wrong with me."

Listening, Jenny was shocked at the bitterness in her mother's voice. She put her hand in her mouth and nervously wiggled her remaining front tooth.

Her mother said, "You must think I'm just lazy, that it's all in my head—like I'm crazy or something!"

"Now, sweetheart, I don't think that at all," Clyde said softly. "I have an idea. Next week is the kids' spring vacation. We'll drive to Indianapolis to visit Grandma. It will be a vacation for you."

"I always like going home. But can we afford it?"

"Don't worry. I'm judging gymnastic meets so that'll be a little extra. I'll stay at Grandma's just on the weekends and drive back and forth. Maybe you should consult a new doctor in Indianapolis."

She sighed heavily. "He'd only say the same old thing. I'm thirty-seven years old and they've been saying there's nothing wrong since I was sixteen. I felt so bad that year I had to drop out of school. And the next year it happened again. They kept me out so long I couldn't catch up and ended up two years behind."

"If you hadn't been behind, we wouldn't have met at college."

"And maybe you'd be better off, Clyde."

"Nora, never say that again! We've been happy. I'm proud to have you for my wife."

"And I'm so lucky to have you, Clyde. We did take each other for better or worse, but with me, you're certainly getting the worst."

"Now, honey, don't think like that."

Nora sighed. "It's not natural to be so tired all the time. When I was sixteen, it was the same old refrain. 'Nothing wrong, you just need a spring tonic.' I had a bad chest cold and pleurisy and their spring tonics didn't help. It's not in my head, Clyde. I don't know what's wrong with me, but something is!"

Indianapolis reeled from an unusually hot spring and the fans droned in the living room of Grandma's stucco bungalow. Clyde left early Sunday morning and drove home, planning to return the following weekend.

On Thursday morning, Nora took the trolley for a return visit to the new doctor, and Dale walked to the library a block away. Fay, a little girl who lived next door, came over to play. The two seven year olds went down to the cool dark basement.

For hours Jenny and Fay colored, played jacks, and then finally turned to paper dolls. Jenny had just picked up a fancy dress to place on her favorite Joan Crawford figure, when from upstairs she heard the front door open and close and the murmur of voices.

Suddenly the air was split by a scream. "No! Oh, Nora, no!"

A chill ran through Jenny. Her hand stopped in mid-air and her frightened eyes met Fay's. Frozen, the two playmates hardly breathed. Alert, they listened intently. After a few seconds, the voices droned on again, but they couldn't make out the words. Jenny couldn't seem to move.

Fay's eyes widened. "Jenny, why did somebody scream?"

Scrambling to her feet, Jenny said, "I don't know. Let's go find out."

The two girls crept quietly up the steps and, when they reached the top, pushed open the door and tiptoed to the edge of the living room. Grandma saw them and said hurriedly, "Fay, I'm sorry. It's time for you to go home."

"But...." Fay stood still, waiting for an explanation, but none came. Grandma quickly ushered her out the front door.

As the door closed behind Fay, a flood of uncertainty and fear swept Jenny and she ran to her mother for comfort, starting to throw her arms around her.

Nora put out her hands and pushed her child off. "Get away, Jenny. Stay away." She burst into tears. "You can't come near me any more!"

In shock, Jenny looked into her mother's white face. Then she felt her grandmother's hands on her shoulders, heard her voice above her head, "Nora, dear, don't be so sharp." Turning Jenny around, Grandma said, "Come with me, honey," and guided her to a chair far from Nora and drew Jenny onto her lap. Tenderly, she smoothed the straight fine hair. "Your mother is very sick."

From across the room Nora said, "Mama, I'm almost glad to know I've really got something."

"But, Nora, not this!"

"I knew they were wrong, Mama. My being so exhausted was never in my head. All the time it was in my chest!"

"Jenny," Grandma said quietly, "Your mother has a disease that's called tuberculosis, and it's catching. That's why she can't kiss you or hug you any more. We don't want you or Dale to get it. Please try to understand. I know you will. You're a bright little girl."

Jenny felt frightened, empty and lonely. Something terrible was happening. Grandma was rubbing her back as if that would smooth away this awful calamity. But it didn't. She felt like the bottom dropped out of her stomach. Afraid to ask, she wondered, *Is Mother going to die?* Nervously, she wiggled the loose tooth with her tongue.

Now Grandma's mouth was close to her ear. Jenny could feel her breath, smell her lavender soap and powder. "Your lives are going to change. But you can learn to float above the troubles."

Jenny looked up into her grandmother's brown eyes. Her own blue eyes darkened and her back straightened. Soberly, she nodded. She wanted to be taken care of, but instead she said, "It's all right. I'll help with everything. I'm a big girl."

That night her tooth fell out and, despite that very bad day, three tooth fairies remembered her.

The next night, Jenny had a dream. In it, she stood beneath a lighted movie marquee next to Gary Cooper while a crowd of fans cheered them. Happily she bowed, Gary hugged her, and she felt thrilled.

But when she smiled, she faced horror on every face. The dream turned into a nightmare. She wanted so much to look pretty. Turning to a mirror, she saw her mouth was a gaping black hole. All her teeth had fallen out!

She woke into lonely blackness, drenched in sweat and despair. How could she ever be a movie star if all her teeth fell out? How could she pursue her dreams if Mother needed her?

On the weekend, when her father returned to Indianapolis and heard the news, he said, "Nora, now that we know, we'll have you well in no time."

With a wan smile, she said, "Oh, Clyde—always the optimist. The doctor said it might take a long time, but you seem to have your own timetable."

Grandma stood in the background, her face creased with worry.

Frowning, Clyde said, "So, what do we do? What's the treatment?"

"The doctor said there's really no known cure. Just good food, and rest."

"Anything else?"

Nora shrugged. "I have to go to bed right away. I can walk to the bathroom, but that's all. I have to eat liver, and take a raw egg in a glass of tomato juice every day."

He made a face. "Ugh."

Nora said, "Clyde, if I have to do that to get well, I will. The main thing is to keep the children and you from getting it. You'll all be x-rayed now, and every six months."

"Of course."

"They'll check everyone in my family. It makes me feel like a villain. You'll have to boil my dishes and silverware for twenty minutes. I have to cough into a tissue, fold the germs inside, put the tissue in a paper sack which you must burn." She turned away. "I can't kiss or hug the children—or you."

"Now, honey, when you get well you can."

Her voice caught, "It's spring, 1931. Who knows when that will be?"

# 12. A Bird in the Hand

For the next months, Nora carefully followed the doctor's instructions. Thankfully, no one else she had been in contact with had the disease. The family had no idea where she had gotten it. She wondered if Uncle Jake, now deceased from a heart attack, who had had a cough they thought was from painting houses, could have had TB, but now there was no way of knowing. Clyde's and the children's x-rays were clear.

They hired an older woman to help weekdays with the housework.

One evening, Clyde came bursting into Nora's room. "I've got a great idea," he announced. "We're going to raise canaries. I've just bought sixteen birds."

"What?" exclaimed Nora.

"Look, we have a nice big warm basement. People love canaries because they're so cheerful. One of the men who comes to the Y was getting rid of his because he's moving away, so I bought them, cages and all. Most cages contain a male and female."

"Oh, Clyde." Nora shook her head.

Jenny and Dale helped their father carry in the cages. He hung one in the living room and one in Nora's bedroom. The others went down into the basement where they were placed on Clyde's long work benches.

Jenny watched the birds. They jumped from perch to perch, sharpened their beaks on the cuttlebone. Some warbled beautiful songs.

"The bright yellow ones are the males," her father said. "The brownish ones are the females."

"I love them!" Jenny exclaimed.

"Are they going to have chicks?" Dale asked.

"Eventually. We'll put in the materials and they'll build nests and pretty soon—more canaries."

They went upstairs where Nora rested on the couch. "They do sing beautifully," she said, "but those cages should be kept spotless."

"I know. The kids and I will do it."

"Do they have names," Jenny asked, "or can we name them?"

"You can name them, but don't get too attached, Jenny. We're going to have to sell them to make money. I can see it now. Pate's Pretty Perchlings. Why, in no time, we'll be on Easy Street!"

A few days later, Nora said, "Clyde, I love hearing those birds sing, but why did you buy so many? How will we ever make the money back?"

"Don't worry, come spring we'll have babies."

"But you haven't sold any yet, have you?"

"Not yet, but just wait."

"What are you doing with that old newspaper?"

He looked up. "I'm cutting a lining for the bottom of a cage."

"Why don't you stack a bunch of papers and cut out several at a time."

"Good idea."

"Not only that, you could put the stack in the bottom of the cage and, when one gets dirty, just lift that one out, and there'll a clean one underneath."

"Great! Nora, with your ideas, we'll make a go of this business."

Finally came the day tiny eggs appeared in the nests and Jenny and Dale watched anxiously until the chicks hatched, scrawny and naked.

Clyde beamed. "You're getting a wonderful education."

He sold a few birds, but within weeks, two birds were found lying on the bottom of their cage—dead. Not long after, half the fledglings had died.

The children held a funeral in the back yard and gave the birds an elaborate burial.

Watching them out the window, Nora said, "I don't know if this was such a good idea," and dragged herself back to the couch.

Clyde said, "Well, one good thing—our kids are learning about life."

# 13. The Y's Big Show

With no money coming in from the canaries, Clyde cast about for other ways to increase their prosperity and pay the help. One day he came home from work, brimming with enthusiasm. "I don't know if it was me or the whole staff that came up with the idea, but the Y is going to put on a festival next month and you children are invited."

"What's it for?" asked Dale.

"To tell the public what a great organization the YMCA is. Did you know I know Harold Keltner at the Southside Y? He heard an Ojibway Indian say the Indian father teaches his son forest skills and the meaning and purpose of life, so Keltner started the Indian Guide Program. We need to inform people about our programs and show what goes on at the Y. Our festival could bring in new members. It'll be as good as a three-ring circus and put the Y on Easy Street."

The following month found Dale and Jenny crowded onto bleachers in the swimming pool area of the Y with a mob of other spectators. Sunlight reflected off the water and the air smelled of chlorine. "There's Daddy," yelled Jenny.

An announcer proclaimed, "Ladies and gentlemen, the St. Louis Northside YMCA presents a Festival of Athletes. Did you know that basketball, volleyball and racquetball were all invented at Ys? So was Indian Guides. The Y's swimming program is outstanding. Caveman drawings have depicted swimmers, and an Egyptian pharaoh ordered his children be taught to swim. In 1906 George Corsan taught swimming strokes on dry land. Three years later the Y campaigned to teach all boys how to swim. Being able to swim can save your life. It's fun too. Now to our show! Our youngest boys will perform the back float, the American crawl, the sidestroke and the backstroke."

"Wow," exclaimed Jenny as twenty boys demonstrated the techniques.

Again that voice: "Ladies and gentlemen, our next exhibit is diving which should be taught only by qualified instructors like Clyde Pate. Here's Clyde."

Daddy executed a swan dive. He climbed back up to the high tower. The diving board made a resounding thump when he flew up into the air and executed a jackknife. Next, he ran down the board and threw himself up into the circle of a half-gainer.

The audience applauded. Then the voice announced, "Now, Mr. Pate, who has over 500 hours of life-saving and holds an American Red Cross medal, will demonstrate saving a drowning man."

A figure swam out into the deep end of the pool, flailed about, and yelled, "Help!" He went under the surface. Clyde dove off the side of the pool, pulled up the man, and swam back, carrying him to safety with his head above water. Reaching the pool's edge, he hauled him out, laid the man down, raised his arms and simulated pumping water from his lungs. Then both men rose and bowed. The crowd roared in appreciation.

Next, the spectators all moved into the gymnasium. After they had all settled onto the bleachers, a voice announced, "Now, the gymnasts."

A group of boys appeared. They pushed mats into place, hauled out parallel bars, and maneuvered pulleys that dropped ropes and rings from the ceiling.

The announcer said, "Ladies and gentlemen, there are four styles of gymnastics, Danish, Swedish, German and American. All strengthen muscles, and improve posture, balance, and agility. You will see flying rings, flying dismounts, somersaults, and vaulting off the leather horses. Clyde Pate's gym class will execute numerous maneuvers."

Dale and Jenny applauded furiously and watched their father and the men.

The gymnasts trotted off. "Now folks, we'll dim the lights and you'll see re-creations of Greek sculpture which idealized the human body."

The lights went out. Then came the noises of equipment being removed. Suddenly a spotlight illuminated a naked man seated on a bench, chin on fist, elbow on thigh. The muscles of his body gleamed gold. Dale whispered, "That's Rodin's 'The Thinker.'"

The next pose was two wrestlers, also greased gold. Then Rodin's "Adam" was followed by Michael Angelo's "David." Silence. The spectators seemed stunned.

The lights came up. "This concludes our Festival of Athletes," the announcer said. "This is Lou Barrington inviting you to take care of your body, mind and spirit. Join the YMCA."

The audience rose to its feet with thunderous applause.

At home, Nora asked Clyde whether he was tired.

"It's a good tired. The performances couldn't have been better. We should get hundreds of new memberships."

But they didn't. The crowd appreciated the free show, but kept their money tucked in their pockets.

# 14. Ominous News

The canary business continued to be unprofitable. Clyde sold four, but two more birds died.

"Clyde," Nora asked, "what could be killing the canaries?"

He shook his head, "I don't know, but we still have a few left."

She thought a moment, "I wonder if it could be the soft coal we burn in the furnace. Miners used canaries to warn of bad air."

"If it was that bad, I would think all the birds would be dead."

Putting down her mending, Nora said, "There must be some reason."

"Maybe. The pet store wasn't much help. Do you suppose some birds just have stronger constitutions than others? We'll just have to wait and see—and hope."

But soon it was Nora who had run out of hope. After her next appointment, the doctor requested Clyde accompany her for a return visit.

Dr. Swartz got right to the point. "Nora has been ill for two years and her x-rays show more damage." He drew a deep breath. "If you don't move away from St. Louis—in a year Nora will be dead!"

The Pates stared at him in shock. On the street below, trolleys rumbled and cars honked. A siren wailed close by. Nora pressed a handkerchief to her face trying to block out the odor of disinfectant and medicine, trying to shield herself from the doctor's words.

Dr. Swartz broke the silence. "You need to get away from the bad air here. St. Louis burns too much soft coal." He looked at them sympathetically and spoke gently. "Nora needs sunshine, and fresh, dry, clear air. I recommend you move to Phoenix, Albuquerque, or Denver."

Nora's hand fluttered to her heart. "So far away—hundreds of miles."

"When?" Clyde asked.

"As soon as possible."

"Not till after school's out," Nora protested.

"Don't wait any longer than that. You've got to get out of this bad air."

Nora's face was deathly pale. She whispered, "I'm one of the canaries."

The doctor looked at her, puzzled. Then he understood and nodded. "You must go."

"Not till Mama and my family come for a visit. Please!"

Dr. Swartz stood up. "I know it's a big change, but it's for the best. I'll refer you to a doctor in the city of your choice, but go as soon as you can."

Clyde's face was taut. "I'll give the Y notice, and we'll have to rent our home."

"How long will we have to stay?" Nora's voice was subdued, resigned.

Dr. Swartz turned away. "I don't know."

"When can we come back?" Nora pressed.

He hesitated and then sighed. "Maybe not for a while."

But his eyes said, *Maybe never.*

# 15. Where Will They Go?

As Shakespeare said, when troubles come, they come "*Not single spaced, but in battalions.*"

After some deliberation, Nora and Clyde decided Denver was the most appealing place to go, but then Jenny broke the shin bone in her left leg roller skating and, for six weeks, had to wear an ankle-to-thigh cast. The canaries were nearly a total loss. Only one small male survived—and he wouldn't sing.

They planned to leave by the end of summer. From her bed, Nora tried to direct the cleaning out and packing for the move, but quickly became exhausted.

Bursting into the house one day after work, Clyde cried, "Listen, here's what we're going to do."

Everyone looked up.

"We're going into business." He waved a letter. "Guess what? Harry and Rose are coming to Denver, too, and Harry's going into business with me!"

"Harry's coming too?" But then the joy left Nora's face and she asked warily, "What kind of business?"

"Making ready-prepared products. It's a totally new idea to save housewives work."

"Clyde, people don't have the money to spend on a scheme like that."

"Yes, they do. A man at the Y has been highly successful with this. To start, the products aren't going to be that expensive. What we'll do is to pick over, pre-wash and package red beans, white beans, pinto beans, split peas and lentils. We'll get a house in Denver with a big basement, and I'll do all the work down there, while Harry will do the selling. We've got it all worked out. I didn't want to say anything until it was all set. Isn't that great? No more long hours at the Y, and Harry and Rose will be in Denver right there with us."

"Won't a business take a lot of cash?"

"Not so much. I have money coming from the Y, and there'll be rent from our house. We'll do fine. Wait and see. Why, soon we'll be on Easy Street."

"Oh, Daddy," Jenny said, "you always say that."

Clyde laughed. "If I say it often enough, Jenny, it's bound to come true!"

That evening Clyde ran his finger along a red line he'd marked on the map from St. Louis to Denver. "This is the route we'll take."

"Why Denver?" Dale asked.

"Of the three choices the doctor gave us, Mother and I think it sounds like the prettiest city with the best climate.

From her place on the couch, Nora added, "Besides, I have a cousin and her husband, who live there and own a drapery shop. They're looking for a house for us. But I hope we don't have to stay in Denver long. It's so far from Grandma, and I hate to leave this house."

Clyde said, "I'm sure the renters will take good care of it until we get back." He grinned. "Man, I'm going to love it out there—hunting and fishing, and you kids can pan for gold."

Alarmed, Nora tried to sit up. "Clyde, hunting for gold is gambling. Don't you children get interested in that. Your father's cousin had a fine position as an engineer at the telephone company, but when he was transferred to Colorado, he got gold fever and quit his job. Now he and his wife live in some little shack up in the high peaks."

"Boy, that sounds great!" Dale exclaimed. "I'd like to hole up someplace in the mountains and be a writer."

Nora drew a deep breath. "Don't dream impractical dreams, Dale. Fred never found gold, they have no money, and are getting on in years. It's sad. Unfortunately, we certainly are in no position to help them."

"Now, Nora," Clyde said, "we'll be all right."

Turning her worried face away, Nora murmured, "Will we?"

Nora's mother and two sisters came from Indianapolis for a brief visit. Soon movers loaded the van and Clyde handed the keys to the new renters. At last they got into the car, turned and looked back at the big house in a final farewell.

Jenny positioned her leg in the back seat of the black Model A Ford and re-read the date the doctor had written on her cast—*August 3, 1933*. Nora reclined on the seat next to her, her legs resting in Jenny's lap.

The car doors slammed and the Pates set out across the miles toward hope and health.

Everywhere the country still reeled from the impact of the Great Depression. The day before Franklin Roosevelt was inaugurated, the banking system had collapsed and banks were closed for four days. Roosevelt desperately attempted to allay fear and rescue the economy with an alphabet soup of federal organizations. But conditions remained grim.

Over the past few years, Clyde's salary at the YMCA had been repeatedly cut ten percent. Fifteen million people were jobless. Now, because of the move, Clyde became one of them. He'd managed to scrape together some cash, but feared it wasn't nearly enough.

In Kansas City, the Pates visited Harry and Rose. Moving to Denver, too, they planned to follow in a week or two. The Chevrolet plant had laid off Harry and he looked forward to joining Clyde in the business.

Jenny was filled with excitement. "I feel like a pioneer," she bubbled.

Once on the road, the miles went on and on. At first they sang favorite songs like "Sweet and Low," "Skip to My Lou," and "Down in the Valley."

When they tired of that, someone would read a Burma Shave sign. *"Peanut raced 'cross the railroad track. His heart was all aflutter. The train came barreling down the track. Now he's peanut butter."* Soon someone would spy another series of the signs. *"In this world of toil and sin, your head goes bald, but not your chin."* Everyone would burst into laughter. Miles farther on Dale yelled, "Here comes another one. *'Missed the turn, car went whizzin'. Fault was hers'n, funeral his'n."*

After the laughter died down, Dale said. "I'd like a career writing Burma Shave jingles."

Then they grew quiet and thoughtful. They'd left behind the greenery and rolling hills of Missouri and now stared out at the flat expanses of Kansas. Evidence of hard times loomed everywhere—boarded-up stores, tramps camping by railways, abandoned barns surrounded by deserted fields. Grime coated everything, and blowing dust sometimes obscured the road. Out of the murk would come tumbleweeds almost rolling into the car, only to blow away to settle against some broken, leaning fence.

Before long, they traded the brown dust of Kansas for the red dust of Colorado. Finally, at one point the clouds made a tunnel and, at the far end, Jenny could see the faint blue outline of mountains. They were nearly there! What would their new life be like? How soon could they go home?

# 16. Will Anything Be Better?

When the Pate family arrived in Denver, Grant and Ellen Mills took them to the hill that overlooked City Park Lake and pointed out the blue mountain range that stretched across the western horizon.

Grant pointed, "That southernmost peak is Pike's Peak, the high mountain in the middle is Mt. Evans, and the snowy ridge in back there is the Never Summer Range."

Clyde's eyes gleamed. The children drank in the scene with pleasure and amazement. Nora took a big breath. "The air is so fresh."

"And the highest point there to the north is Long's Peak," Grant continued.

Clyde chuckled. "That range of mountains is impressive. I'm glad we decided on Denver."

Jenny instantly fell in love with the mountains, the shadowed foothills, and the snowy peaks.

A week later the Pates moved into a rented house that the Mills had found and shown to Clyde. As he helped Nora up the front steps, she said, "This reminds me of my childhood home in Indianapolis." Inside, Nora looked around. "I like the porch across the whole front, although it does make the living and dining rooms dark."

Clyde said, "Jenny will have the downstairs bedroom in back, next to ours, with the bathroom between. The upstairs is only half finished, but the big bedroom in front will be your mother's when she visits. Dale wants the back room and adjoining sleeping porch. It'll be cold sleeping out there, but that's what he wants to do."

"Dale likes to be different." Nora laughed, then sobered. "You're setting up your business in the basement?"

"Yes. The produce and the boxes were delivered yesterday. Our official name is Pate's Prepared Produce."

"That sounds good."

"Here are your pajamas." As she undressed, Clyde put her clothes away. "I'll open the window."

Nora peered outside. "What big leafy cottonwood trees in the back yard, and look at all the squirrels!" She breathed deeply. "I love this crisp air." Turning, she got into bed.

Clyde drew up her covers. "Ellen Mills says it's so clean here, the houses hardly get dirty."

"That would be a big help." She coughed into a tissue. "Oh, Clyde, I wish I could do the work. I used to like to clean." Gasping for breath, she said. "Honey, I need my prescription filled."

"Right. Isn't this location great? It's a half block from the street car line, and on the corner are a drugstore, market, and several other stores. We'll be happy here, Nora, and you'll soon be well. I'll go get your medicine."

At the drugstore Clyde handed the prescription to the man behind the counter. The pharmacist was a bespectacled fellow in a crisp white coat. After studying the paper a moment he said, "My wife will fill it. He passed the paper to a capable-looking brunette and turned back to Clyde. "I'm Alvin Mack." He extended his hand. "You must be new in the neighborhood."

"Yes, sir. I'm Clyde Pate." The men shook hands. "We moved here from St. Louis."

"Denver's a great place. If you don't like the weather, just wait fifteen minutes—it'll change."

Clyde chuckled. "Really?"

"This Park Hill section is a nice part of town. Your family will enjoy City Park, just a mile west of here. In summer there are band concerts, and the fountains in the big lake change colors. In winter there's ice-skating."

"Sounds great."

"You got kids?"

"Yes. Jenny's nine, and Dale's almost fourteen."

"Everybody loves Denver. Beside the three big city parks, we have mountain parks too. Good for picnics."

"Any fishing?"

"Plenty of streams, but the close ones are pretty fished out."

"I love to fish and hunt. I'd like to put some food on the table myself."

"Times are tough here, like every place. Denver's a health and tourist town. Not much other business. Do some sight-seeing. Don't miss the capitol dome—plated with real gold, or the Tabor theatre, named after the big miner, or the Unsinkable Molly Brown house on Pennsylvania Avenue."

Clyde nodded. "Say, Mr. Mack, do you sell groceries here?"

"No, but Dexter Foods is right next door. Small but mighty convenient." He collected a small bag from his wife. "Here's your prescription. That'll be $1.95."

After Clyde paid, Mr. Mack said, "Drop in again. Anything we can do to help, just let us know."

\* \* \*

Jenny entered fourth grade in September, still on crutches with her entire left leg in its cast. The teacher assigned students to help Jenny enter and leave class before the other children. Jenny appreciated the help, but felt even more self-conscious than usual.

Three weeks after the cast was removed, Jenny suffered a terrible fall down the front steps—landing on the cement sidewalk and breaking her left arm.

When she appeared in school with her arm in a cast from wrist to elbow, she felt really mortified. But finally, her arm healed too.

Jenny's parents said nothing about the new bill but she felt bad to cause so much trouble.

Later, one evening while preparing dinner, Clyde called the children to the kitchen. "I'm starting something special and you both will be important members. I call it the GMWS club."

"What does that mean?" asked Dale.

Eyes a-twinkle, Clyde said, "Guess."

"Get Many Wonderful Snacks," suggested Jenny.

"No," Dale said. "I bet it's Go Mountains Wednesdays and Sundays. We're going to the mountains aren't we—mountains with bubbling streams, pine trees, and wild animals? Hey, that's a great club."

Clyde's face was somber. "That's not what the initials stand for." He brightened. "But we'll go to the mountains sometimes. This is different— an important club."

Jenny and Dale waited expectantly. Finally Jenny could contain her curiosity no longer. "What does GMWS mean?"

With a big breath, Clyde said, "Get Mother Well Soon."

Together Jenny and Dale breathed a deflated, "Oh."

Jenny wondered how soon "soon" would be, but seeing her father's expression she cried, "We'll help, Daddy. We always do."

As promised, a few weeks later, with Nora reclining on pillows in the back seat of the car, the family drove into the mountains for a picnic.

While Nora dozed on an army cot, Clyde fished for trout. Dale and Jenny climbed the hills, fed crumbs to chipmunks, and collected interesting rocks. After lunch, Nora told the children, "Gather wood off the ground and fill the trunk. Winter's coming and we can save on heating bills."

All day long Clyde cast his fishing line back and forth moving far out in the rushing stream in his waders, but at the end of the day, he'd caught no trout, nothing.

"Aren't you disappointed, Daddy?" Jenny asked.

But Clyde exclaimed, "No, I've had a wonderful time!"

This was one of his last pleasant days. Slowly, his perpetual optimism faded. He and Nora waited anxiously for the rent check from the Ferguson house. Clyde tried to reassure Nora, "They'll pay eventually. Times are hard."

Dale began delivering *The Denver Post* and Jenny saw him hand his collection money to her father, who hung his head and muttered, "I'll pay you back, son." But later Dale told Jenny he never did.

One day Nora told Jenny, "The next time you wash a flour sack, bring it to me. We'll make it into a pillow case, and I'll draw a design on it and teach you to embroider. I brought all my thread when we moved."

So Jenny's mother taught her all the embroidery stitches—the Lazy Daisy, the satin stitch, the feather, the chain stitch and French knots, as well as the blanket stitch, blind hem, and the running stitch.

Before long, flour sacks became not only pillow cases, but towels, aprons, garage curtains and even doll clothes. Jenny savored spending time with her mother.

When jigsaw puzzles became the latest rage, Nora said, "Jenny, you've been wanting a jigsaw puzzle. Mix up flour-and-water paste, and glue this old magazine picture onto some cardboard. When it's dry, cut out pieces and, you'll have your puzzle."

Nora constantly tried ways to make her children happy, but every time Jenny asked for a toy or some clothes, Mother said, "It's just a fad, dear. Wait until tomorrow." But when Jenny asked again, she got the same answer. Finally, Jenny stopped asking and even stopped wanting anything.

Once the ice cream truck rounded the corner and Jenny's playmate, Essie cried, "Let's get ice cream. Ask your Daddy for a nickel."

Jenny said, "I can't."

"Sure you can," Essie said, "just beg. Beg!"

Jenny said, "At our house we don't beg." She knew the family had no money. Not even a nickel.

One midnight Jenny crept down the basement steps seeking her father. "Daddy?"

He turned suddenly, "Jenny, what's wrong?"

"I can't sleep. I dreamt that my teeth were falling out. Will you come lie down with me? Please?"

Clyde put down the box he had been filling with split peas. "Sure I will, honey. You go on up to bed. There's nothing to be afraid of." But his frown deepened and he turned back to his work.

Jenny crawled into bed. Waiting and listening, she heard the leaves outside rustle, the house creak, the clock chime one, two. She waited and waited, but her father never came. He used to read her stories. He used to stretch out atop the bedspread, and sometimes even fall asleep beside her, and she could feel the warmth that emanated from his body like sunshine. When he was near, she felt safe. A tear trickled down her cheek. He didn't keep his promise. He just stayed in the basement working. Burying her face in the pillow, she knew it was no use to even ask him any more.

A few days later when Clyde picked up another prescription, he talked openly with Alvin Mack. "My wife's worried. She says that I can't do it all—cooking, housework, my business, plus waiting on her. Do you know anybody we could hire to help?" He hesitated. "I can't pay much."

Mack thought a few minutes. "Say, I think I do. An elderly couple live in an apartment over the market. Sad. They thought they'd retire with plenty, and lost everything in the Crash. He does a little handyman work, and I'll bet she'd be glad to help you out. If she's interested, I'll send her over."

When Clyde told Nora he had a line on household help who could walk a half block to their home and wouldn't have to stay overnight, she was pleased. After hiring workers in Missouri, she was confident in her skill at judging people.

From the time she had first been sentenced to bed rest, she had determined to still be a good wife and mother, planning everything, even instructing the children in character-building proverbs like, "Vanity is a sin." "To thine own self be true." "A penny saved is a penny earned."

A dietician major in college, Nora prided herself on her nutritious, varied menus and her skill at providing protein when they couldn't afford meat. It took a lot of energy, for she had to figure out the prices of all their food. Sometimes it exhausted and discouraged her, and some days she was cross and scolded everyone, but a housekeeper would be a real blessing.

Clyde said a Mrs. Balor was coming for an interview this afternoon at four when Jenny could answer the door.

At the appointed time, Nora fluffed her hair and sat up in bed. The woman was prompt. Jenny showed her to the bedroom doorway and left.

Nora saw a short but strong-looking stocky woman. Appearing to be in her sixties, her gray hair was arranged in a no-nonsense cut.

"Mrs. Balor, I'm Mrs. Pate. Please sit down."

She sat. Clyde had told Nora how the Balors had lost everything and the woman's face told the story of pain and despair. Nora wondered if she'd be too negative to have around. "Mrs. Balor, you know about my illness?"

"Yes. Alvin Mack told me."

"We're very careful. I've been ill over two years and no one in the family has gotten sick. You're not afraid?"

"No." Mrs. Balor's gray eyes were clear and intelligent. "I understand you want housework and cooking done."

Nora decided she liked this somber woman. "I was thinking of afternoons five days a week. I need you to get my lunch about twelve thirty and prepare the evening meal and do housework in between— washing, ironing, cleaning. You'd get two meals a day and $20 a month."

Mrs. Balor nodded. "That would be satisfactory."

"Our older boy has a paper route and does the yard work, so he can't help much. Jenny's not quite ten, so I don't want her to work too hard and get sick, but she'll do the dishes so you can go home after you eat your dinner."

Mrs. Balor nodded.

Nora wished she would smile. "I plan the menus, and my husband does all the grocery shopping, so you won't have that responsibility."

"Good."

"Mrs. Balor, one other thing. I may be bedridden, but I'm not helpless. I like to control my household, so I hope you won't mind my telling you what to do. I need that. I hate to be regarded as a 'no-good' invalid."

"It must be awfully hard for you, Mrs. Pate. I won't mind. It's your house. When would you want me to start?"

"Tomorrow?"

"Fine." She rose. "I'll be here at twelve thirty." She turned back. "Oh, one other thing. You said I'd have dinner here. I don't eat much. I was wondering, after I serve all of you, could I take my meal home and share it with my husband?"

"Of course you can. I'll see you tomorrow."

Mrs. Balor started the next day, but all the time she worked, she rarely smiled—perhaps because she rarely got paid. Along with the rest of the country, the Pate's problems kept getting worse.

Jenny heard the whispers behind closed doors, saw the drawn

expressions on her parents' faces. It was Dale who told her they had lost the house in Ferguson, and would never go back, that the business had failed, that Uncle Harry had gone to work selling Heinz products and that their father tried to get on with the YMCA, but there were no openings. He wasn't trained for anything else, and was pounding the pavements looking for work.

Finally, her father came home full of excitement. "Tell you what I'm going to do. I'm going to sell life insurance. That's something every family needs, a product I can believe in. I'll be on commission, but the good thing is, once you sell a policy, as time passes, you get more commissions on those same policies. They call them renewals. Lots of salesmen build up real big renewals. And one of these days I'll sell a really big case, and we'll all be on Easy Street!"

Jenny noticed no one in the family said anything. They'd all heard that line before. In a few weeks it became obvious that the Pates were living on Poverty Place because, though her father was selling, no one was buying.

The neighbors shared their daily newspaper and sometimes Dale had papers left from his paper route. Nora instructed the children. "I want you to make logs out of newspaper. Crumple a bunch of papers, roll them up into a log shape and tie them with string. Then soak them in water in the basement wash tub. When they're wet through, put them on the floor. When they're totally dry, they'll burn like wood in the fireplace. That'll save money."

So, that winter while blizzards raged outside, the mountain wood and paper logs burned cheerily inside. Jenny loved the beauty of the snow frosted landscape.

As usual, Nora made the menus and priced them out from the grocery ads. On Saturday when Clyde was ready to go to the store she handed him the list. "It comes to $5 for five people for the week. Now that's good planning!"

Shamed, he pulled silver dollars from his pocket. "Honey, I've only got $3."

Reaching up, she said, "Give me back the list. I'll whittle it down." Erasing items, she wrote in new ones. "We can do without the roast and instead have eggs a la goldenrod, chipped beef, and red rarebit." Then, she said softly, "I think we should try to borrow a little money from Mama."

Clyde's face crumbled. He owed everybody—the doctor, the druggist, even Mrs. Balor, who kept working because she at least received two meals a day. He felt it shameful to owe money, and even more shameful to borrow, but what could he do? "Borrow from Mama?" He raised his head. "But just this once." But he knew it wouldn't be just once, because if they didn't borrow they wouldn't eat.

# 17. Who's No Good?

Just fourteen, Dale was a lanky, self-conscious, awkward teen. Under a mop of straight brown hair, his thick glasses made his blue eyes look even smaller. Benny, his paper route manager, heard from another carrier about the family's hardships and thought it was too bad he couldn't give the youngster a route in a better part of town. The solemn tense kid couldn't charm his customers out of good tips the way some carriers did.

Dale's route in the older section of Denver west of East High contained many apartments. He had to get off his bike and hand-carry the papers through the buildings.

One night he came home, stored his bike in the garage, opened the back door, and wearily climbed the steps into the kitchen. In the living room he sank down on the worn gray couch. Fuming, he told his father. "Four customers in that apartment on Downing Street skipped town. I'm out a month's papers for each one. I wish I had a better route."

Clyde sighed. "I know, son. It's the times. Things have to get better soon."

Dale sighed. He realized the seriousness of his mother's illness, his father's inability to make money, and the severity of the Depression, so he continued working with glum resignation.

He buried his concerns in reading Jack London and Richard Halliburton, listening to Rachmaninoff and Debussy, and dreaming of being a great writer some day. At junior high, typing was one course he really liked. He found he excelled in it, motivated because he knew typing would help any writer. Reading books, and dreaming of writing himself someday, made up for the drudgery and disappointments of his paper route.

Jenny envied his having a bicycle, adventuring far from home, and being able to give their Dad money every month; however, Dale attacked his route with stoic conscientiousness, and little satisfaction.

Not only did customers disappear without paying, Denver's weather was volatile, meaning Dale had to ride through high winds, hail, small floods, and blizzards.

One night he came in, his raincoat dripping with water, his cheeks red with cold, his galoshes sloshing with slush.

His father looked up. "Bad night outside."

"Yeah." Dale seldom smiled these days.

"Think of all the good you're doing, son. Despite rain, hail, sleet and snow, the U.S. mail, and *The Denver Post* will get through." He laughed heartily.

When Dale said nothing, Clyde looked up in real concern. "I was just trying to cheer you up. Spring's coming, son. The weather will soon be better."

"I bet," Dale said bitterly.

He had a right to be bitter. Snow in late May broke tree branches all over the city making the streets impassable in spots. Still Dale faithfully delivered *The Post.*

In June he was surprised to receive recognition from the newspaper for being a faithful carrier, and inside the envelope was five dollars. Dale stared into Mr. Lincoln's face and grinned. What a welcome sight! He hadn't seen that face on a bill for a long time!

With summer, Clyde sold several small policies and, with renewals coming in, was able to borrow from the company against them. Things seemed to be improving.

Then, one Saturday afternoon in July when Nora was lying on the couch in the living room for a change of scenery, the doorbell rang.

Jenny answered it and, when she came back, Nora looked up from darning socks. "Who was it?"

"The Better Brush Man. I sent him away." Jenny said. "You said last time, you didn't want anything. He wanted to see you, but I told him were an invalid."

Nora's face crumbled. "Don't say that."

"Say what?"

"That I'm an invalid. I despise that word."

"But, you are, aren't you?" Jenny hadn't meant to hurt her feelings.

Her mother's face contorted as she struggled not to cry. "Just say I'm ill."

"I'm sorry, Mom. Please don't be upset with me."

"Do you know what invalid means?"

Jenny's heart went out to her mother. She was having a bad day. Though she never complained about being sick, she sometimes got in a bad humor, like now. Her voice went on, not waiting for Jenny to answer.

"'In' means no, and 'valid' means 'good.' Invalid means 'no good.'" Her face contorted and her voice dropped. "I'd love to do all the housework, if I only could. Do you realize I don't even have the satisfaction of a hard day's work? I don't want to be considered no good!"

"I'm sorry, Mom. You're good."

"People probably think I'm not. What do I ever do? What difference do I ma—" Glancing at Jenny's stricken face she broke off. "Forgive me, honey. I try not to complain, but... Forget what I said. Go on with your game. What are you playing?"

Jenny hesitated, wondering what comforting thing she could say. She couldn't think of anything. "I'm playing jacks."

Nora nodded. "I used to like jacks."

Jenny went back into the dining room and sat down on the floor in the vacant spot between the table and the front door. Sunlight slanted through the big west windows and dust motes danced in the rays. The jacks made a little metallic tinkle when she scattered them across the shiny hardwood floor. Jenny's hands were big and well coordinated. It gave her pleasure to be so good at jacks. She was up to the sevens when she heard the front door open.

Looking up she saw Dale standing in the doorway, face white, weaving slightly, holding up his right hand—a hand covered with brilliant red blood. Blood oozed from his fingers, ran down into his sleeve, splattered in bright red drops on the floor. Blood!

Jenny screamed.

In an instant Nora scrambled up off the couch and rushed to Dale's side.

Bolting to her feet, Jenny jumped up and down in fright. "Oh no, Dale, no."

Coolly Nora said, "Calm down, Jenny. Run and get the small green pan and the big bottle of antiseptic from the bathroom closet. Hurry."

Jenny ran.

Quickly Nora threw one arm around Dale. With the other, she pulled out a dining room chair. "Sit down."

Dale's face was a white, his eyes large in disbelief.

"Put your arm on the table. Lean your head over. You need blood to your brain. Lean over, son, so you don't faint. That's the way. What happened?"

"Something seemed wrong with my bike, so I reached down. Stupid, stupid! I put my hand down when I was riding along fast. I caught it in the chain."

Nora blanched and felt sick.

Jenny returned with the pan and a brown bottle. Nora grabbed the pan, and poured in the antiseptic. She took Dale's arm. "This is going to sting, but it has to be done." She plunged Dale's bloody hand into the liquid which turned pink. The tips of the fingers were pulpy, chewed up.

Dale grimaced, clenched his teeth, and perspiration broke out on his upper lip.

Nora turned. "Jenny, listen carefully. Phone Mrs. Palmer next door. Tell her Dale mangled his fingers and—can she take him to Doctor Milstein right away? Then call Daddy. Tell him to meet Dale at Dr. Milstein's. Go!"

When Jenny got back from phoning, her mother was mopping Dale's brow. His skin looked translucent, and he gulped for breath. He wobbled.

Nora steadied him. "Jenny, bring me a full glass of water, the salt shaker and a teaspoon. Hurry."

In a moment Jenny was back. Nora stirred salt into the water and held the liquid to Dale's lips. "Drink this."

He made a face but obeyed.

"All of it," Nora urged.

"What's that for?" Jenny asked.

"It's for shock. Keep your hand in the antiseptic, Dale. Do you feel any better?"

He managed a nod.

When the doorbell rang, Jenny dashed to answer it. Mrs. Palmer took in the scene, hurried to the table and looked into the pan. She drew back in horror.

"Jenny," Nora instructed, "get some towels to protect Mrs. Palmer's car seat."

Then Mrs. Palmer put her arm around Dale. "Here, I'll help you out."

"Jenny," Nora instructed, "run alongside and hold the pan so Dale can keep his hand in the liquid."

In a moment Mrs. Palmer and Dale were gone.

Anxious hours later, Daddy brought Dale home. His right hand wore a big bandage and he still looked pale.

"Better lie down in your room, son. I'll go with you." Clyde said.

When he returned, Nora looked up anxiously. "What did the doctor say?"

"The thumb and the little finger are okay. He only hurt the middle three fingers."

"But they looked as if they'd been chewed up in a meat grinder," Nora cried.

Jenny asked anxiously, "Will Dale be all right?"

"It took some stitches, but no bones were broken. Doc will check him each week."

"So often?" Nora was frightened. "Why?"

"Just a precaution."

"There's danger of infection, isn't there? He could lose his fingers, couldn't he?"

"But he's not going to."

Nora was like a bulldog, worrying a bone. "He could even lose his hand."

"Now, Nora, don't borrow trouble. He'll be all right. I called his route manager He won't be able to carry papers for a while, but they'll take him back when he's well."

Nora thought—no money from the papers, and more doctor bills. Just when things seemed a trifle better, the world turned around and smacked them down again. But the thing that mattered most was Dale's hand. What if he couldn't type—and him wanting to be a writer?

A few weeks later, Clyde and Dale came back from the last visit to the doctor. Everyone trooped into Nora's bedroom where she was reading her Bible.

"Time for the unveiling," Clyde said.

"Where's the veil?" Jenny asked, trying to be funny.

"Here, Mom, look." The whole room stilled. Then Dale thrust his right hand in front of his mother, held it up and then turned the palm toward her.

Nora gasped. The fingertips looked slightly pink. There was a small dent in the middle finger, and it looked a bit misshapen but, otherwise, the fingers appeared normal.

"Why, you can hardly see any scars," she exclaimed.

"I can type," Dale said. "Dr. Milstein had me try on his typewriter. It felt a little funny, but it didn't even hurt much."

Nora was all smiles. "I'm so happy. Dr. Milstein did a wonderful job."

"He's not the only one," Clyde said. "Doc said if you hadn't acted so quickly and put Dale's hand in antiseptic right away—everything might have been different. He said 'Clyde, you be sure to tell your wife she did good. She did very, very good.'"

"I did? Yes, I guess I did." A radiance filled Nora's face. "Why, I guess I'm not no good after all."

# 18. What's Burning?

As the sun slipped behind the mountains, the autumn night came down rapidly on Denver—dusky and cold. Children playing on Dexter Street had kicked their last can and hollered, "Olly, olly, ox-in free," and run home where windows were glowing squares of golden light and families gathered around dinner tables.

In the kitchen, Clyde finished making Nora's sandwich and handed it to Jenny. "Take this to Mother." As she started to go, he asked, "You finish your ice cream?"

Jenny said, "Yes, Dale and I ate ours. Are you coming?"

"I'll be there as soon as I dish up mine." He chuckled. "I love Sunday night. It's the best night of the week."

Jenny nodded and went off with the sandwich.

Clyde heaped up his bowl. The family always ate their big meal at one o'clock on Sunday so in the evening each person ate whatever he wanted.

Their snacks were often bowls of popcorn, or an apple and a handful of cookies, or a couple of pieces of cake or, best of all, bowls of ice cream. Although Nora planned healthy meals during the week, Sunday night the Pates could have their favorite treats.

After licking the scoop, Clyde put the empty ice tray in the sink.

Made with cream skimmed from the top of the bottle, the concoction, frozen in the ice box, was never as creamy as store bought, which they couldn't afford. But Nora had found a recipe for peanut butter ice cream which was satisfyingly rich, especially with home-made chocolate syrup.

Jack Benny was coming on, followed by Charlie McCarthy. For those evening hours, Clyde could laugh and forget all his troubles. How he loved those shows!

Carrying his dish into the living room, he turned up the radio and sank into his chair. The program was just starting.

Just then, Nora sat up straighter, "Clyde, I smell something. Something's burning."

"It's fall. Probably somebody burning leaves."

"That doesn't smell like leaves to me."

Reluctantly, Clyde rose. "I'll check." He set down his ice cream and quickly toured the downstairs and then the second floor.

Coming into the room, Clyde looked at the questioning faces. "Our house is okay. It must be outside. Maybe somebody's ashpit."

"I wonder what it could be," Nora said.

Picking up his bowl, Clyde took a spoonful. "Don't be so worried, honey. I'll look around." Dish in hand, he wandered to the big glass front window and looked out.

"Good Lord." He set his dish on the window sill. "Back in a minute," he yelled. Clyde bolted out the front door, raced down the steps, and dashed across the street.

Nora stood up. Then she saw it. Through the Yates's big front window she could see orange flames. The parents and their two teenage boys stood on the sidewalk, staring at the fire inside as if under some hypnotic spell.

Up and down the block, people gathered on porches and sidewalks, watching.

Jenny heard the familiar rumbling breathing. Her mother was standing beside her.

"Oh, no!" Mother exclaimed. "Look at that." Turning, she called, "Dale, call the fire department. Yates's house is on fire." She leaned on Jenny. "Help me out onto the porch. I have to see where Clyde is. Where did he go?"

When they reached the porch, their neighbor, Mrs. Palmer came running up. "Oh, dear, the Yates. Isn't it too bad? Hope it doesn't spread. Here, Nora, let me pull up a porch chair for you. Shouldn't you be in bed?"

Nora sat. "Where did Clyde go? What's he doing?" All eyes stared at the house with the burning flames.

"There he is," Jenny called. "He's going up on their porch. He's almost to the door. He's standing there, right at the doorway, looking in. The smoke's all around him."

"Look," Mrs. Palmer said. "I can hardly see him. Where is he now?"

Nora's face paled, "I saw him go in. He went inside."

"Why?" Jenny cried in anguish.

Her mother's face was grim. "He always wants to help."

Mrs. Palmer muttered, "And you in your condition."

No one spoke. The night seemed strangely still.

Dale ran out on the porch. "At first the line was busy. But I finally got through. Somebody had already reported it. I'm going over there."

"No, you are not." Nora grabbed his sleeve and, reluctantly, he stayed.

They could see more smoke, and then the flames seemed to move away from the window. More smoke, and then there were flames in the doorway. The fire moved. An enormous wing chair with flaming upholstery stood in the open front door. It seemed stuck there. When the smoke swirled, they could see a dim figure behind the burning piece of furniture. The flames licked higher. In the gray veil of smoke, the figure bobbed back and forth.

Suddenly the chair burst through the doorway with Clyde behind it— pushing, poking, wrestling the big wing chair across the porch. With a giant kick, he sent it tumbling down the steps.

Then Clyde ran around to the side of the house. In a moment, he returned with the garden hose and sprayed the chair, soaking every inch until the last red ember sizzled out.

The Yates stood lined up on the sidewalk, still as bowling pins. Neighbors all around watched Clyde in astonishment, but no one else had moved to help.

Clyde inspected the chair again, ran around and turned off the hose, and then came trotting back across the street.

Nora rose as he came up onto the porch. "Oh, honey, I was so worried."

He grabbed her in a firm embrace. "It was just a chair on fire. If I'd left it inside, the whole house would've gone up."

"That was wonderful, Clyde," Mrs. Palmer said.

"Thanks."

"I'm glad it all turned out okay." The neighbor stood awkwardly a moment and then said, "Nora, Essie says you make ice cream from top milk. I sure would like the recipe.

"I like the peanut butter best," Clyde said.

"Peanut butter ice cream? Never heard of that."

"I'll write out the recipes later and send Jenny over with them."

"Thanks. Bye, bye." Mrs. Palmer went home.

Nora brushed the sooty sweat from Clyde's face. "Are you all right?"

The children pressed around him. He grinned. "Heck, I'm fine. I smell a little smoky, don't I? And I sure need to wash my face and hands."

"That was marvelous of you, Clyde, but I was so frightened. You shouldn't have risked it." She put a hand up to his hairline. "Look at that. You singed your hair in front. Are you sure you're all right?"

He dabbed at his forehead with a dirty hand. "Sure, sweetheart. Somebody had to do something. Oh, look. Here comes the fire truck."

As they watched, two firemen leaped off, ran up and inspected the chair, three others raced into the house. In a few minutes they came out and all five huddled around the chair and inspected it again. Then all five trooped into the house. Finally they emerged again. After saying a few words to the Yates, they clambered back on the truck and it lumbered away.

"Huh," snorted Dale. "That was fast. You did their job for them."

"Daddy, did the Yates say 'Thank you?' for saving their house?" Jenny asked.

Clyde drew his children into his embrace. "Listen, kids, you don't do stuff to get thanked. You just go ahead and do the right thing."

They all went back into the house—Nora back to lying on the couch, Jenny and Dale to their chairs near the radio.

Clyde washed his hands and face and then picked up his bowl from the living room window sill and went to his easy chair. He sank into it and looked down into his dish. His face fell. "Doggone it. It's all melted!"

Nora smiled. "Get more, Clyde, you deserve it."

"There isn't any more." He sat a moment, staring into the bowl. After a minute his face lit up and he laughed, "Oh, well, ice cream soup!" He took a spoonful, smacked his lips, and then turned to the radio. "And Jack Benny's still on. Like I say, Sunday night's the best night of the week!"

# 19. Story Gems

Days fluttered by like turning calendar pages. In May, Nora shuffled down the hall from the bathroom toward her bedroom. Reaching the doorway, she clutched the frame, gasping for breath as if she had run ten miles instead of walking ten feet. She had so much to do today, and already she felt exhausted.

Before she'd fallen ill, she'd been a meticulous housekeeper. Now, every time she was in the bathroom, it seemed natural to wipe a few spots off the basin, then thoroughly scrub it with cleanser while sitting on her small metal stool. Energy permitting, she cleaned the toilet, and swabbed out the bathtub with the long-handled brush.

It always began the same way—with intending to do just a little, but working more and more, until she ended up spent and coughing. Moving to Denver was supposed to make her well, but she wasn't well yet. Periodically, she'd improve, only to worsen.

Today having cleaned the bathroom, she tottered to the bed, and sank back against the pillows, too tired to pull up the covers.

Jenny turned from dusting the big dresser. "You all right, Mom?"

"I'll be fine." Resting, she gazed out the window. An unseasonable May snowstorm had covered everything in a soft blanket of white and brought memories flooding back.

For an instant, she was once again twenty years old, feeling vibrant, skating down a frozen river in Indiana with Clyde's arms holding her close—and all around—limitless horizons, expanses of glittering snow, and tree branches outlined against the blue sky like fingers coated with frosting.

Oh God, how she longed to leave this bed, these four walls, this house, and skate and play tennis and frolic in the sunlight. How she yearned to twirl in a grassy meadow and drink in the towers of white clouds and distant blue horizons. But she couldn't. *Will I ever again?*

She drew a quivering breath. *Enough of that!* Right now she had important things to do. Slowly, she slid the hospital table across her bed. They had bought it soon after the doctor said she must have bed rest. That had been five years before, in 1931. Five years ago—and she wasn't any better. Picking up a pencil, she began making the menus and the grocery list for Clyde.

Jenny, now nearly twelve, came to the bedside carrying her mother's purple velvet jewelry case. "Mom, can you show me your jewelry again? Please."

Nora debated a moment. She needed to get the menus ready, but she smiled tenderly at her daughter and pushed her papers out of the way.

They had few pleasures. Movies were too expensive. They read, listened to the radio, played games. Jenny so delighted in this ritual with the jewelry, she simply had to make time for it.

"Pull up that chair, sweetheart. Never stand when you can sit. Remember, it's important to save your energy. We can't have you getting sick."

When Jenny was settled and eagerly leaning forward, Nora slowly opened the purple velvet case. Against the gleaming white satin lining, her jewelry glistened.

"Remember, Jenny, never love possessions too much."

"I won't. It's the stories I like. Tell me the stories again."

"Are you going to be a writer like your brother?"

"Maybe. I don't know."

Picking up a brooch, Nora handed it to Jenny. "My grandparents gave me this cameo on my sixteenth birthday."

Jenny laid the piece on her palm, thinking how in a few years, she'd be sixteen. Smiling, she traced the face of the woman carved there. "She's beautiful."

"Mama and Papa often gave us jewelry to commemorate special days. This opal ring was for high-school graduation." Nora slid the gold ring onto Jenny's finger.

As she tilted her hand back and forth, Jenny's eyes sparkled at the changing colors. "Your family must have been rich."

"Not exactly, but quite comfortable until Grandpa made a mistake." She retold the old story. "He was part owner of a wooden box factory. One day a man appeared and told him cardboard boxes would soon replace wooden ones. He urged Grandpa to buy the new machinery he was selling to convert the plant to paper boxes. Grandpa couldn't believe flimsy cardboard could replace wood, so he refused to buy.

"By the time he realized he was wrong, his competitors had all the business and the new machinery was horribly expensive. The wooden box factory went broke. Shortly afterward, he died. He was only sixty. Mama always thought he died of a broken heart."

"Do hearts really break?"

For a moment, Nora didn't answer. "Sometimes it feels like it. Listen, we'd better hurry. I have to make everybody's to-do list, and the grocery order."

Jenny slipped off the opal ring and put it in the box.

Nora said, "When I was sick at sixteen, this gold chain and pendant cheered me up. And this ring has a real pearl, from an oyster, and here's the matching necklace. Remember? Daddy asked his best friend to buy souvenirs for me on his trip to Japan, so he brought back the pearls and the kimono you dressed up in when you had mumps."

They both laughed. Jenny bent her blonde head and, as always, her mother slipped the pearl necklace over it. The youngster fingered the smooth beads a few moments, then reluctantly pulled it off and handed it back.

Sun streamed through the window, glittering off the gold and precious stones, touching the brown and blonde heads bent close together.

One by one, Nora lifted the pieces, handling them with the care of a diamond merchant and recounting the stories—the marcasite ring and pin bought from a German actress, the ruby-and-diamond brooch, and earrings carried by covered wagon from Ohio to Indiana, a star pendant set with pearls, Grandma's gold pin-on watch whose carved case popped open when Jenny pressed the round stem.

Last, Nora showed Jenny an oblong mosaic pin whose tiny pieces portrayed a white flamingo surrounded by pink flowers.

Holding it up, Nora said, "Daddy bought me this on our honeymoon at Lake Geneva, Wisconsin." Her eyes, above the dark circles, glistened in memory. She sighed. "Someday, you and your brother will inherit this jewelry. She closed the case. "Now, let's put it away, please."

After Jenny put the velvet jewelry box on the dresser, Nora said, "Honey, please bring me the *Homemaker's Best Cookbook*. I have to finish the menus for next week." Jenny fetched the book and deposited it on the hospital table.

Nora leafed through it. Trying to give her family attractive meals with good nutrition when they could rarely afford meat, took time and effort. *We must get the protein we need. Protein rebuilds cells—important for a family living with TB.*

She had to keep everyone well, and make sure they had strong bones and teeth. The hardest part was estimating the prices, so when Clyde went shopping he had enough cash.

By the time Clyde finally got home, it was dark. Dale had come in hours ago and was upstairs reading. Clyde bounded into the bedroom and gave Nora a big smile and a kiss on her forehead. "How's my girl?"

"Fine. You've been gone a long time."

Sinking down on his twin bed opposite hers, he sighed. "I ran a few errands and then I made a couple more calls this afternoon."

She waited, hoping against hope for good news.

After a minute, his body sagged. "People want to buy insurance, Nora. They know they need the protection, but don't have the money." He sighed. "At least the ones I see don't."

She looked away. *Once again he hasn't made any sales.*

His eyes were sad. "Nora, I hate to tell you this, but you know the Lochners at the end of the street—the ones with four kids?"

Nora nodded. "Yes, what about them?"

"You remember I tried to sell Don a policy last month, but he said he couldn't afford it—and him working a steady job." He shook his head. "Today I heard he was killed in a car accident."

She gasped. "Why, that's terrible. What are they going to do? Four children!" Making a quick decision she said, "Clyde, take them the burnt sugar cake Mrs. Balor made today. I know it's everyone's favorite, but we can do without dessert to help them out."

"It's tragic they didn't buy a policy," Clyde said. "The men I saw today didn't buy one either. Ah, well, we can't get discouraged."

Nora's eyes went to a couple of loose threads at his neck. That shirt was beginning to fray. She'd have to turn the collar—another tiring task. Pumping the treadle sewing machine wore her out. Maybe she could teach Jenny how to turn collars.

"Yes sir," Clyde said. "Someday I'll sell that big one."

He was always so optimistic. But the big sale never materialized—even though he worked so hard, walking all over downtown Denver to save gasoline, and wearing big holes in his socks. He'd probably gone without lunch again today too. Clyde was a wonderful man. Holding up a paper, she said, "I finished the menus."

His smile faded. "How much?"

"You know I try to limit it to five dollars a week."

He took the proffered paper, then sat there immobile. He hated to tell her. Outside, a car droned past, dogs barked, and children called to each other. Clyde moved to her bed. He stood there fidgeting. "Nora— something else."

She looked up. The face looking down at her was not like her optimistic, hopeful, smiling husband. Her heart sank. "What? We still owe Dr. Milstein?"

"Yes. And the druggist and Mrs. Balor and the landlord, and we can't afford this house. We have to move."

"Again?" Nora's pencil rolled across the bedside table and clattered to the floor. Eyes sad, she glanced out the window. Chattering noisily, a squirrel scampered across the lawn and she could hear him claw his way up the big cottonwood.

Nora turned back to Clyde, her face bleak. "Close the door. We need to talk, and I don't want the children to hear us."

The following week, when Jenny dusted her mother's furniture, she went to the dresser and stopped expectantly. Picking up the jewelry box, she carefully carried it to the bedside table, smiling in anticipation. When her mother got back from the bathroom, they'd look at the jewelry again. Heart beating wildly, unable to wait, Jenny stroked the purple velvet and then slowly lifted the lid.

She gasped, reeled—as if from a blow. She stared in horror. The box was empty! Empty—except for the blue mosaic pin—the honeymoon pin. Gone were the cameo, the sparkling rings and brooches, the marcasite set, the gold watch. All gone!

At a gasp behind her, Jenny whirled. "The jewelry, Mother. Where is it?"

Slowly, Nora moved to the bed and sank down. This dreaded moment was upon her. "Sit here, honey." She patted a spot beside her, wishing she could hug Jenny close and cover her with comforting kisses, but she couldn't risk giving her TB. "I'm so sorry, sweetheart. We had to sell the jewelry."

"Sell it!"

"Yes. Sell it—all but our wedding rings, and the mosaic pin. It wasn't gold—wasn't worth much. These things happen when times are hard. Our whole country is having what they call The Great Depression."

"But, Mother...."

"I'm so sorry. I always wanted you children to have my jewelry some day. But they were only stones and metal, and we can always remember how beautiful they were. Nothing can take away the memories. Just close your eyes and see those pieces."

Jenny shut her eyes, then opened them. "It's not the same."

"I know." Nora squeezed her hand. "The Bible says not to store up your treasures on earth. We have so much. We have each other. And you know what? Someday you'll have beautiful jewelry. Never stop hoping."

Her eyes teared. "One day I'm going to be well." She sighed. "And one day, Daddy will sell a great big policy." Her voice grew soft and dreamy. "And someday, we'll all be living on Easy Street."

# 20. Will Mother Hate
# the Little House?

From her front window, Gwen Palmer watched Dale, and Nora's brother Harry, scurry through the pouring June rain into the cab of the rented moving truck. Clyde followed, shoved a broom and dustpan into the back, slammed the door, and then jogged up her porch steps.

Opening the door, she let in a gust of wind and pebbling droplets. "Come in, Clyde. How discouraging to have rain on your moving day."

"Oh well, we're almost ready to pull out. We'll miss that place. Nora and I have always lived in big houses." His face was tired. "You wanted to see me before we left?"

"Yes. I've enjoyed knowing you folks." She smiled sheepishly, thinking how afraid of them she'd been. "I have something for you. Just a minute."

She came back from the kitchen carrying two big paper sacks. "There's meatloaf and a jar of pickled beets, and this other is potato salad, and a cake. They might help out."

As she handed the bags to him, his eyes lit up. "That's mighty kind of you. And thanks again for taking Dale to the doctor that day. What a scare that was."

"I'm glad his hand is all right."

"It's fine, and a good thing too. He's working on a dude ranch this summer. Leaving in the morning."

"What fun for him!" Mrs. Palmer exclaimed. "He'll be a regular cowboy."

"We hope so. I met the ranch owner through work. Dale learned to ride a horse at my aunt's farm in Minnesota when he was about ten. I hope he'll do all right. He's not exactly a cowboy—more like a book boy." The paper bags of food rattled as he grasped them closer.

"You look tired, Clyde."

"Who, me? Na-aw."

"Your jacket's all wet. Don't overwork and get sick."

"Oh, I'm never sick. The kids call me 'The Iron Man.'" Sniffing the sacks, he said, "Sure smells good. Thanks a lot."

"Glad to help."

"I've got to get going." At the door he turned. "Maybe Essie can come over and play with Jenny sometime. It's not far."

Gwen hesitated, "Maybe—we'll see. She started piano lessons, and she'll have to practice, you know."

He nodded. "Sure." A tight look crossed his face. "I understand."

She stood awkwardly and then said, "I hope Nora likes the new house."

With a sigh, he said, "Me, too. Thanks again."

As she watched him go out into the rainy evening, she thought—*Clyde Pate is the glue that holds that little family together. What a blessing!*

After eating dinner at Harry and Rose's, it was dark by the time the Pates arrived at their new house. They pulled into the small garage in the alley, and Clyde held an umbrella and helped Nora hurry up the drenched walk and into the kitchen. As he turned on the lights, Clyde steeled himself for Nora's reaction to the house, a house half the size of any they'd lived in before.

Leaning heavily on his arm, she gulped for air and noticed hardly anything. He closed the umbrella and they all took off their wet coats. "I'll hang these up later," Clyde said, putting them on a kitchen chair.

Dale said, "The red linoleum around the drain board is brand new. The landlord let Dad pick it out."

"It's certainly bright." Secretly Nora thought it a little wild, and it made the blue-and-gray checked floor look dingy.

Clyde went ahead, switching on lamps. The dim yellow glow illuminated a long room that served as both the living and dining rooms. Even he thought the furniture looked worn. "Here we are," he said, afraid of her opinion. "Most everything's in place."

"Good." Nora rested with a hand on the big round table. "You men worked so hard. Wish I could have helped."

"Just a few more boxes to unpack," Dale said. "We put them in the basement."

Gasping for breath, Nora said. "Fine. It's been a big day. I'm going to bed. I'll look at the house tomorrow."

Clyde steered her around the dining table and through another doorway. "Our bedroom here is right off the dining room."

Nora nodded, but said nothing. The two children trailed behind. Jenny blurted, "Everything's so small!"

Turning, Clyde said, "Your room is down the hall, Jenny, and then comes Dale's. At the end of the hall is the bathroom."

"I wish I could have a bathroom right off my bedroom," Nora said bleakly, sinking down onto the twin bed.

"Someday we will. Here, I'll help." He pulled off her shoes. "You kids turn in. Dale has to get up early tomorrow."

The children threw their mother kisses, and called goodnight.

Clyde helped Nora off with her clothes.

"Hang everything in the closet, honey. You know I like things neat."

"I will." He caught his breath and grimaced as he moved, but she didn't notice.

She pulled on her nightgown. "I wish somebody would design attractive, comfortable clothes for people confined to bed all the time. I hate pajamas that are so mannish, and these nightgowns bunch up under me."

"Maybe someone will." He put her clothes away, and then helped her to the bathroom. When they got back, Nora said, "I feel so bad about the piano, especially for Jenny's sake. She so loves to sing."

"I know. But there's no room for it here, and the bellows for the player mechanism were broken." He turned away hiding a flash of pain that made him grit his teeth.

"Oh Clyde, I miss the way I used to play and you'd sing. Remember?"

"Yeah, honey, I do."

"It seems a lifetime ago." Looking around at the twin brown iron bedsteads, the old dark dresser, and windows covered only with shades, the words just popped out. "It looks so gloomy." A gust of rain drummed on the window.

"One day we'll have a big house again, and another piano, and we'll play and sing together like before. Get some sleep now. Things will look better in the morning."

When Nora awakened the next day, she saw it was seven o'clock. Clyde's bed was empty and already made. They couldn't afford Mrs. Balor any more. When Nora sat up, she realized that her bed was beside the window. It was so close she reached out, pulled the string and rolled up the shade herself.

Across the small porch, she could see a giant elm tree on the parking strip, the street, and houses on the other side, all drenched from yesterday's rain. On Dexter Street, her view had been limited to their back yard. Here she had a window on the world!

The door was closed, so she rang her bell. In a minute, Clyde opened it. "An egg for breakfast okay?"

"Yes." Then her face broke into a smile. "Why, I can see the dining room table from my bed. I'll be able to see you all eating when I'm not well enough to get up for meals. This is wonderful."

"I'll walk you down to the bathroom."

"No, let me try by myself. I'll call if I need you."

He went back toward the kitchen, but stopped, frowned, and put a hand to his back.

As she slowly stepped into the dining room, Nora drew a breath. Through the big windows streamed golden sunrays. "It's so cheerful!"

Clyde turned. "I hoped you'd like it. A contractor built it for himself, and I guess he liked sunshine. The living room, dining room and kitchen face south. They'll be sunny all day."

"How nice! The Dexter house was so dark. Oh, I feel better all ready."

But when she came back from the bathroom, she noticed that the bright light also showed up the shabby furniture and little worn rug lost in the middle of the living room floor.

She got into bed remembering her enormous childhood home in Indianapolis where the channel-back loveseat and matching chairs upholstered in soft burgundy velour sat in the parlor, the home where all the furniture wood was glowing solid cherry, where Mama's oil paintings of country landscapes graced the walls.

The colonial house in Ferguson was large too. She and Clyde had spent so much building it, they had little left for furniture. They had bought cheap items, thinking nice ones would come later—but what came later were the Crash, The Depression, and illness.

In her opinion the walnut-veneer bedroom pieces, and the dark oak dining set they'd settled for were ugly. And the wine and blue drapes she'd made for the Ferguson house were skimpy single panels. And now here they hung, worn limp strips framing the big sunny windows. For a person who so loved beauty, it was hard not to have a nicely furnished house, especially when she was cooped up inside day after endless day.

Then loneliness swept her. She hoped a letter from her mother would come soon. Here in Denver, they had few friends, and now with this latest move—they didn't yet even know the neighbors.

Jenny came running in, fluffed up her pillows, and then brought her breakfast tray. As Jenny set it down, Nora exclaimed with delight. "Where did the flowers come from?" A cheese glass was filled purple violets and white lilies of the valley.

"They're growing on the north side of the house. I went exploring outside before you were up."

Nora's spirits lifted. "Aren't we lucky, Jenny! Our new house has sunshine and flowers, and I can see you all at the table." When she saw Dale, her eyes misted. He'd be gone all summer.

After breakfast, he set down his suitcase, and came to her bedside to say goodbye.

She looked at him sternly. "Be sure your underwear gets washed every week."

"I will."

From her bedside cabinet, she took a small package. "Here are some postcards and stamps. You be sure to write us. You may even find story material at the ranch."

"Maybe."

"Inside are some hard candies too."

"Swell, Mom!"

"And Dale," she went on, "be pleasant and do your work without complaining."

He nodded.

"And ask for some prunes if you—"

"I know. Gee whiz, Mom. I've gotta go, Daddy's waiting." He threw her a kiss.

Standing at the back door, Jenny watched them drive away. Dale was so lucky. She wished she was a boy. He got to do everything, go every place, and she had to stay home with Mother.

She hoped she'd sleep better tonight. Last night she felt lonely and the new bedroom seemed strange. She lay awake a long time listening to the wind moaning around the house outside and boards creaking inside. When she did sleep, she'd had another dream that all her teeth were falling out.

They'd moved on Friday and today was Saturday. When Daddy got home from taking Dale, he would go grocery shopping, and she should wash, and maybe unpack some more. She'd probably be glad to go to bed tonight.

She was glad to go to bed. The room didn't seem so strange. She felt tired and fell asleep almost immediately.

But then through the black unconsciousness, she heard her name called from far away. "Jenny!" The voice came closer. "Jenny!" Then she felt a hand shaking her shoulder. "Jenny, Jenny, wake up. I need you."

Opening her eyes, she saw her mother's figure standing over her—a dark silhouette against the light from the hall. Outside she could hear it storming again. She tried to come awake, tried to think. What was her mother doing out of bed in the middle of the night? The fragrance of Mother's powder was close and she could hear the familiar whistling breath.

"Get up and help me, Jenny." Her mother's voice was calm but firm.

Jenny scrambled out of bed with a gasp of alarm, but her mother put a hand on her shoulder. "Stay calm and don't panic. Put on your robe and come help me. Daddy's sick."

Jenny struggled into her robe and slippers and pattered after her mother down the hall. "Do you want me to call the doctor?"

"We can't call anybody. The phone won't be connected till next week."

The clock chimed two.

As Jenny neared their bedroom, she heard her father groaning—making horrible cries of agony—of terrible pain.

# 21. What's the Matter with Daddy?

Jenny followed her mother into her parents' bedroom. Goose pimples pebbled her arms, raised by her father's moans and cries of anguish.

The room seemed unreal. Her mother's bedside lamp threw giant shadows of the two of them against the flowered wallpaper as they leaned over Clyde's bed. Jenny stared down at her writhing father.

This seemed strange. For years now, she had become accustomed to her mother lying in bed. Now it was reversed. Mother was standing up, and Daddy was lying down. He couldn't be sick. He was the strong one. Consumed with fear, she cried, "What's wrong, Daddy?"

His usually jolly pink face was white and contorted with pain. "God, no-o-o-o-o." He gripped the sheet with his fists, rolled his head from side to side in agony.

"Daddy! Oh, Daddy!" Jenny cried. She felt her mother's hand grip her shoulder.

"Honey, that won't help."

Turning, Jenny saw her mother's stricken face, but her voice was commanding. "We have to stay calm."

"What's wrong with him?"

Nora's voice was level. "I don't know." Bending over the bed, she put a hand to Clyde's forehead. "You don't seem feverish. Where does it hurt, dear? Could it be your appendix?"

"No, no." The words grunted out from between clenched teeth. Outside thunder rolled and lightning flashed.

"If only the phone was connected. If only Dale were here."

"I'm here, Momma."

"Yes, Jenny, I guess you'll have to be the one. Run next door to the neighbors and ask them to call the doctor."

"No!" Clyde insisted. "Listen to the rain. It's pouring. I won't have her going out in a storm in the middle of the night to a stranger's door. Absolutely not! Oh God, I need the bedpan."

Jenny cried, "I'll get it." She nearly slipped and fell, running down the hardwood hallway to the linen closet. In a moment she was back. Her mother took the white enamel pan from her.

Her father looked up. "Jenny, leave the room."

"Close the door after you," her mother said.

She waited in fright outside the closed door. The dim living room looked lonely. The clock on the mantel kept ticking, ticking. Gusts of wind shook the house, rain poured, and wind hummed around the cracks.

At last the door opened and her mother handed out the pan. Jenny hurried to the bathroom. Wrinkling her nose, she emptied the liquid into the toilet. It smelled funny, different from her mother's. She'd often emptied her mother's pan. She gasped as she saw this urine was pink. *Oh, no. Daddy must be bleeding inside.*

After washing out the bedpan, she set it under the bowl, thinking they might need it again, and hurried back to the bedroom, hearing her father's cries as she drew closer. They sounded worse.

"Jenny, bring me the green pan filled with lukewarm water and a wash cloth," Nora said.

When Jenny was back, her mother said, "Please pull my bedside table over here."

Her mother set the pan on it. "Now get the stepstool from the kitchen. I need to sit down by Daddy's bed. After that, bring the aspirin bottle and a glass of water."

At Jenny's anxious face, Nora said, "Stay calm, Jenny. We're doing all we can."

When Jenny returned, she set up the stool beside the bedside table. Then her mother instructed Jenny to put an aspirin on her father's tongue. Nora held Clyde's head up and he drank a gulp of water. "Again."

Jenny put a second tablet in her father's mouth.

He swallowed, then groaned and cried out.

Jenny started from the room. "I'm going next door and have them call the doctor." Lightning whitened the shades. The rain cascaded down in a deluge.

"Come back here, Jenny!" Clyde called.

"But somebody's got to help."

"You stay here. I want you here in the house. Nobody can do anything for me. I've got to do it myself." He groaned. "Oh, God, the pain's so bad. Nora, I don't like Jenny to see me like this. Get her out of here. Jenny, go to your room! Oh-h."

"Mother?"

"Do as your father says." She sponged Clyde's face. "Now, isn't that better?"

He turned his head away. "Oh, just leave me be."

Nora turned and took Jenny's hand, "Come along." Outside the bedroom, she said in a low voice. "Daddy's never ill, but when he is, he's impossible. He acts just like a sick dog that wants to crawl into a corner to die."

"Die!"

"I didn't mean that. It's just an expression. Daddy's not dying. It's just—I mean—don't pay attention when he's cross. That happens when you get sick, you know. You say things you don't mean."

"I'm going next door." Jenny ran across the living room and flung open the door. A gust of moisture hit her face.

"Shut the door! The rain's coming in. I'm afraid for you to go out there. Look! The streets are flooded. I can't worry about you as well as your father."

Jenny was surprised at the strength it took to push the door closed.

Nora said, "Maybe there is something we can do. Come."

They went to Clyde's bedside, where he lay white and groaning. Nora said, "Honey, perhaps my cough medicine might help. There's codeine in it."

Clyde said, "I'll try anything."

"Jenny, I need a spoon."

When she brought it, Nora said, "You hold up his head." She poured a spoonful of cough syrup into Clyde's mouth."

When he quieted, she turned to Jenny. "Listen. This is important. Never give one person's medicine to someone else. You never know how they'll react to it. But this is an emergency." She glanced at Clyde. "It should help some, but it may not last."

The little room smelled of Clyde's sweat, the sweetness of the medicine and Nora's lilac bath powder.

Suddenly Clyde called, "Bedpan!"

Jenny ran with winged feet, returned, handed the pan to her mother. Again the door closed and she waited outside.

Finally, the door opened and the pan was handed out. Jenny hurried to empty it. She shuddered. The dribble inside was bright red blood. Quickly, she cleaned the pan, carried it back and said, "I'm putting it under the bed." Pulling her mother aside she whispered, "Why is he bleeding?"

Daddy groaned. "I'm passing a kidney stone."

"Oh, dear Lord," Nora sank onto her bed in a coughing spell. "I'll go next door myself and phone the doctor, or Harry, or somebody."

"Don't you dare! You could never make it." Another moan. "I'm passing this stone—now—myself. Nobody can help. Just leave me alone. Go to bed, Jenny."

Jenny grasped her mother's hand, "Let me stay."

Her mother nodded and motioned to the chair at the end of Clyde's bed.

"You can't do anything, Nora. Get in bed. Rest."

"All right." Coughing, she picked up her medicine and got into bed, and took a dose. Her spell finally passed. Then she got up and wiped Clyde's face.

He said nothing, gritting his teeth, clenching his fists.

Sitting in the dim light at the end of her father's bed, Jenny tried to puzzle things out. Her father's body looked small on the bed, and something inside Jenny crumbled. *Daddy's always been the strong one. But he can get sick too. He could die.*

Her father had been the one who made her feel safe, feel everything would be all right. He was the sunny one, always smiling, always making big promises.

With a jolt she realized—*Daddy's promises don't come true.*

She watched her mother's white hands dip into the basin of water which streamed down silver as she squeezed out the liquid. She noticed the blue veins and the pale freckles. Jenny saw those hands gracefully move to her father, and then she noticed the loving glow on her mother's face as she tenderly wiped away the sweat of pain.

Her mother—calm, efficient, always knowing what to do in a crisis. How cool she'd been when Dale mangled his hand.

Then Jenny thought of all the menus her mother made, all the plans and to-do lists. She smiled remembering all the proverbs, like: "Pride comes before a fall." "Pretty is as pretty does." "Use it up, wear it out, make it do, or do without."

She realized how much her mother had taught her—patient instructions on embroidery stitches and how to darn. Recently she'd said she'd teach Jenny to turn collars and cuffs.

She remembered hearing her mother's voice, "Clyde, we must sell the piano." She recalled how her mother had said, "Clyde, we need to talk. Close the door." And after that, the jewelry was gone. Her mother, tonight saying, "I need you, Jenny. Stay calm. Don't panic."

Something inside Jenny shifted. She realized for the first time that it was her mother who, despite being sick, despite being in bed all the time, was always working, doing things, accomplishing things. Her mother was a strong person too!

A fresh new sensation of feeling safe sifted over Jenny like falling snow. The girl relaxed into the chair and her head nodded.

Later, rousing, Jenny realized she must have drifted off to sleep. Her mother was now leaning over her father, helping him drink from a glass.

"Send Jenny to bed," Clyde said. "I wish this room was soundproof."

"It's all right, dear. Make as much noise as you want." Turning to Jenny she said, "Run along to bed. You've been a big help, but I can manage now. If I need you, I'll ring my bell."

With one last glance at her father, Jenny pattered back to her own room. Crawling between the cold sheets, she soon realized why he had sent her away. Now his cries were louder and more dreadful. Trembling, she curled into a ball and squeezed her eyes shut.

The clock chimed four. The rain still poured and blew violently against the windows. Daddy's groaning continued. Wide awake, the little girl shivered. She didn't care what Mother and Daddy said, when it got to be seven o'clock, it would be light and people would probably be up. Then she'd go pound on somebody's door—anybody's—and get help.

Although she felt like a wrung out dishrag, she couldn't sleep. Tossing and turning, she cupped her hands over her ears, tried to shut out her father's cries. They were getting louder and louder. He screamed. Mother shrieked. Then silence.

Jenny bolted from bed and raced to her father's bedside. He lay silent, motionless, his face covered with drops of sweat. "Daddy!"

His lips finally moved. "It's over. Turn your back."

Obediently turning away, she heard her mother say, "Clyde, what are you...."

"It's all right, Nora. Get in bed. Turn on the overhead light, Jenny, I want to show you something."

Looking at him closely, Nora said, "Are you sure you're all right?"

"Now I will be. It's over. I'm mighty sore, but this is heaven compared to what I've been going through. Here Jenny, stick out your hand."

"Clyde!" Nora sounded shocked.

"It's all right. I just washed it off in the green pan." Taking Jenny's hand, he placed an object on it. When he took his hand away, she bent to see what it was.

"That's my kidney stone."

It felt hard—was heart shaped—a quarter of an inch long. Jenny squeezed it and felt the hard roughness prickle her hand. It hurt. Peering closer, she saw it consisted of tiny, sandy-looking crystals stuck together, each flat surface reflecting the light and each little square sharp as a knife. Tannish brown, it looked like a rocky burr. No wonder her father had suffered so!

Clyde said almost proudly. "That's the varmint right there. A big sucker, isn't it? The reason it hurt so much, Jenny, was it traveled from my kidney, down through the urethra and out the penis."

"Clyde! You shouldn't say those words."

"Now, Mother, what else are you going to call them?"

"Where did it come from? How did you get it?" Jenny asked.

"I don't know." He sighed. "But I sure don't want another one. Put it in my water glass there, Jenny. You can bring me another glass of water. When I see the doctor I want to show him that rock."

Pulling the sheet up under his chin he said, "Think I deserve to stay home from work."

Gently Nora said, "Honey, it's Sunday."

"Oh, then it's all right. I feel like I've lost a week or two. I'm so tired, and sleepy. I think we should all catch a few extra winks.

Nora got in bed, wheezing and exhausted. Jenny fetched her father another glass of water, stood and studied the stone in the other tumbler, and then turned out the light.

Her father turned over and chuckled. "That was a real chore to get rid of that boulder. Reminds me of a mountain peak. But I sure don't want to pass any more chunks of the Rocky Mountains!"

# 22. The Neighbor's Secret

Not long after her father was fully recovered, Jenny climbed into the low, beckoning arms of the willow tree in the front yard next door. Lately, enamored of pioneer stories, she pretended to be a frontier girl scouting for Indians. Tiring of that, she became a beautiful Southern belle, flirting with a handsome imaginary suitor admiring her from the lawn below.

The sun sent shadows shifting on the grass and a breeze rustled the leaves. Mourning doves cooed nearby and Jenny felt all was again right with her world. She burst into song. *"Beautiful dreamer…"* Singing came naturally, and she sang everywhere—in the yard, around the house, and doing laundry in the basement. Hand resting on the rough bark, she sang happily in the willow tree.

*"Starlight and dewdrops…"* turning, she caught a glimpse of a woman coming out of the little white cottage: the neighbor who owned the tree!

Guiltily, she broke off in mid-song and scrambled down, turning to dash home.

"Wait!" called the woman. "Don't run off."

Jenny stopped, turned back, and braced herself for a scolding.

A small woman wearing a silky blue dress moved toward her. Short sandy hair sprinkled with gray curled across her forehead above blue eyes. "I want to talk to you."

Squirming uncomfortably, Jenny thought this petite person was older than her parents, but not as old as her grandmother.

"I'm Mrs. Wheatley," the neighbor said. Her eyes traveled over the girl's cheap dress and worn shoes. "What were you doing in my tree?"

Gulping, Jenny said, "Playing."

"Playing what? You looked like you were acting. Were you?"

"Ye-s-s-s."

"I see." Mrs. Wheatley nodded. "You're Jenny aren't you?"

"How did you know?"

"Your landlord told me." She didn't offer her hand. "Now, I would like to meet your mother."

Apprehension enveloped Jenny. She was going to tell her mother on her. Besides, people shunned their family because of the TB. Cautiously she said, "My mother's sick."

Mrs. Wheatley said somberly, "I know. I would like to see her now"

"All right. You can wait inside while I ask her."

They went into the house. When Mrs. Wheatley sat on the shabby couch her small feet barely touched the floor. Her gaze traveled around the room, resting on the pathetic rug and then the skimpy drapes. She shook her head.

Jenny appeared, ushered the visitor into her mother's room, and left them talking.

When the neighbor had gone home, Nora rang for Jenny. "Mrs. Wheatley seems very nice. She said you could play in her tree any time."

After that first visit, Mrs. Wheatley dropped over almost every day, bringing magazines, flowers, or treats. Nora appreciated the woman's kindness but wondered why she had such a sad demeanor. At first they discussed Roosevelt's latest Fireside Chat, operas, or a book Mrs. Wheatley had read and promised to loan her.

Nora assumed her neighbor was a childless widow because she never mentioned her family. Both relished their conversations yet, more and more, Nora felt her neighbor harbored some mystery. Over time, the two women began to confide in each other.

One afternoon, Mrs. Wheatley startled Nora by saying, "I have three grown boys," and added wistfully, "I would have liked a girl. I so enjoy Jenny's singing."

Nora smiled. "She's always cheerful, just like Clyde, and she can be so funny, even when she's sick. When she had mumps, her cheeks swelled so much that her eyes were only slits. So she put on white socks and my blue Japanese kimono embroidered with dragons and cherry blossoms, then tottered out with the kimono trailing, bowed and chanted, 'So happlee meet you. I visit you from countlee of Japan.' She had us all in stitches." She sighed. "I wanted more children, but Clyde didn't, maybe because even back then I tired so easily."

Mrs. Wheatley said, "I didn't want any more because my husband was always tied up with his work."

*Ah! She mentioned a husband.*

Mrs. Wheatley went on. "Earl owns a Cadillac dealership. He came from money and has always made money."

Not wanting to probe, Nora said, "Before the Depression, Clyde did well at the YMCA where he taught athletics. I know he misses it terribly."

It seemed as if a floodgate had opened. Mrs. Wheatley said, "You know, Nora, I married too young. Earl rather swept me off my feet. Then I was delighted when he took me to Europe on our honeymoon."

"How I'd love to see Europe!" Nora exclaimed. "Clyde and I married during the great 1918 flu epidemic and had to settle for a weekend in Wisconsin, but I loved it and Clyde was wonderful."

"Despite the marvels of Europe, one day I sat at a table in St. Mark's Square in Venice and looked across at my husband and realized the man sitting there was totally different from the man who'd courted me." Mrs. Wheatley's eyes misted.

Nora tried to offer comfort. "I have to confess I had my doubts about Clyde."

The neighbor looked up in surprise. "You did?"

"When he was about eight, he and another boy put torpedoes left over from Independence Day on the railroad track. They actually stopped a train."

"Oh, my."

Nora hoped Clyde's stories would lighten the mood. "The boys got caught, and when the railroad detective appeared at their house, Clyde's father said he'd punish Clyde himself. He didn't want his boy to go to jail."

"What did he do?"

"He whipped Clyde, and for a month made him sit all day down at his barber shop."

Mrs. Wheatley smiled. "That must have been agony for an active little boy."

With a laugh, Nora said, "One time I asked Clyde if that's where he got his patience because he's the most patient man in the world, and he said maybe so."

"Stopping a train!" The visitor clucked. "Boys will be boys."

"Clyde was still pretty wild in college. He and his gang turned over an outhouse."

"I've heard of boys doing that."

"But at the time, the old man was in it."

Both laughed.

"Then one night Clyde led a cow out of the college agricultural barn and left it on the steps of Main Hall."

"What a prank! Was he disciplined?"

"The college was forgiving. Clyde played football, you see, and other sports—which is probably why he didn't get expelled. And he taught swimming at YMCA camps every summer, which probably made a good impression."

"He doesn't sound so bad."

"I hate to tell you. The worst thing about Clyde was the letters he wrote me during summer breaks."

Mrs. Wheatley frowned. "What was wrong with them?"

"He couldn't spell or punctuate—still can't. His family spoke German at home, like mine did until the World War. Because of prejudice against Germans, we were afraid and stopped. None of us had trouble with our English, but Clyde did and still does. Maybe it's because of his childhood."

Mrs. Wheatley listened with full attention.

"Strangely enough, Clyde's mother also had TB, so she took him to Hamburg, Germany, when he was three, and left him with her sister while she went into a sanitarium for two years. His aunts, uncles and little cousins there all spoke only German, so now he just spells words the way they sound. I once broke up with him over it. His letters made him seem so—uneducated."

"And then?" Jane Wheatley asked.

"Well, when school started again, I realized how wonderful he was, and how much I loved him, and I told him so." Remembering, her face turned soft. "His job at school was ringing the bell for chapel. Baldwin Wallace is a Methodist college and, that day after I told him, my, how he rang that bell!"

"You're very lucky. Clyde seems like a fine man, and you've told me you both enjoy the arts. I love music and theatre and museums. My Earl is only consumed with making money." Hastily she added, "I know I'm fortunate on that score but—" She raised sad eyes. "It wasn't so bad when we lived in California because there I had friends with similar interests. I loved it—the artistic world, the climate, the scenery." She paused and looked down at her dainty hands. "I don't believe in divorce."

Nora nodded. "Nor I. No wonder you miss California. I miss the trees and greenery of Indiana and Missouri."

"Earl couldn't resist the business opportunity in Denver. I had to leave so many friends."

Nora's eyes misted. "I understand. All my family, except my brother Harry and his wife, are in Indianapolis." She brightened. "Mama's going to come visit us soon."

"I'm glad you have a mother. My parents are deceased and I was an only child." She was silent and then said. "Earl and I weren't getting along, so two years ago I designed a little house and had it built next door—especially for me—so I could get away and read, go to art galleries and museums, and listen to music."

"I see." Nora took a breath. "Where are your husband and your boys now?"

"Earl and Larry, my youngest, live in a big house only three miles away. The middle one has just married and my oldest boy is away at law school. Larry is talking of enlisting in the army. Earl supports that decision, but I don't because things seem so uncertain in Europe."

Nora shook her head. "I wouldn't like my son in the army."

Standing, Mrs. Wheatley said, "Earl and I aren't divorced, you understand, simply separated."

"Oh." Nora sighed. Now she understood. "I'm so sorry for your pain."

Mrs. Wheatley looked startled. Studying the reclining figure in the bed, she said, "And I'm so sorry for yours!"

One day, Mrs. Wheatley invited Jenny to come next door to see her home. Jenny moved carefully about the rooms, admiring each beautiful item—the sparkling glass chandelier, shiny pink upholstery on curvy chairs, a silver tea service glittering on the small buffet. All the furnishings were scaled to fit the proportions of the little house and Mrs. Wheatley's small stature. Looking at the luxurious items, Jenny was breathless with admiration, but she realized that all the finery didn't make Mrs. Wheatley happy.

One day, Mrs. Wheatley sat on a chair across from Nora. "I was wondering if you might do me a favor."

"I can't imagine what we could do for you, but we'll try."

"I have some furniture that's going to be ruined if it stays in the basement of our big house much longer. When we moved to Denver from California, we couldn't fit everything in. I was wondering if you'd mind using it. You could give the items a nice home here. There's a long narrow couch that would go fine where your divan is."

"I...I don't know," Nora said uncertainly.

"My men can bring the sofa and a few other things over in their truck. Why not give the pieces a try? You would really be helping me out."

"I think you're just being nice, and what if we soiled or damaged something?"

"It wouldn't matter." Mrs. Wheatley suddenly made a decision. "In fact, if you like, you can just keep all the pieces. It would save me the trouble of getting rid of them. Please accept. Would this Saturday be convenient?"

Nora's eyes moistened. "You're being very kind."

"Not at all." Mrs. Wheatley went to the bed and took Nora's hand. "Getting to know your loving family has made me miss mine." Her face lit up. "Nora, I've decided to move back in with my husband. All this time Earl's called me every evening to see if I was all right. I have so much to be grateful for. All through our marriage, he's never missed a big event. One Christmas he gave me a car, and for our anniversary, a mink coat. He is kind and thoughtful and generous."

Nora thought of the bath powder Clyde gave her last Christmas and the box of stationery for her birthday, but she was sure she was just as happy as Mrs. Wheatley.

The tiny woman's face glowed. "We do have three boys together. I'm very grateful for the lovely life he's provided me. So, I'm renting the cottage to a divorced friend and her son. I'm going back home to Earl."

The following Saturday, after the Pate's old furniture had been moved to their basement and the new was all in place, Nora walked slowly out of her bedroom to see the change. The long narrow turquoise couch made the room appear more spacious. A small gold brocade chair stood nearby.

In the dining room, four curved-back chairs enhanced the round table. What an improvement! Nora quickly got over her embarrassment at being given things. She nearly cried with pleasure and appreciation. What a gracious, caring neighbor! The entire family was thrilled too.

That wasn't all the generous woman did. She persuaded Clyde to cut the legs off the buffet and place it in front of the window, which left room for Mrs. Wheatley's mahogany china cabinet.

Just before Mrs. Wheatley moved out of her little house, she presented a package to Clyde, who was mowing the lawn.

"Clyde, these are white ruffled curtains for Nora's bedroom windows. They're washable, so they don't need expensive dry cleaning. They'll brighten up her room. I don't see how she stands being in bed all the time—or how the rest of you stand it either."

He took the package. "I don't know how to thank you."

"I've found it great fun. I like to decorate. And, Clyde, when you can manage it, ruffled curtains in the other rooms would be nice."

"We'll keep that in mind."

She handed him a card. "That's my husband's. You sell auto insurance, don't you?"

"Not yet, but that's a great idea," he said enthusiastically.

Her eyes twinkled. "Maybe you and Mr. Wheatley can do some business."

They did do business and, after a few successful months, Clyde took Nora looking for carpeting and curtains. The effort left her so exhausted she had to sit down on a chair in the showroom. She fell in love with a soft green rug, but settled for a dusty rose carpet so they could afford ruffled curtains too. The whole family loved the prettier house.

It was good Jenny liked ironing, because it became her task to wash and iron all the curtains—fourteen pair—twenty-eight panels. But when she did, she sang, and dreamed that someday she'd be a singing star.

# 23. The Whiskey Mystery

One of the few highlights in Nora's quiet life was letters. One morning when the postman's brisk step reached the porch, no one was home to fetch the mail. She felt too tired to walk to the living room, too weak to pull open the heavy front door. She'd have to wait hours until Jenny got home from playing at a friend's house.

Sitting up, she called to the postman, "Farley!"

He came to the window and peered through the screen, "How are you today, Mrs. Pate? Letter here for you from Indianapolis."

"Probably from my mother. She writes every week."

"Postcard from your son at the ranch too."

"Finally! We've been worried. He hasn't been writing much. Oh dear, I can't wait to read it and I'm not feeling well today."

"Wish I could come inside and hand it to you, ma'am, but it's against regulations."

"I wouldn't expect you to do that." She leaned toward the window. "I wonder. If I unhook the screen, could you pass the mail through to me?"

"Sure."

The hook moved easily. "There." She pushed the screen open and Farley slid her mail through the crack.

"Ma'am, that works fine. From now on you'll get a window delivery." He ran down the steps, turned, and gave her a grin and a wave.

Eagerly, Nora read Dale's card. Frowning, she thought, *I'll bet he's homesick*. The description of the Wyoming ranch didn't contain his usual

111

vivid words. He reported he wasn't a cowboy, liked he'd dreamed of being, but a houseboy. *He doesn't like it.* With a sigh, she set the card on her bedside table and tore open the letter from her mother. As she read, her face froze.

Just then Jane Wheatley came up on the porch and called to her through the screen. "Are you up to a visitor?"

Nora hesitated and then said, "Come in. I was just reading the mail."

Jane sat in her usual chair. "You're upset. What's wrong, Nora?"

"Nothing." Nora dropped her mother's letter on the covers.

"Is it bad news? Would it help to talk about it?"

At first Nora merely looked away, then finally said, "I hate to say this, but it's my brother Silas. He's been drinking and gambling and Mama says it makes her feel like a failure. I know how she feels. Sometimes I feel like a failure as a mother too. What can I do for my children?"

"Now don't say such a thing. You mother them from your bed. I've seen you teach them a lot about good manners and honesty and nutrition and germs."

"But is that enough? Clyde and I can't have any social life. I feel like both the children have trouble making friends and, when they try, some people shun them because they are afraid of my TB." She wrung her hands.

"Now, Nora, maybe some folks are that way, but those wouldn't be worth bothering with. You've lived on Holly Street only a few months. The children will have friends in time."

Nora sighed, picked up the letter and smoothed it out on her tray table.

After a moment, Jane said cautiously, "You say your brother drinks. Most men do. Perhaps your mother is exaggerating."

Nora said firmly, "Our family doesn't drink at all. My grandfather was a Methodist minister. We were all raised to be teetotalers. Silas didn't used to drink. I think it's utterly tragic that Prohibition failed!"

"Most people like a drink or two," Jane said. "There's nothing so wrong with that."

"You don't understand. Once Silas goes to a bar, he doesn't come home for hours. He lost his last job, so our uncle gave him one at his drugstore, but lately he hasn't been showing up for work."

"Perhaps he's just a young man rebelling. Maybe your folks were too strict."

Nora made a face. "He's not so young. Although he served in France during the war, he never saw any combat. He's married now, with a child. As for being too strict with him, my father was anything but that!"

"He wasn't?"

"Before I was born, Papa desperately wanted a boy because they already had my older sister, Madge. Papa was awfully disappointed when I came along. Then three years later, here comes Silas—with olive skin, dark hair, dark eyes, just like Mama. Papa was ecstatic."

"Oh, my," Mrs. Wheatley said.

"Silas used to be so handsome, so full of vim and vigor and laughter, but now—he's so dissipated. It's funny. Out of us six children, the three dark ones like Mama, are good looking, energetic and strong-willed. We three blonds, like Papa, are thin-skinned and timid and shy." She shook her head. "No, Papa was never strict with Silas. He spoiled him absolutely rotten."

Standing, Jane Wheatley went to Nora and took her hand, "How hard on you to have a favored little brother. But he'll probably straighten out. Now, worry won't change anything, or do anybody any good."

"I know. I'm just having a bad day. From Dale's postcard I don't think he's happy at the dude ranch."

Jane clucked. "Poor boy, maybe he's homesick. He'll get over it."

"And then there's Jenny."

Her visitor's eyebrows shot up. "You are worried about everything. Jenny? She always seems happy, always singing."

"I worry about making her work too hard. She does so much around here. And she has to go everyplace by herself. I can't even go shopping with her—not that we have any money. And the worst yet—she's such a tomboy. She even says she wants to be a boy."

Mrs. Wheatley laughed. "Smart girl! She simply recognizes that boys get to do things girls don't, like Dale going off to the ranch. Tomboys turn out fine. I wouldn't worry about Jenny."

Nora frowned. "But I do. Even on Sundays, Jenny's all alone. Clyde hates to leave me, so when Dale isn't here, she even has to go to church by herself."

With a smile, Jane said, "Some people don't even send their children to church. Now, keep your spirits up. Things will look better tomorrow."

The following Sunday at church, Jenny sat on the hard pew and felt her mind drifting away from the minister's sermon until she heard him say, "You sinners must repent!"

Indignantly, Jenny thought *I am not a sinner! I do everything Mother and Daddy tell me. I'm a good little girl!*

Unless, unless, was it sinning to eat what she wasn't supposed to? A funny feeling started in her stomach. Maybe she was a sinner after all. But she got so hungry for sweets. She didn't have many toys, or a bicycle, and only three school dresses. There wasn't money for her to be in Girl Scouts. The family hadn't had a vacation since Mother got sick, and she and Dale had seen only one movie last year. What did they have in their lives but food? The more she thought about it, the hungrier she felt.

When she got home, she'd hunt for the brownies Daddy made yesterday. He put them in a big can and, because of her, he hid it. He knew she often got into the sweets and stole some, so he always spirited them away.

She shouldn't eat so much, but she couldn't seem to help it. After Daddy made cake, Mother said to cut it in sixteen pieces. Mother counted on that cake for four meals, so if Jenny snitched an extra slice, she always got caught—but cookies or brownies were something else. Often nobody noticed if she took a few. She could hardly wait.

After lunch and the boring dessert of canned peaches, Mother and Daddy went into the bedroom and closed the door to take a nap. Jenny waited. Outside, a bird chirped and a car roared down the street. Inside, the house was silent. She tiptoed to her parents' door and listened. All was quiet. *Good, they must be asleep.*

Jenny slipped into the kitchen, closed the swinging kitchen door, and carefully opened all the cupboards on the left side of the sink, starting with the highest one that went clear to the ceiling, hunting, hunting.

*Where did Daddy hide that can?* At the thought of the dark chocolate squares dusted with powdered sugar, her mouth watered. Lunch was mighty skimpy, and she felt ravenous.

*Nothing in the left-hand cupboards.* Quietly, she moved the stepstool to the right, pulled open the high ceiling cupboard door and stared in surprise. There stood a big casserole dish they seldom used, and next to it a tall brown glass bottle a third full of liquid. *I never saw that before.* Carefully, she lifted the bottle to the countertop.

The cork made a pop when she untwisted it. She paused, heart pounding, afraid her folks had heard. Bending, she sniffed, then wrinkled her nose. *That smells awful!* Holding it at arm's length, she reached for the cork, pushed it back in, and stood puzzled.

*What is it doing there—as if somebody hid it?* She turned the bottle and read the label—whiskey.

*Whiskey? That's alcohol, isn't it? How strange! Mother and Daddy always said never drink alcohol. Why is a lot gone when nobody drinks? Whose is it? Maybe they use it for medicine. I've heard of that. I'll ask somebody about it.* After setting the bottle back on the shelf, she continued searching for the brownies.

At last she found the hidden treasure pushed way back in the corner under the sink. Silently, she pulled out the can and pried off the lid. The wonderful aroma of chocolate engulfed her. She rolled her eyes in pleasure. Guiltily, she crammed a piece into her mouth, then rapidly devoured three more. Taking the dishcloth, she wiped up telltale dribbles of powdered sugar, replaced the lid on the can, and returned it to its hiding place.

All the next week, feeling frightened and worried, she wondered about the whiskey. If she mentioned it, her parents would guess she'd found the hidden brownies and helped herself. Maybe that was a sin. Still, she had to ask about that bottle. When nobody in the family drank, who could be drinking it? *Is it Dale's?* She was afraid to say anything—and terrified not to.

Then she thought, *If the bottle is Dale's, the folks should know.* But every time, just as she'd be about to bring it up, something or someone would interrupt, and the moment would be gone. No one had caught onto the missing brownies, and on Thursday she ate several more. Days passed without her ever posing questions about the liquor or getting any answers.

The longer she waited, the harder it was to ask, and she persuaded herself to forget about it.

A few weeks later on a Saturday, her mother was just returning from the bathroom, when Jenny heard Farley whistling. "I'll get the mail, Mom," she called, and raced to the door. Coming back, she recognized the handwriting. "Letter from Grandma," she said, "I'll open it for you."

After slitting the envelope, she handed it to her mother, who'd gotten into bed.

"What does Grandma say?" As Jenny watched, she saw her mother's face fade from pink to stark white, her jaw drop, her chest heave. Then she coughed violently and struggled for air. As the spell subsided, her eyes closed, and her body sank back against the pillows. She lay there limp, almost lifeless.

"Mother! What is it?"

"Get Daddy," she said weakly.

Jenny dashed out back where her father was washing the car. "Daddy! Daddy, come quick! Something's happened! Mother needs you!"

He dropped his wet rag, ran up the backstairs and into the bedroom, with Jenny following. Nora looked up, her blue eyes dull, her lips pinched, and silently handed him the letter.

As he read, his face turned gray. Stiffly, he moved toward the doorway. "Wait outside, Jenny." His voice sounded different—strangled. He waved her into the dining room and closed the bedroom door, shutting her outside.

Jenny stood wide-eyed, stomach churning, listening. The sounds were low, muffled. Once she thought her mother was crying. Her mother seldom cried, but now Jenny heard the small noises become deep choking sobs and that frightened her. Then her father's voice murmured, but she couldn't hear what he was saying. A long silence, more sobs, then more murmurs.

At last he came out. Behind him, she could glimpse her mother sprawled immobile on the bed. Daddy closed the door and took Jenny's arm. He led her to the couch and they sat side by side. She could smell his shaving cream and sweat. Her heart pounded so loudly she could hear it in her ears.

"Is Mother all right?"

"Yes, honey, it's just that she's very upset." He took her hand in his big warm one. "We think you have to know, Jenny." His voice was low, hesitant. "We've tried to teach you right from wrong, haven't we?"

"Yes, Daddy."

"We've always told you that it's wrong to steal, haven't we? That you mustn't take what belongs to others, even if you intend to put it back?"

"Yes, Daddy." She felt the flush flame up her neck and bloom across her face. *Was he talking about the brownies?* She didn't think finding she'd stolen sweets would make everyone this distraught. No, it must have something to do with Grandma's letter.

His face was still shadowed. Frowning, he swallowed and seemed to search for words. "We've always said don't try to get something for nothing—that you should work for what you want. You know that don't you?"

"Oh, yes, Daddy."

"It's wrong to make bets and to gamble. That's trying to get something for nothing."

"I know." She nodded vigorously.

"Jenny, sometimes liquor muddles the mind and makes people do things they wouldn't do otherwise. Alcohol is a terrible thing—terrible." He sat lost in thought. Then he turned to her and ordered, "Never marry a man that drinks!"

"No, Daddy, I won't. But what happened? Why is Mother upset and why are you telling me all these things?"

He clenched his teeth and looked away. "It's your Uncle Silas."

For a long time he didn't say anything else. Jenny waited and waited. Finally, he spoke again in that strange pinched voice. "Silas drank and gambled."

Jenny nodded. "I knew that."

"The trouble is, he kept trying to win back the money he lost, but instead, he kept losing more. The people he owed put pressure on him—unbearable pressure—to pay up. He didn't have any money and he owed a tremendous amount—so he—he embezzled money from the drugstore—from his own uncle who had hired him in the pharmacy to help him change his life."

"What's embezzle?"

"Stealing. He took a lot of money from the drugstore, thinking he'd pay it back, and tried to cover up what he'd done. Then, instead of paying off his debts—he went and gambled again, trying to make more. He lost it all—every cent."

"Oh, dear."

Clyde hung his head. After a long time, he said so softly Jenny could hardly hear the words, "He was found in a field over in Tarrytown, a little distance from Indianapolis—shot dead."

A gasp escaped from Jenny. She felt dizzy and clutched her father's hand hard.

He went on, "No one knew why he was over there. At first everyone thought the hoodlums he owed the money to had done it when he couldn't pay, but the police said no one else had shot him—they said he'd shot himself. They found he'd left a note for his wife saying she and their little girl would be better off without him.

"Your Uncle Silas committed suicide, and it's about killed your Grandma as well, and now your mother."

Jenny sat immobile, too stunned to speak. Chills ran up her spine and goose bumps raised on her arms. Her head began to ache. She was afraid of death, couldn't imagine someone killing themselves. Her father's voice came from far away, then closer. She felt his hand holding hers.

"We're all bound together, honey, each of us to the other. What you do affects other people. If you ever get in trouble, sweetheart, come to us. We're always here for you."

"Of course I will, Daddy."

After a long time her father said, "Jenny, don't get mixed up with drinkers."

Nora's bell rang and he got up, patted his daughter on the shoulder and went to see what his wife wanted.

Jenny sat there a long time, thinking about Uncle Silas. He was such a handsome, smiling man with a hearty laugh. She'd liked him a lot. Every time they went to Indianapolis, they saw him and his wife and cousin Lisa, who was four years younger than she. Though they seldom saw him, Uncle Silas was often mentioned—his funny jokes and high spirits. He carried the same blood she did. Jenny didn't cry. Some hurts went too deep for tears. Like her mother, Jenny seldom let herself break down.

Then she thought of the bottle of liquor in their own house. Hurriedly she went to kitchen, closed the door, and climbed up to the cupboard. She grabbed the whiskey, clambered down, and set the bottle on the counter. When she twisted the cork out, it made a little pop and the wicked smell scorched her nostrils. She didn't know the sinner, but she'd fix them!

When the swinging door swished, she turned, still holding the whiskey. Her father bellowed, "What are you doing with that?"

Heart pounding, eyes big, Jenny clutched the bottle to her chest. "Nothing." They stared at each other. Then Jenny said, "I was going to pour it down the sink."

Daddy snatched the whiskey from her. "Have you been drinking this?"

"No. I haven't even tasted it. The smell hurts my nose."

"That's good." He gripped the bottle so tightly his knuckles were white.

Looking up, Jenny asked timidly, "Whose is it?"

First he was silent, and then softly said, "It's mine."

"Yours? But you said to not ever drink."

"I know, Jenny. I don't very much, just once in a while. I've had this bottle over a year."

Her face crumbled. "You drink? But you always said not to. I thought you didn't."

"I know, but once in a while a man needs relief, to forget everything, to dull the pain. Sometimes a man feels he has to have a drink."

Jenny stared at him in shock. Smiling, jolly, sunny Daddy? She'd never known he was ever sad, ever distressed. Now he looked—embarrassed and guilty. She was all mixed up. "You said not to, but you did! You always said to face things and be brave."

Sheepishly he said, "I know. I shouldn't have drunk, even a little. I'm sorry, Jenny." He looked at the bottle. "You don't need to pour this down the sink. The reason I came out here was to do that myself, to get rid of it—once and for all." He tipped the bottle and the amber liquid flowed out, gurgled into the sink, swirled around the drain and disappeared. The pungent smell permeated the room.

He threw the empty bottle in the wastebasket and said, "I never drank that much, but from now on, I won't drink at all. Don't you worry."

"I won't." She believed him.

"And, sweetheart, promise me that you'll never turn to liquor, or go around with people who do. And if you get in any kind of trouble—always know your mother and I will help you. Promise?"

She threw her arms around him. Despite all the sadness, something had changed for the better. "Yes, I promise."

# 24. Can Dale Win over the Cowboys?

Still recovering from the shock of her brother's death, Nora tried to distract herself by thinking about Dale's trip to the dude ranch.

On that Saturday, Clyde had taken Dale down to the Brown Palace Hotel to meet the ranch owner, Mr. Warring, who was driving him to the ranch.

Shaking hands, Dale was dazzled by the silver-haired, bronzed-skinned, hulking figure wearing a brown Stetson and scuffed cowboy boots.

Warring introduced the man beside him. "This is Olly, my foreman."

A wiry, bowlegged, weathered fellow stepped forward. After they shook hands all around, Dale hugged his dad and clambered into Warring's big car.

Then the dusty black Buick headed north.

Dale settled back, enjoying the ride. "How far is it?"

"About 600 miles."

They drove steadily, only stopping for lunch and a few minutes of exercise. The sun slipped over the horizon. They had passed the Rocky Mountain range and now drove through the barren prairies of southern Wyoming. When they pulled up to a shabby, roadside restaurant for dinner, it was still hot. Dale was grateful that Mr. Warring was paying all the checks.

Night fell, and on they drove, stopping again around eight for coffee. Then they started down a dark two-lane road. No street lights illuminated the blackness. Occasionally the yellow eyes of an oncoming vehicle hurtled toward them. Dale drifted off to sleep.

When they reached a tiny town with one gravel street, Dale saw a sign "DuBois—Population 200."

"Only twelve miles to go," Warring declared, and they turned off onto an even darker, winding road.

Close to midnight, they bounced over the dirt ruts and under the sign announcing "TBW Ranch." Olly led Dale to the bunkhouse, pointed to an empty bed and warned him not to disturb the sleeping cowhands.

In the morning, he was awakened by a speaker blaring, *"I'm back in the saddle again,"* and recognized Gene Autry's voice singing the familiar tune.

Before the record ended, a buxom, matronly figure with wispy blond hair and a sunburned face boomed from the center of the sunny, bunk-lined room, "Rise and shine, boys. Up, you get. It's five-thirty already. Hey you, boy, I'm Mrs. Swearingen." She motioned to Dale. "Get your duds on and help me in the kitchen. Shake a leg!"

Dale found the log building which contained the kitchen. When he appeared, Mrs. Swearingen gestured to an enormous table. "This here is where the help eats." Dale looked around in interest at the gigantic pantry containing dish cupboards. Bustling over to the black, wood-burning stove, the cook ordered him to fetch the cream from the enormous refrigerator, and pour syrup from the pan on the stove into pitchers.

When he had done his tasks, Mrs. Swearingen pointed with a wooden spoon out the window at another building. "That there's the lodge."

Peering out, Dale said, "It looks big."

"You want big, why this whole ranch is big, boy. Spreads over 29,000 acres—about forty-five square miles. Most of it's rolling low foothills."

"Mr. Warring must be mighty rich."

"The name is Thomas Boyd Warring, and he's heir to the Warring Iron Works. At the end of the World War, he discovered he had two million dollars, so he took three trips around the world and toured every state in the Union. On his way to Yellowstone, he fell in love with this place. He runs some cattle and dairy cows and set it up as a dude ranch. Spends most summers here."

Dale was impressed.

"Now, fetch me the wood outta that bucket, boy."

Dale obeyed, mouth watering at the bacon and eggs sizzling on the stove.

"Step outside there and ring the bell for breakfast," the cook instructed.

When Dale stepped back inside, the cowhands rushed past him to the table. Mrs. Swearingen thumped him on the arm so hard it hurt. "Set down and fall to."

Dale consumed huge amounts of oatmeal, bacon and eggs, pancakes, and coffee doctored with rich cream. He listened as Olly bragged to another cowboy, "Warring's barn is the biggest in the state. Cost 100,000 bucks and its floors are made outta concrete."

"Why does he need such a big barn?" asked Dale.

"It's gotta be big," Olly went on. "Why, he's got thirty cows and thirty-five horses stabled in there.

"Collects saddles too," Olly said, between slurps of coffee. "English, Western, and a few bucking saddles. Them last has got really high backs." He glanced over at Dale and grinned. "Himself rides a thirty-nine-year-old mare—loves that horse like a daughter."

"Thirty-nine seems awfully old for a horse." Dale ventured, and then thought Olly winked at the other cowboys. Uneasily, he wondered if being so young, and a city boy, that these cowhands might tell him tall tales. He felt wary, unsure of what to believe.

"You ride, sonny?" Olly asked.

"Yeah. I learned on my aunt's farm in Minnesota." He wished they wouldn't call him sonny.

Olly nodded, "Old farm animal, huh? Betcha it wasn't no buckin' bronc." He howled with laughter and, working at his yellow teeth with a toothpick, he rose.

Dale jumped to his feet. "I'm ready to go, sir. I sure am looking forward to working with the horses and cattle."

"That so? Well, now, that's sure too bad, 'cause, sonny, you ain't gonna be workin' with me, you're to report to Mrs. Swearingen for your duties. What helps me is men!"

"Oh." Dale's heart sank. He thought he'd get to be a cowboy this summer and ride a horse every day. Mr. Warring had only told his dad that they needed help at the ranch. Dale had jumped at the chance to work here. He was almost sixteen, and jobs were hard to come by for men, much less boys.

Although he was disappointed not to be a cowboy, Dale thought he might be doing other interesting things. Milking cows would be fun, and pitching hay. Forlornly, he watched the cowboys amble out.

"You, boy," came the cook's booming voice. "Bring them dishes out here, all of 'em. We got lots of work to do before I have to feed the dudes. Step on it."

Dutifully, Dale cleared the table. "Olly said you'd tell me what to do."

"That's right. Start in by washing those dishes. Then you'll set the tables in the adjoining dining room, be a waiter, and clean up after the guests finish. You'll be washing a lot of dishes. When you get done there, I'll take you over and show you around the big house."

Scurrying about, Dale hoped maybe there would be something more interesting at the main house for him—playing cards and games with guest kids maybe, or telling them historic stories about the West. He'd studied up on a few since they came to Denver. Or maybe he'd have time off till lunchtime, and he could write letters or read. Mr. Warring had said the big house had a library with a lot of books.

While drying and putting away the everyday dishes, he came across several sets of china in beautiful, intricate patterns. Noticing him lingering there, Mrs. Swearingen called, "Them are from countries Mr. Warring visited. You be careful," Mrs. Swearingen yelled. "Tomby's mighty proud of them."

"Who's Tomby?"

She laughed. "Boss's name is Thomas Boyd, we all call him Tomby. Nice man, 'cept for his temper. Don't you never cross him."

"No, ma'am. I wouldn't think I'd have occasion to."

When they were finished in the kitchen, she led him to the Big House, an enormous log building with a vast living room and a fireplace he could have stood up in. An elk head with enormous antlers hung on the far wall. Reaching the second floor, they stood on a balcony overlooking the living room.

The cook waved an arm. "Those are all bedrooms lining the outside walls. You'll stay mighty busy. First, you put clean linens on any used beds. Then you're to vacuum and dust the whole place. See there's plenty of firewood laid in all the fireplaces."

"Where do I get the wood?" Dale asked.

"It's stacked at the side of the house. And you'll be helping me at lunch and supper. If you have any extra time, there's picture glass and windows to wash, or come to me and I'll find something for you to do. You'll be off on Sundays after lunch for the rest of the day. The supplies are all in this broom closet and the linen closet next to it here. You know how to make a hospital corner on a bed?"

"Yes, ma'am, my mother taught me."

"Smart boy! I'll be watching you, but I guess you'll do. Scoot now."

With a sinking heart, Dale attacked his duties. He wasn't going to be a cowhand. Instead, he was going to be a househand, a male waitress, a maid—duties any girl could do. Nuts! He didn't like it at all. Peering out the window, he could just make out the gurgling stream bordered with cottonwoods and pines. He could hardly wait until Sunday. His hopes for a fascinating, exciting summer had vanished. He'd have to write his mother, but he was so disappointed, he wouldn't say anything about his feelings.

He had just finished making up a four-poster bed in a large room with gold wallpaper when the cook appeared at the door. "How you doing?"

"Fine."

Going to the bed, she raised the heavy red bedspread and nodded. "Good corner. This here's the Queen's Suite. Tomby's mighty proud of these couple of rooms cause two years ago Queen Marie of Romania stayed right here. She liked this mahogany Victorian furniture and the three-way mirror on the vanity. Nice lady."

*Wow*, Dale thought. *That would be good story material.*

But he had no time to write and that evening at dinner, he was kept hopping waiting on eighteen guests including the forest ranger, the mayor of DuBois, and a Wyoming State Senator, along with their wives.

He overheard that the guests' fee for a week included room, board, and all-day horseback trips. Wistfully, he thought how nice it would be to have money.

Refilling Tomby's coffee, Dale heard him laugh and tell about a Kansas City lawyer who'd visited last summer and drank a pint of whiskey every weekday and a quart on Sundays. He then said another guest took drinks every two hours—just like medicine. Dale certainly wouldn't mention that on his next postcard.

When he finally crawled into bed each night, Dale was exhausted.

The cows were milked twice daily, and Dale helped put the milk through the cream separator. Then he poured the cream into five-gallon cans which he lugged to the cooling room.

When Mrs. Swearingen told him to pour the skim milk into the creek, he cringed. As he poured the white liquid into the clear bubbling stream, he decided not to describe that on his postcard. *How we could use that milk at home!*

Instead, he wrote about having cream for cereal and coffee, and the rich ice cream Mrs. Swearingen made. He liked the chocolate best and ate huge mounds of it, trying to fill his stomach which always felt like a bottomless well.

Breezes wafting through the sunny days carried the aroma of pine. Through the cool nights, he could hear the rushing of the nearby stream. The full moon cast a silvery light over the buildings nestled in the meadows surrounded by cathedral spires of pines.

When the last dishes were done, Dale wandered by the big house, casting an envious eye through the open door at the flaming fireplace and the dudes playing cards bathed in golden pools of light. He could hear the tinkle of ice and gales of laughter. The smell of roasting marshmallows lingered as he plodded wearily to the bunkhouse and collapsed into bed.

One morning after Dale had eaten breakfast and started to clear the table, Olly said, "Here, we'll help," and the cowboys kept stacking dirty plates in his arms until he could hardly carry the load. Dale kept saying, "That's enough." But they kept laughing and said, "Sonny, you're a big strong boy. You can carry them." Cowboys flanked him on either side and wouldn't let him put any dishes down.

While he arched his back in desperation, they shoved him and his heavy load toward the sink, and then—swish—his feet flew out from under him. Dishes sailed out of his arms. He hurtled to the floor with a resounding crash. A last piece of shattered china tinkled to the floor.

"Oh, no," Mrs. Swearingen groaned. "They probably heard that all the way to Cheyenne. You're in for it now."

He lay sprawled on the linoleum feeling dampness on his back when he heard a shout, "What the hell? Who did that? I'll have your bloody scalp! You'll pay. You'll pay for that china." Through the door barreled the boss. "What the—?"

As Dale lay there looking up, he saw Tomby's feet fly out from him, saw arms flailing. He could see daylight between the body and the floor. Then the boss came crashing down on top of him.

"Owww," Dale and Tomby cried out together. They both lay stunned, staring at each other.

"Oh, boy," the cook muttered, dishcloth in hand.

Finally, Tomby scrambled up, jaws clenched, face red. He slowly looked around at the carnage, then down at Dale. "Well!" he said. "Well, I'll be damned!" He glared at the boy and shook his head, but then he put out a hand and helped Dale up. "So, you fell down, huh?"

"Yes sir," Dale said, holding his breath. "I slipped. I didn't mean to."

Warring said, "Neither did I!" He looked down and pushed at the broken plates with his shoe, then bent and examined the floor. "Water," he said. Looking around, he noticed a big teakettle steaming on the front burner of the stove nearby. "Swearingen," he bellowed. "That steam's settled on the floor—made it mighty damn slick. See it doesn't happen again. Pick up these pieces, boy." He started to the door and then turned back, "You hurt?"

"No, sir. I'm sorry about the plates, sir. I'll pay."

"Pay? Son, you're only making thirty bucks a month."

"I'll pay, sir, when I get my first check."

"You'll get paid for your three months all together at the end of your hitch, and I'll figure out then how much you owe me." He strode out.

Dale wondered how much he'd deduct for the china. He wouldn't find out until the end of summer. Not wanting to worry his mother, he didn't write home about that episode either.

He did write about the beautiful weather and the fact that it always seemed windy. "Blows about as much as these talkative cowboys," he wrote. "Don't worry, Mom. I'm too busy to be homesick."

Nora worried aloud about Dale's working too hard and wondered if he was happy, but Clyde said experiences, good and bad, were essential to growing up.

Dale's weekly cards sometimes described the scenery, sometimes related comical character sketches of fragile dudes who could hardly walk after a day on a horse. He gave mouth-watering accounts of buffalo meat and venison and the fancy desserts served at every meal. He said he liked to hear the cowboy's tales, but didn't know if they were true. They had told him Mrs. Swearingen's husband was descended from a famous saloon keep in Deadwood. Finally came the card Jenny had been hoping for. It said, "This Sunday I get to ride a horse."

That Sunday afternoon the sun beat down and the barn smelled of manure and hay. As Dale waited in the yard, he felt an ominous foreboding at the way the cowboys were acting. He saw them winking at each other and, sure enough, the horse they brought him was a wild-eyed black named Midnight. When Dale tried to mount, the horse danced around in circles with Dale, one foot in the stirrup, clutching tight to the saddle horn. Once he swung his other leg over and was seated, the horse reared—then bucked. Dale reined him in tight and tried to show him who was boss, all the time saying, "Settle down, boy. Settle down."

Just when he thought he had the animal under control, Olly slapped Midnight and he lit out at a gallop with Dale hanging on, praying. "Whoa," Dale hollered. "Whoa!" Behind him he could hear the cowboys whooping and laughing. "Whoa," Dale kept yelling, but the horse must have thought he was yelling, "Go!"

He went.

Dale managed to stay on, and finally savored the rocking rhythm of the horse's flowing stride and the wind blowing through his hair. He felt pretty proud of himself, but by then they were over the hill and the cowboys couldn't see them, couldn't even know how later the horse followed his commands, how he turned obediently, how he docilely cropped grass when Dale dismounted to have his snack near a chuckling stream.

He rode all afternoon and by four o'clock he thought Midnight had become his pal. He stroked the big black nose, patted the dark coat, mounted and started for home.

Suddenly, the horse took off galloping full speed, pounding under a tree whose branches nearly knocked him off. Dale ducked just in time. Midnight only slowed when they were in sight of the barn. To his chagrin, Dale saw all the cowboys perched in a row on the fence, chewing on strands of hay, hats pushed back, watching the approaching horse and rider.

"Behave, Midnight, behave," Dale muttered. But when Midnight got to a post right in front of the cowboys, he passed so close the pressure hurt Dale's leg. "Stop it," he said, only to have the horse find another post. *He's trying to scrape me off,* but Dale succeeded in staying on. When he finally got the horse to the barn and dismounted, he thought he wasn't going to be able to walk. Riding Midnight on the last dash home was like getting spanked over and over.

As he hobbled off toward the bunk house, he heard the cowboys yell, "Hey, sonny, have a nice ride?"

Some things about that ride, he failed to include on the postcard home. He did write about one of the cowhands who bragged that he could pitch hay either left or right handed, insisting this enabled him to do more work than any of the other men—and with less fatigue.

The ranch never had a full roster of guests but TBW didn't seem to mind. In late summer, a Boston banker, his wife, and five teenage daughters arrived for two weeks.

Dale was very conscious of the giggling girls and soon was smitten by the redhead named Mindy. When he waited on her at the table, he bent close. She smiled at him, but didn't speak.

He couldn't stop thinking about her. On Saturday night when the hired help all piled into a big truck and rode into town, Dale went along. DuBois consisted of only five buildings. One was a big ballroom where a four-piece jazz band's music flooded out into the night. The general store and the barbershop stayed open until ten, so Dale spent a precious fifteen cents on a haircut.

On Monday, Olly, who directed the activities of the guests, had the five Boston girls hoeing weeds from the large gravel driveway for hours. Dale was astonished to hear the girls' comments as they worked. Physical labor was so unusual for them, they considered it great fun.

That night after his dishes were done, Dale hung around outside the Big House, hoping for a glimpse of Mindy. When he looked in the door, she glanced up from her cards and smiled. He quickly darted away and was throwing a few rocks around outside when he heard footsteps on the porch.

He turned. Mindy was coming toward him. She said, "Hello."

"Yeah, hi." The blood rushed to his face.

"I'm bored. Do you want to take a walk?"

"Sure. But hadn't you better tell your folks?"

"I already did."

They walked and talked and sat on some rocks by the stream. He pointed out the Big Dipper stars glittering like diamonds in the black velvet sky. On the way back, he reached out and lightly held her hand. He wished he had the nerve to kiss her, but he was afraid.

That night he had trouble sleeping. He didn't write home that he was in love.

But the two weeks of Mindy's visit passed too quickly. She gave him her address in Boston and promised to write. He couldn't believe he was so lucky. He gave her his address in Denver. As he watched their rented car pull away, he felt his heart would break. When would he ever see her again? The rest of the summer was more tolerable because he could remember the smiling freckled face and that flaming red hair.

One day the cowhands found a barrel full of several large hunks of meat swimming in brine. It was from an elk killed the previous fall. The meat smelled spoiled, but TBW ordered Mrs. Swearingen to spice it up and serve it anyway. Dale, thinking more of Mindy than food, didn't think it tasted so bad and, surprisingly, nobody got sick.

In a few weeks his stint here would be over. It had been an interesting and different summer. He did have one regret, though. He felt the cowboys were unfriendly, really didn't like him, and always made him the butt of their jokes. And they always called him "Sonny."

Dale had developed another problem—one his mother had cautioned him about. Maybe it was from being tense, or missing Mindy, or too much food, or always rushing.

The next morning, at the breakfast table, he decided he'd have to do something drastic—like taking his mother's advice. He didn't have any milk of magnesia.

Still, feeling really hungry, he gobbled three helpings of scrambled eggs, nine pieces of bacon, and seven biscuits.

Watching him, Olly said, "Sure a shame you don't have any appetite."

Dale didn't say anything—just started eating a big bowl of prunes like his mother had instructed.

Suddenly, he realized all eyes were on him. Olly and the others started yelling the numbers as he ate each prune.

"One! Two!"

Dale didn't smile. He just kept eating.

The cowhands got clear up to twelve and Olly leaned over and said, "Say, sonny, what'd you do with them prune pits? Swallow 'em?" Everybody roared with laughter.

Dale pushed the bowl to the side. He looked at Olly, let his eyes run over the rest of the cowhands' faces, even glanced over at Mrs. Swearingen. She was standing at the stove, watching.

Slowly Dale opened his mouth, reached in, pulled out a prune pit, held it up high and then dropped it onto his plate with a little "plink."

All eyes were riveted on him, and then the group, as if on cue, yelled, "One!"

With a flourish of his hand, Dale pulled out a second pit and with deliberate showmanship dropped it on the plate.

They yelled, "Two!"

One at a time, he slowly pulled each pit from his mouth and dropped it. Every time, the pit made that funny little noise when it hit the plate.

The cowboys yelled the count after each little plink. "Three!" "Four!" "Five!"

When they'd called, "Eleven!" Dale paused. The room fell silent. If a stirrup had jingled it would have sounded like a cymbal. Outside, the wind sighed in the pines and a horse neighed. Dale waited and waited.

At last, he pulled back his shoulders, shook his hands out like a magician, and, with a flourish, put his right hand into his mouth and paused. With exquisite deliberation, he pulled the final pit from between his lips, held it overhead—and then let go. The object hurtled down and landed on the plate with an emphatic "pul-link!"

Then he looked up and grinned.

"Twelve!" the cowboys all yelled together. Then somebody hollered, "My God, the kid kept all them pits in his cheeks, all twelve of 'em—think of that—in his cheeks—just like a dad-blame little squirrel!"

Suddenly a roar erupted. They all screamed and laughed and stomped their feet. Jumping up, they clapped each other on the back.

A cowhand ran to Dale and punched him on the shoulder. Another put out his hand and said, "Be honored to shake your hand. Yessiree, put 'er there." Olly pushed his way through the crowd gathered around him and astonished Dale by grabbing him in a hug. "Best entertainment we've had in weeks. Hey, you're okay, kid. You're okay."

After that morning, many asked him questions about the books he read at night. Now they'd wave at him, grin and give a thumbs-up. Dale couldn't believe it. He guessed they really did like him. Best of all, now they called him "Kid" instead of "Sonny."

His last day came. He'd grown a couple of inches, put on eight pounds, and his voice had deepened. When he lined up for his pay, Mr. Warring looked up. "Son, I'm forgetting those broken dishes. This is your full pay, plus a $40 bonus."

"Gee, thanks, sir! I've had a great summer!"

"Glad to hear it. Now, get your duds, son, and climb into the Buick. It's time to drive you home."

# 25. Dale Gets Caught

At first Jenny was thrilled when Dale returned home from the dude ranch. The whole family listened raptly as he recounted the details of his summer adventures.

But Jenny's happiness soon faded. She'd always thought Dale a great brother, and, even though they seldom discussed their poverty or Mother's illness, there had always been an unspoken bond between them. When nobody else had time for her, Dale talked about books he was reading, listened to her funny stories, or played games with her. Now everything had changed.

Dale had grown taller, tanner, thicker. But worst of all, from little hints, she realized he liked girls!

Now he spent a lot of time in his room, writing. Jenny saw letters addressed to a girl in Boston, and teased him about the returning pink, perfumed envelopes.

One day when she went in to dust his room, Jenny was startled by the appearance of a small book open on his desk. *What's this?* The handwritten black printing on the page looked very odd. Curious and puzzled, she dropped the dust cloth on the desktop and picked up the notebook, leafing through the pages. All were written in the same peculiar strokes. Baffled, she stood studying the printing that reminded her of hieroglyphics.

Just then Dale clunked into the room. When he saw her, his face turned red. "What are you doing with that book?"

"Nothing," she said, feeling guilty.

Eyes blazing, he yanked the small volume out of her hands. "You have no right to look at my journal."

"Then don't leave it open on the desk."

"Then don't come in my room."

"Then dust your own room." She picked up the dust cloth and threw it at him.

He dodged and the rag dropped to the hardwood floor at his feet. Then his face changed and became thoughtful. "Could you tell what it said?"

"No. I didn't know it was your old diary anyway. I don't read other people's diaries and don't you read mine! It's just the printing is so different, I was curious. Besides, I couldn't make out a single word, if that's what they are."

Dale's shoulders relaxed. "You couldn't read it?"

"No. What kind of writing is it? It looks like you copied Egyptian or something."

Smiling, he rubbed his hand across the small black cover. "It's code, a secret code. I made it up myself."

Jenny's mouth dropped. "Why?"

"Why do you think? So nosy little sisters can't read it."

"I bet it's about your girlfriend. Nyah, nyah. The one you write to in Boston. Is it lovey dovey poetry? Oh, sweetie, my sugarplum, I love you so much."

He scooped up the dust rag and threw it back at her. "Dust my room. You have to. It's your chore. I did mine. I've already cut the grass. Now get busy and keep your eyes off my journal. If you have to know, it's a journal like writers keep." Clutching the little black book, he stomped out of the room.

As she dusted, Jenny stomped too. *He doesn't have to be so mean about it. Him and his dumb code.*

When she was finished, Jenny went out into the back yard to play under the big weeping willow tree. She carefully cut a square out of the side of an empty round oatmeal box to make a cradle, and then headed behind the garage into the alley to gather blossoms and buds from the hollyhocks growing there to make hollyhock dolls.

When she rounded the garage, she saw three boys sitting on their heels, leaning against the garage wall, laughing and talking. Above them spiraled a blue haze.

"Dale!" she exclaimed, aghast.

Startled, he looked up.

But she had already turned and flown pell mell to the house and up the kitchen stairs. Her father was putting away groceries while her mother rested on the couch.

"Daddy, Dale's smoking! Out in the alley. I saw him. He's smoking cigarettes!"

Clyde's hand, clutching a can of creamed corn, stopped in midair. Nora struggled to sit upright. "Oh, no."

Just then Dale swaggered up the stairs and into the kitchen, whistling.

"I saw you. I saw you smoking," Jenny yelled.

"Tattletale!" Dale's words came through clenched teeth and, as he passed his sister, he jabbed her in the ribs.

"Owww. He punched me. Aren't you going to punish him? Aren't you?"

Everybody ignored her. Her father went on putting away groceries and Dale ambled into the living room, smiling with superiority, and picked up a book.

Nora wore a worried frown. "Is that true, Dale? Were you smoking?"

"Sure. I roll my own, like Dad. The cowboys showed me."

"I'm disappointed in you," Nora said.

Clyde came into the room. "And where did you get the tobacco?"

"I took a little of yours."

His father's voice wasn't even angry, "Without asking?"

"It'll stunt his growth, won't it?" Jenny cried.

Clyde tried to hide a smile. Dale was almost six feet tall. "You took my tobacco?"

Sheepishly Dale said, "I didn't think you'd want to give me any. Gee, Dad, I didn't take much. I figured you'd never miss it. Hey, I like having a smoke—just like you, Dad."

Sternly Nora said, "Your father is an adult. You're sixteen. I suppose you've been smoking all summer long."

"Not all summer, Mom, just a few days before I came home."

She shook her head. "Smoking is out of the question. It's not good for you and you can't afford it. We will have to—"

"Now, Mother, I'll take care of it."

Dancing around, Jenny said, "He's going to get punished, isn't he?"

With a stern look, Clyde cut her off. "That's enough, Jenny. I'll take care of it."

"He deserves something really bad. Besides, he hit me."

"Jenny, go out to play. Now!"

When her father's voice got that edge, Jenny obeyed. She went out into the back yard muttering, "It isn't fair. Dale gets to do everything."

The next morning as they sat around the breakfast table, Clyde put down his spoon and looked at his son. "Dale, your mother and I have discussed your taking up the weed, and we have a few conditions. One, you'll have to buy your own tobacco and wrapping papers, so you'd better look into some sort of employment to support your smoking. Of course, the money you made this summer goes into a fund for college. Two, you can't smoke inside the house because of your mother's condition, and three, if you insist on taking up this habit, you must not do it secretly.

"Never do anything that you wouldn't do in front of your parents, or God. Therefore you're to smoke out in the yard where we can see you. I don't like deception. A person of character doesn't sneak around."

"Daddy, if Dale can smoke, why can't I?"

Nora sighed. "Jenny, only fast girls smoke. Now you just forget it."

"Gee whiz. Aren't you going to do anything to Dale for stealing Daddy's tobacco and smoking?"

"Jenny!" Now Mother's voice had that dreaded sharpness. "Your father said he would take care of it."

Clyde pushed his chair away from the table. "All finished, son? That ranch sure gave you a big appetite. Finish up the pitcher of orange juice. It's good for you."

Dale gulped the rest of the juice. When Clyde rose from the table, Dale got up too.

Taking the boy by the arm, Clyde said, "Smoking is rather coming of age, Dale, so you might as well do what men do. I've decided to give you a real treat. We're going outside to have something special together—a cigar."

Beaming, Dale said, "A cigar! Wow!" He swaggered triumphantly as the two went out the front door.

Jenny bristled. "Mo-ther!"

"It's all right, Jenny. It's none of your affair. You get busy and clean up the dishes. Take mine, too, I'm finished."

Grumbling under her breath, Jenny took the dishes and carried them to the kitchen, then cleared the table. At the sink she banged pans and silverware to display her pique. After putting her mother's dishes and silver in a big pot of water to be sterilized, and rinsing the other dishes, she went back to wipe the dining room table.

The front door banged. She glanced up to see Dale rush in. Holding his hand over his mouth, he zoomed past her and raced down the hall toward the bathroom.

Staring after him, Jenny said, "Oh!" She'd read of such a color in books. Dale's face was absolutely green. Then she heard him in the bathroom, losing his breakfast.

Jenny made a face.

Her mother looked pained.

The screen door squeaked open and banged shut. Her father came in and strolled into the sunny living room. No one commented. They all just listened to the sounds down the hall.

Clyde looked at Jenny's horrified face. "That was the punishment, Jenny. Most effective thing I could have done."

"But, you did it on purpose!"

"Jenny, Shakespeare once wrote, 'I must be cruel, only to be kind.' I'm praying that cigar will keep Dale from ever smoking again." He smiled at Nora. "I told you I'd take care of it."

# 26. What Did Grandma Bring?

In early September, Grandma arrived by train for a month's visit. She had ridden sitting up in the coach all the way from Indianapolis. "Now I think that's pretty good for a seventy-two year old," she said, eyes twinkling.

In the past two years, Jenny had grown taller than her five-foot grandmother. Nor would a stranger ever guess they were related. Jenny had blue eyes, white skin and blonde hair. Grandma had dark brown eyes, olive skin and, beneath the gray, chestnut hair.

As soon as she and Clyde came in from the train depot, Grandma went to the couch and took Nora's hand. "My dear, how are you feeling today?"

"About the same. Oh, Mama, I'm so glad to see you. Are you all right?"

"Yes, I am. No amount of grief will bring Silas back, and I've cried enough. We have to live for the living." She sank down in the big chair. "Come here, children." She set down a flowered carpet bag. "I've brought presents. Dale, this book is for you."

When he unwrapped it, he exclaimed, "*White Fang!* Oh, thanks, Grandma. I like Jack London's books and I haven't read this one yet."

"Jenny, this one is for you. You remind me of the little girl in this book."

Opening the gift paper, Jenny saw a green book with gold lettering. "Oh, *Pollyanna.*"

"You haven't read it have you?"

"No, Grandma. Thank you so much."

Grandma took out another book which was unwrapped. "This is for both of you. *Knock the T out of Can't.* It suggests you keep trying when things seem impossible. Here, Dale, you can read it first."

With a smile, Nora said, "Mama, how nice of you."

"Well, dear, I didn't forget you. You've written sometimes that you'd like to do something outstanding, something of real consequence." She handed Nora a package. "This contains crochet hooks, a pattern for a bedspread, and the thread."

"Mama, wasn't all that thread awfully expensive?"

"No. It's ordinary, everyday string. Bedspreads from string are all the fashion now, with The Depression, you know."

Nora opened the crackling paper and looked up, all smiles. "The string's a pretty color, sort of ivory. The pattern picture shows a beautiful design. This will certainly keep me occupied. How nice."

Clyde came back into the room from carrying the suitcases down the hall.

"I didn't forget you, Clyde. Here's a present for you."

He received three pairs of socks. "Thanks, Mama, I really needed these. Say, I'm sorry you'll have to sleep in the big double bed with Jenny."

"I don't mind," cried Jenny.

"I don't mind, either," Grandma said.

That night, when they went to bed, Grandma told her, "If I snore, wake me up."

Grandma did snore—a great rumbling sound. Jenny hesitated, but finally she shook her grandmother's arm. "Grandma, you're snoring."

"Oh, I'm sorry," Grandma turned over and Jenny pulled up the covers, but in a few minutes, Grandma was snoring like a motorboat.

Shaking her, Jenny called, "Grandma, you said to wake you up."

Grandma raised up. "What's the matter? Am I snoring?"

"Yes, ma'am."

"I'm sorry. Just wake me up" She turned over.

Jenny stretched out and pulled the sheet under her chin. In no time at all, Grandma was snoring like a train engine. Heaving a big sigh, Jenny knew it would be useless to wake her again. *I don't care. I love having Grandma here.*

Later on, the family went on a mountain picnic with Harry, Rose, and their little girl Jody. Harry brought Heinz baked beans, ketchup and pickles. Rose brought a big tin of oatmeal cookies and another of brownies. Daddy proudly made a fire under the grill at the camp spot and soon hamburgers were sizzling. Jenny dished up the potato salad she'd made at home. What a feast they had beside the roaring mountain stream!

Harry and Clyde were full of funny stories and, after everyone ate, the giggling began when they swiped each other's hats. Harry wore Grandma's, Clyde wore Jenny's. Dale took Nora's and then everyone switched.

The shadows grew longer. The aspens' silvery green leaves rustled and shimmered in the wind. Overhead stretched tall pine trees which scented the air. Jenny and Jody looked for pretty rocks, while Dale fed a chipmunk bread crumbs.

Jenny sat down on the blanket and asked Grandma to tell stories about her family. After thinking a minute, Grandma said, "Well, when I went to school, my brother Clarence, was in the same class and the teacher said, 'Oh, are you twins?' and we said, 'No, we're brother and sister.' And she asked, 'How old are you?' And I said, 'I'm eight.' And Clarence said, 'I'm eight too.' The teacher said, 'Now that can't be.' I said, 'It can, too. We're six months apart.'"

Jenny was confused. "But it takes nine months to make a baby."

Grandma nodded. "Our teacher was really mixed up, too, so we had to explain."

Jenny leaned forward, mystified.

Grandma Baldwin chuckled. "My father and his brother married sisters. They both had several children and then they both went off to fight in the Civil War. While they were gone my mother died, and Father's brother was killed in the war. Papa came home to find he was a widower, and his sister-in-law a widow. Before long, Papa married his brother's wife. So my aunt became my step-mother and together the new couple had eleven children. We were all cousins, and then we also became stepbrothers and sisters. People really got confused, especially our teachers."

"That's a funny story," Jenny said.

"I'll tell you another one. One day when I was eighteen years old, my mother told me to finish the Sunday dishes promptly, because Ally was going to come over and play the piano with me. So, I hurried with all my chores. I hadn't remembered meeting Ally at church where I played the organ, and wondered if she was a new girl in town.

"I finished up in the kitchen and hung up my apron. Just then I heard the doorbell ring and I went into the parlor, but there was no girl waiting there. Instead, I saw a tall, handsome young man my age.

"Mama said, 'Ella, this is Ally Baldwin.' I shook his hand. 'I thought you were a girl.'

"I thought he'd be mad, but he only laughed and said his name was Albert but everybody called him Ally, and he was sorry if I was disappointed, that our parents thought that we should play the piano together and maybe later perform at church."

"And then what happened?"

Grandma smiled in remembrance. "We played the piano together a lot, and we did perform at church, and three years later, we got married. That was your Grandpa. It's too bad he died when you were only a year old, Jenny. I still miss him."

"I wish I'd known him, Grandma. Look at the pretty rocks Jody and I collected. I like the ones with the sparkles. Is that gold?"

Grandma took the stones and examined them closely. She shook her head. "No dear, I don't think it's gold. It's something else." She handed back the rocks.

"I don't care that it's not gold, Grandma. I'm thankful anyway, for everything. I love the *Pollyanna* book. I'll always try to play the Glad Game."

"I thought you'd like it. The wind is getting chilly. Nora, are you warm enough?"

From her cot, Nora called, "Yes, Mama. Jenny, you children better gather up plenty of wood for our fireplace. There'll be snow this winter."

After Grandma went back to Indianapolis, Jenny convinced her neighborhood playmates to put on a show in her friend Hilda's basement. Hilda and Irene danced, Walt played his drums, George did magic tricks and Jenny sang "Let Me Call You Sweetheart." Parents said they were good, and Jenny delighted in being on stage again. Maybe someday....

# 27. What Happened at Midnight in the Cemetery?

Fall in Colorado was beautiful. In the mountains, the aspen and pine blazed gold and emerald against a sapphire sky. In the Pate's yard, squirrels whisked up and down the trees, and bronze leaves whirled down and curled up on the ground as if trying to stay warm against the coming chill of winter.

After school, Jenny raked the rustling leaves into elaborate houses and dreamed about Halloween. Now she was in seventh grade and attending Smiley Junior High School just a half block north of home.

As she walked to school on windy days, tumbleweeds blew in from the prairie and piled up against the steel fence that rimmed the school yard. Jenny liked to stand on that corner and look eastward. She could see miles of sky stretching far away. On the horizon beyond a slight rise, lay the airport. Sometimes planes roared overhead using the street at the end of the block to guide them in a straight line toward their runway. She'd look up at the thundering silver birds overhead and wish she could be up there, being a pilot or a stewardess. She longed to leave home, to experience excitement and glamour—to be somebody!

Dale attended East High School. He rode his bike there every day and Jenny wished she could have a bike. She wondered if her solemn, silent brother didn't yearn for excitement too. He probably found it in the fictional world. Daddy caught him reading forbidden pulp mysteries and

Westerns. At school he liked English class best because sometimes the assignments were to write stories.

Jenny skipped down the street. Halloween was coming. She could hardly wait. The handouts of candy, cookies, or candied apples provided rare treats.

She would have liked a pretty princess costume, but knew the family couldn't afford it. Sewing was too exhausting for her mother and material too expensive. Jenny settled for rigging herself up like a gypsy with a scarf tied over her head. She made necklaces of popcorn, and rolled up paper into ornaments and strung them on long threads. Then she selected the largest paper sack she could find to hold her booty.

"I'm meeting Hilda and Irene," she told Dale. Her friends lived down on the corner. "You can't go Dale," she taunted, "because you're too old."

"Who said I wanted to? Besides I have my own plans for tonight."

"Come to dinner," Clyde called. "You can't go trick or treating until six, Jenny."

The family gathered around the dinner table. Clyde passed the boiled potatoes to Dale. "Why don't you go with the girls, just to make sure they're safe?"

"Daddy," Jenny cried, "don't let him tag along."

"I can't," Dale said. "I have homework. Plus, Mrs. Lopez wants us to do research and write a story, so I've decided to go out to Fairmont Cemetery tonight."

Clyde looked up from his salad, "The cemetery? How are you going to get there? Jenny will be gone, and I don't want to leave Mother alone to drive you over there. Kids will ring the doorbell constantly, and she can't be jumping up to answer the bell."

"I'm riding my bike."

"But, Dale," Nora said, "It must be five miles!"

"I ride four miles to school every day."

"But," she protested, "not at night. Motorists can't see you in the dark."

"I'll leave here about eleven-thirty. Won't be much traffic then. I want to wander around the graveyard right at midnight to get atmosphere for a ghost story."

"I don't want you to go."

Clyde looked up. "Jenny'll be home by then, son. I'll take you."

"No, Dad, bicycling there will be part of the adventure. I can take care of myself."

His mother frowned. "I'm against it, Dale"

"Now, Nora, on second thought," Clyde put in, "Dale's getting to be a young man, and men have to go out into the world, have to test themselves. He'll be all right."

"Gee, Mom, I just want some background for my story. Writers have to do unusual things. Look at Richard Halliburton. I bet his mother didn't tell him he couldn't go."

"Nora, I'll wait up to make sure he gets home safe."

Reluctantly, Nora finally agreed.

Jenny finished her chocolate cake with mixed feelings. She thought the escapade was a dumb idea. Still, she admired Dale for his courage—to go to the cemetery on Halloween at midnight! But then she reconsidered. "Do you expect to see a ghost, Dale?" She turned. "Do you believe in ghosts, Mom?"

"Of course not."

"Do you, Daddy?"

"There are no such things."

"Do you think you'll see some, Dale?" Jenny probed. "Are you going to talk to the ghosts tonight?"

"I don't know. I guess I'll find out, won't I?"

When supper was over, Dale disappeared and Jenny went to put on her costume. When she reappeared she asked, "How do I look?"

"Fine," Nora said.

As Jenny picked up her paper sack, the doorbell rang. Her friends had arrived. The three girls compared costumes and twirled in front of Mr. and Mrs. Pate. Giggling in excitement, they gathered their bags and waved goodbye.

"Be careful," Nora called.

When the girls reached the bottom of the porch steps, a wavering white apparition jumped out from the bushes calling "Whoo-ooo-oo." Shrieking, the trio ran back up onto the porch.

Pulling off the sheet, Dale laughed. "Scaredy cats!"

"We are not! You're mean. I hope a ghost gets you!" Jenny yelled as she and her friends started off again.

"Silly, there aren't any such things as ghosts." Dale trotted alongside them.

"Then why are you going to the cemetery?"

"I told you. I have to write a story. See you later."

Dale went back into the house, where he studied a while and then prepared a notepad and two pencils for his escapade.

All evening Clyde answered the doorbell, and handed out penny suckers which were all the family could afford. A little after nine, the kids stopped coming.

Soon, Jenny came home and happily dumped her loot on the dining room table and cheerfully shared her treats.

From the couch, Nora asked Dale, "You're still going to do this crazy thing?"

"Yeah, Mom, stop worrying."

Rising and walking slowly toward the bedroom, Nora said over her shoulder, "I'm going to bed. Jenny, it's time for you to go too." She turned back. "Be careful, Dale. Cars won't be able to see you at night."

"Then neither will the ghosts." Dale laughed.

After sweeping her candy back into the paper bag, Jenny went to Dale. Reaching into the sack, she extracted three candy bars. "Take these along, Dale, in case you get hungry." She brightened. "Or maybe you can bribe a ghost."

"Boy, are you silly." But Dale took the candy and watched his sister walk down the hall. Jenny had her good points. He turned to see his father had spread a city map out on the table.

Clyde said, "Let's map out your route to the cemetery. Don't deviate from well-traveled, well-lighted streets, and stay away from bushes and dark spots."

"Okay." Dale bent over the map.

Tracing a line with a finger, Dale said, "I'll go down Holly, turn left on Montview, up to Quebec and then right on Quebec."

His father nodded "Good. How will you get into the cemetery?"

"Climb the fence."

"Well, just see you don't disturb anything or leave any trash."

"I won't."

"How long are you going to stay?"

Shoving his thick glasses back up on his nose, Dale shrugged. "Long enough."

Clyde folded up the map. "Do you need this?"

"No. We've driven past the place lots of times."

Clyde walked to the window and looked out. "It's getting cloudy and I hear the wind moaning. Might even storm. Let's see—with time for you to get there and back, and a half hour or so inside—let's see, if you're not home by one-thirty, I'll come looking for you. Don't deviate from our route. Turn on your headlight so cars can see you."

"Don't worry. Say, you did crazy things when you were young—like stopping a train with a torpedo on the track, and leaving a cow on the college steps."

"I shouldn't have been so wild, and I got whipped for it."

"Is that why you and Mom never spanked us?"

"I don't believe in corporal punishment. At the Y we had training in psychology."

Finally, Dale noticed the clock, jumped up and pulled on his jacket. "Time to go." He opened the front door, looked out into the black, blustery night and hesitated.

"Sure is dark," Clyde said.

"Maybe the moon will come out again."

"Might storm."

"Yeah, it might." Dale made no move to leave.

"You know, you don't have to go, son. You could stay home."

"I know." He lingered, then he buttoned his jacket, grinned at his father, ran down the steps, and got on his bike.

Clyde changed into his pajamas and sat in his big chair reading. Once he dozed off and roused, shook his head, went to the kitchen for a glass of milk and a handful of oatmeal cookies. He checked the clock again and sank back into his chair.

Shortly after midnight he wondered where Dale was at that moment. By this time he should have clambered over the spiked top of the wrought iron fence and dropped down inside. Clyde shivered, picturing the boy wandering among the tombstones. *Maybe he hears voices whispering in the wind. Maybe he's shuddering in fear at shadows moving across the dying grass.* Perhaps because it was Halloween, Clyde's imagination ran wild. *Maybe someone saw the lone cyclist pass under the pools of street lights and pedal off into blackness—and kidnapped the boy. Or maybe he's been hit by a car and is lying in some ditch helpless and bloody. I shouldn't have let him go!*

He straightened. *Were those thoughts, or was I half asleep and dreaming? Not let him go? No, he's almost a man. I've been sheltering him too much. A father has to let his boy experience life, has to let him grow up. In just a few years he'll be out on his own.*

The mantel clock read twelve forty-five. Clyde walked to the window and looked out. *It's black out there.* He paced the floor, sank into his easy chair again, and opened the paper.

Suddenly the front door burst open and Dale dashed into the room, panting.

"You're back!" Clyde jumped up and threw his arms around his son, surprised to feel him shaking through his jacket. "Dale, are you all right? Did you get there?"

"Yeah." He half-stifled a moan.

"Did you get over the fence okay?"

Dale gulped and nodded.

Clyde stood back, holding the boy at arm's length. Chills prickled up Clyde's spine. Dale's face was pasty white, his eyes wild.

"What happened, son?"

Dale let out a frightened cry and kept shivering. Finally, eyes wide, he whispered, "It was terrible—terrible. I'll never do that again."

"It's all right now. It's all right." Clyde took his big boy in his arms and held him if he were a small child. "It's okay. You're home safe." At last he said, "It's bedtime, son."

When Dale peered fearfully down the long dark hallway, Clyde said, "Come on, I'll go with you."

He didn't make Dale brush his teeth or wash his face, just helped him into his pajamas and tucked him into bed. "Get a good sleep. Everything's all right."

A cold hand gripped Clyde's. "Dad," came the whisper, "Dad, there are ghosts. I saw them."

"Now, Dale."

"Don't tell me there aren't any. I saw them, I tell you, and heard them too."

"Okay, son. We'll talk about it in the morning."

But Dale wouldn't talk about it. Jenny pestered but never got a word out of him.

The English assignment to do research wasn't ignored. Dale looked up the history of ice cream in the library encyclopedia and then interviewed the owner of the Colonial Dairy. The story earned him an A.

A week later in the hall at East, Peevey Clark from his English class stopped him. Sidling up to Dale he said, "I never would have thought it. Man, you were great at the cemetery."

"The cemetery?" Dale managed to hide his surprise.

"Yeah. Was it ever black that night! Remember what happened just after midnight?"

"Sure." Dale waited, puzzled.

"Joey and Olaf and I overheard you tell Mrs. Lopez you were going to Fairmont Cemetery to do research for a story."

Cautiously Dale replied, "Yeah?"

"So we got sheets and Olaf's mom's long gauzy scarves and hid behind some gravestones. When we saw you, we waved our material and wailed and moaned, and carried on. I got to hand it to you, buddy. You just stood there and watched. Shucks, you knew it was us, didn't you? We figured that, when you turned around and walked away as calm as could be. Then you disappeared. Where'd you go?"

"Home. I was finished. I'd been there a while before I saw you," Dale lied, trying to look nonchalant. "I just climbed the fence and left."

"We were sure let down that you weren't scared. We thought you'd go off screaming like a banshee. Darn! Our whole shenanigan turned out to be a big bust. Say, did you ever turn in your cemetery story to Lopez?"

Dale shrugged. "Nope. Never wrote anything 'cause nothing happened. Besides, everybody knows—there are no such things as ghosts."

# 28. A Box Full of Sunshine

Jenny liked attending both school and church, but she always felt embarrassed when people inevitably discovered her mother had TB. Occasionally a teacher, or women from the church, would pay a duty call on her mother, but seldom returned.

More and more, Jenny felt confused about where she stood with people. If they weren't friendly, she didn't know if they disliked her, or were just afraid of her. If they were friendly, she wondered if they were just sorry for her. It left her wary and distrustful.

She never told anyone how she felt. Her poor parents had enough troubles. Jenny just wished she could be like everybody else. She still longed to be somebody special.

Dale, on the other hand, tried as hard as he could to be unusual and different. He didn't have many friends either, and liked books better than people. Daddy was everybody's friend. He often said, "People are wonderful!" Jenny wasn't sure, waiting for life to prove it to her.

One spring morning when she went to get the paper off the porch she nearly stumbled over a large cardboard box wrapped in bright yellow crepe paper. Kneeling, she read the tag: *"For Nora Pate. Here is a box full of sunshine. Please open only one gift each day. We care. Your secret friends."*

Struggling with the oversized carton, Jenny carried it to her mother and maneuvered it onto the bed. "Look! Somebody left this on the porch. It's for you."

As Nora read the card, her eyes filled with tears. "How thoughtful! But how can I ever thank them?"

Clyde came in with Nora's breakfast tray of cold cereal and toast, and set it on her hospital table. Seeing the carton, he exclaimed, "What on earth is that?"

"Presents for Mother," Jenny said.

"Where did it come from?"

"I don't know." Jenny shrugged. "It was on the porch."

Nora said, "The card says, 'Your secret friends.' I wonder who they could be."

"A mystery." Jenny did a little dance. "But why didn't they tell us who they are?"

"I don't know." Clyde frowned. "Maybe it's like the Bible verse says, Don't do your good works for the whole world to see."

Unable to wait, Jenny cried, "Open it, Mother. Here, I'll help."

Nora's frail hands and Jenny's strong ones worked at the yellow ribbon and crepe paper. "Be careful, Jenny. Look, we can lift the flaps and not destroy the pretty paper covering the whole outside."

Leaning closer, Jenny peered into the box and gasped. "Look at all the presents!"

Nora took out all the packages, each wrapped in yellow crepe paper, and laid them on the bed beside her. "They're all different shapes and sizes."

Jenny counted, "Fourteen packages," she exclaimed. "Goody! Two weeks of sunshine!"

"How kind! I can't believe it." Nora smiled. "It's not getting gifts, Jenny, that makes me feel so good, it's that somebody thought to brighten my life. Now, I'll put them back inside the box."

After she'd replaced them all in the big Sunshine Box, Clyde squeezed her hand. "Why don't you open one now?"

"Do you want to choose which one, Jenny?"

The youngster reached inside and then snatched her hand away. "No, Mom, you do it. It's your box."

Dale clomped into the room. "What's happening?"

"Somebody gave Mother a Sunshine Box." Jenny's eyes glowed in excitement. "Open a present, Mom."

The family huddled around the bed as Nora selected a small square gift and tore open the wrapping. A gasp of pleasure escaped her. "Look, it's note papers decorated with beautiful pen-and-ink drawings of the mountains. The artist is Lyman Byxbe. Let's see, on the back it says he's famous for his etchings and lives in Estes Park. My, there are six different scenes—two of each. How lovely!" She handed them to her husband.

"These are beautiful," Clyde said, and passed them on.

"Instead of using them, I'm tempted to hang them on the walls, or keep a set to look at. I've always wished for a mountain view from my room. These would be almost as good."

Peering into the box, Jenny said, "I wonder what else there is."

Nora shook her head. "You saw the card, Jenny. We're to open only one each day." Then she sighed. "Those secret friends are awfully nice." Wistfully, she added. "I wish I could do something nice for somebody like they have. When I get well, I will!"

"I'll set your Sunshine Box on the dresser so you can see it all day long."

"Yes, that's good, Clyde."

"I can hardly wait until tomorrow," Jenny said.

"It's something mighty pleasant to look forward to," replied Nora.

Reading the card, Dale commented, "It could be from Mrs. Wheatley and her friends."

Clyde thought a minute. "Or maybe the neighbors."

"There were those two nice ladies from the Methodist church who called on me last summer. Maybe it's from the church."

"Or from school," Dale suggested, "the PTA, or teachers, or even from people down at your office, Dad."

"Whoever it is, they're nice!" crowed Jenny.

"Okay, kids," Clyde admonished. "Excitement's over for today. You need to get ready for school. It looks like we'll have to allow extra time each morning for the Sunshine Box."

Every morning, the family gathered about her bed and Nora opened one package, finding small, thoughtful presents: hand lotion, bath powder, a fancy bookmark, a bag of gumdrops, an embroidered pillowcase, knitted slippers, an address book, a roll of stamps, a slim book of inspirational poetry, a lace-edged guest towel, two tiny glass dishes for jam or butter for her tray.

The family never did find out who those secret friends were who had brought Nora sunshine every day—a break in her routine, a bit of excitement, and pleasant, useful surprises.

After the last gift was opened, Nora said, "Jenny, close the lid and we'll have Daddy put it away tonight. The box might come in handy for something."

The next morning, the box was on the dining room table. Clyde said, "How did that get here? I put it in the basement last night."

"Maybe we didn't get everything," Jenny said.

With a shake of his head, Clyde said, "But Mother opened all the presents."

"You better look inside," Jenny insisted, and Clyde noticed her eyes sparkled.

Clyde set the box on the bedside table. "You better check inside, Nora."

Startled, Nora leaned over and opened the flaps. "For heaven sakes! Here are more packages. This box is magic!"

Nora made a great fuss over opening the first package, three pencils that looked slightly used. The following day the next package yielded a label-less soup can bearing a tiny plant. Nora's smiled. "Somebody else is making sunshine and being nice. Why, there are four more gifts inside. Come here, Jenny." She squeezed her daughter's hand.

"I wonder where they came from—the extra presents." Jenny said. "I wonder who left them."

Nodding, Clyde winked at Nora, "Yes, I wonder who."

Finally, all the little presents were gone, and as Clyde carried out the empty Sunshine Box, he said, "People sure are wonderful—just wonderful!"

Very shortly, the family would ruefully remember those words.

# 29. The Family in Peril

One day Jenny noticed that the pink letters from Boston had stopped, and Dale no longer inquired eagerly if he had any mail.

*Poor Dale*, Jenny thought, *the girl dumped him, and he must have a broken heart.*

On Saturday morning as they did the dishes together, Jenny was consumed with curiosity. "I haven't seen a letter from your girl lately."

"Nope." He ran the tea towel around a cup. "I stopped writing her."

"I thought you liked her."

"I did, till I got to know her." He finished drying a bowl and put it in the cupboard. "Hurry up with your washing, I'm all caught up."

She applied herself to the dishpan. "What happened?"

"Sometimes you can't tell about people. She didn't drop me—I dropped her."

"But I thought you loved her."

"Nope."

"Did she say something wrong?"

"Boy, you're nosy." He sighed. "Yeah, she said something. In one letter she described holding her sister's baby and, at the same time, drinking wine. She and her family like alcohol too much. They're not my kind of people!"

Since it was a warm, sunny day, when they finished the dishes, the children went to help Nora into the yard. She delighted in being outdoors and escaping the imprisonment of the house.

As they helped their mother, they were unaware that three houses down on the opposite side of the street at the Webb's, a lace curtain stirred.

Mrs. Webb, a lean woman with a grim face, stood at the window peeping out. Her dark eyes narrowed. "Look! It's like an African safari. First comes the mister and sets up an army cot in the side yard. Then the boy, loaded down with pillows and an afghan. After that comes the girl, carrying a tray with a jug and a glass." She paused. "Water, I suppose."

She turned to her husband. "Or do you think it's something stronger?" Again she peered out. "Yeah, I wonder. Lookee! Now here she comes, the lady of the house, queen of the roost. Lazy, good for nothing! Lies on that cot all day long reading her books. Disgraceful, that's what it is."

Pushing in beside his wife, Mr. Webb watched the procession. "I don't know. I forgot to tell you, but I heard talk down at the drugstore that the mother—she's sick."

"Hah! Look at her. Don't look sick to me."

"They say she's got TB."

"Consumption?" She snorted. "I don't believe it. Look at those rosy cheeks."

Peering intently, Mr. Webb said, "That could be rouge. Rest of her skin looks kind of pale to me."

Mrs. Webb pushed in, squinting down the street. "People with TB are skinny and that lady's not skinny. She's plump! If you ask me, she's faking it."

He frowned. "I s'pose she could be, but why would anybody want to?"

"To not work. To lie around and have everybody wait on 'em hand and foot all day, that's why." She shook her head. "If you ask me, she's just plain lazy."

He frowned. "But what if she really does have TB?"

Straightening to her full height, Mrs. Webb said, "Then we have to do something about it. It's catching!"

The following Wednesday evening, Nora lay on the couch surrounded by cookbooks, while Jenny and Dale sat at the dining room table doing homework. Clyde, wearing an apron, was cleaning the sink when the doorbell rang.

"I'll get it." Clyde untied his apron, threw it on a kitchen chair, and hurried to the door. When he opened it, he saw two women.

"Mr. Pate?" the tall, skinny one asked.

"Yes." Thinking they were from the church, Clyde, in his hearty, friendly way said, "Come in, come on in."

The strangers stepped into the house.

"Have a seat," Clyde smiled. "We don't have many visitors. It's nice of you to stop by." He gestured toward the sofa. "This is Mrs. Pate."

Nora nodded, sat up a little, and tried to fluff out her hair, mashed down from the pillows on which she reclined.

Pointing to the dining room table, Clyde said, "And that's Jenny and Dale."

The children smiled and nodded.

Clyde went on, "Are you the regular church callers? Jenny enjoys Sunday school, but Dale was gone all summer. That's why he wasn't there. I don't attend church very often because I hate to leave Nora by herself." He sank down into his lounge chair.

The dark-haired visitor shifted nervously, "I'm afraid we're not from the church."

The short one said, "We're from downtown. That's Miss Jones and I'm Mrs. Hill. We're from the County."

Staring at them, Clyde said, "The County?"

They both nodded.

Then Clyde noticed that Mrs. Hill carried a briefcase. His countenance darkened. "Look, we don't need any charity. We're getting along just fine. I don't understand why you would come here. I would never take charity. I would never take taxpayer money!"

Miss Jones looked tense, and Mrs. Hill looked uncomfortable, but she opened her briefcase and took out a folder. "We're not here to offer you money, Mr. Pate."

"Then, why are you here?"

Mrs. Hill looked down, opened her file and pulled out a piece of paper. "You see, we've had a complaint."

"What do you mean? What kind of complaint? What's this all about?"

Looking anxious, Nora said, "Now, Clyde—"

Jumping in, Miss Jones said firmly, "There is a disease in this house—a contagious disease."

Nodding vigorously, Mrs. Hill added, "Your wife has tuberculosis, Mr. Pate."

Silence dropped over the room.

"You think we don't know that?" Ice dripped from Clyde's words.

The two women glanced at each other. The clock ticked loudly. Jenny and Dale raised their heads, pencils suspended in midair. Nora looked frightened.

With a rattle of her papers, Mrs. Hill said, "We're social workers and we don't like doing this any better than you like it, Mr. Pate."

"Doing what? Get to the point."

"We have to think of what's best for the entire family and every person in it. That's the County's responsibility, you understand."

Straightening, Miss Jones spoke firmly, "A sick person can't properly maintain a home, and you have two children, children who are being exposed to a terrible contagious disease."

Closing her folder, Mrs. Hill chimed in, "The County thinks they should not be in this home at all. They should immediately be placed in foster care."

Brilliant red swept over Clyde's face, while Nora's turned even whiter.

Hurriedly, the social worker continued, "We would try to place them together, but we can't always guarantee that."

Dale rocketed to his feet, ran in front of Jenny and threw out his arms protectively. "We're not going any place. You can't make us. We won't go!"

"Daddy!" Jenny screamed.

Nora bolted upright, eyes wide. "No, no, no!"

Jumping to his feet and advancing on the women, Clyde yelled, "Get out of my house!"

The two women cowered, but the tall one said, "Now, now. Maybe we won't have to do that. There is another case plan that could be implemented, but it should take place as soon as possible."

White-faced, Mrs. Hill added, "The—the other solution would be to place your wife in a sanitarium. Put her in a hospital where she belongs."

With a shriek, Nora buried her face in her hands.

Horror filled the room. No one moved. No one spoke. Everything seemed in slow motion. Nora's body visibly shrank. The social workers stared at the family, eyes wide. Dale pivoted and reached for Jenny's hand.

Clyde leaned toward the workers, his head lowered like a bull ready to charge. "What do you think we are? Stupid? Irresponsible? You think we don't know anything?" He shook a fist in Mrs. Hill's face. "We're all under a doctor's care. Why haven't you done your homework? If you had, you wouldn't even be here."

The social workers' faces turned grim. Both started to speak, but Clyde cut them off. "How dare you suggest we don't love our children!" Clyde fumed. "In college, my wife studied to be a dietician. She knows all about germs. In St. Louis, my best friend was a doctor. I almost went into medicine myself."

"But TB is contagious!" Miss Jones cried, tightly clutching her purse.

Clyde stormed on. "We take precautions. We boil my wife's dishes, burn the tissues she coughs into. She doesn't kiss or hug the kids. Dr. Milstein x-rays the children and me every six months."

"But—but—the County—"

"Check with Dr. Milstein. Now get out of this house and don't you ever come back. Get out!" He loomed over them. "Get out!"

The two women snatched up their possessions and scurried out. Clyde followed, slammed the door behind them, then stood staring at the spot, shaking with anger.

Huddled on the couch, Nora looked up and said pitifully, "Don't let them put me in the hospital, Clyde. I don't want to leave you and the children and my home. I've heard what State hospitals are like. I'd rather die."

He patted her shoulder. "Don't you worry. I'll see Dr. Milstein tomorrow and he'll straighten this out. Nobody's going anywhere. Damn County! Damn whoever complained about something they know nothing about. Damn everything!"

In the weeks that followed, uneasiness descended on the little house on Holly Street.

After school, Jenny rushed home, afraid they might have taken her mother away. At night, Dale hovered near Jenny's door before he went to bed asking, "You okay?"

She always said yes, even though she wasn't. She felt frightened all the time and believed Dale was too.

Clyde warned the children not to open the door to any stranger, and sometimes he put down his newspaper and sat in his easy chair staring straight ahead, lost in thought.

But it was Nora who took it hardest of all. She became limp, as if some leech had sucked out all her lifeblood.

Now the family began to catch her doing more and more around the house. Jenny found she'd scrubbed the kitchen sink and was wiping the stove. Dale discovered her dust-mopping the hall. Clyde saw her dusting their bedroom. They all scolded her, pleading with her to not overdo.

They suspected that when no one was home, she ignored their reprimands and valiantly tried to assume more household responsibilities.

The rumbling in her chest became louder, her coughing spells longer. Black circles developed under her eyes and she became quieter. She commented that the library books seemed so heavy. All her smiles and sparkle evaporated.

Finally, she again had to take her meals in bed.

One night Jenny awakened to a terrible sense that something was wrong. Hearing noises, she rushed to her mother's bedroom. Her father was leaning over the bed, and her mother, propped upright against the pillows, was having a terrible coughing spell. When she took the tissue from her mouth, Jenny saw with horror that it was speckled red with blood.

"Jenny, go back to bed," her father ordered. "There's nothing you can do here."

She obeyed, and lying there in terror, she heard her father on the telephone talking to the doctor. He never called the doctor in the middle of the night. She heard him say, "She's hemorrhaging."

After that, the doctor's house calls began again and Jenny heard her father tell him he was sorry about the big unpaid bill, that business had been bad. He said maybe he could borrow against his renewals.

The new cough medicines were expensive. Dale and Jenny hunted up Mother's old menus and planned many meatless meals themselves. The family carried bed trays and bedpans, and for weeks Nora never left her bed.

At last she began to improve and, by Christmas, her sputum became negative at last. "I was determined to get better," she insisted. "They're never going to put me in any hospital."

Later, Jenny asked her father, "If her sputum is negative, why does she still have to stay in bed?"

He took her on his lap. "Because the bacteria have destroyed some of her lungs. When she gets better her body builds hard little shells around the germs so they can't destroy any more tissue. You can live with only part of a lung, but you don't have much energy, and the tubercles—the little shells—can break open and the germs get out and cause more damage, so she has to be extra careful not to have another breakdown.

"Your mother must have a very strong constitution" he went on, "because each time, after she has a relapse, she's able to get better, so much better that tomorrow she's going to eat meals at the table with us."

"Good!" Jenny slipped her arms around his neck. "Daddy, sometime are they going to put Dale and me in foster homes?"

"You still worried about that? No, never. Damn County!"

"Thank goodness." She looked at him quizzically, "Momma says you should never say damn."

"She's right, and your mother never ever swears, but you know what? I'll tell you a secret. Not so long ago I even heard her say, 'Damn County!'"

# 30. The Defender of Drayton Castle

For several years drought plagued the center of the country. The Pates struggled desperately to seal their little house against the dust storms howling in off the prairie, depositing grime for Jenny to clean, and leaving Nora gasping for clean air. Later, grasshoppers stripped away all the greenery in one voracious swoop.

Miniature golf and radio were the inexpensive national pastimes. Some men found work with the Works Progress Administration, but Clyde was too proud to participate in a government program. Nora's health and the family's finances suffered constant ups and downs like the newly popular yo-yo.

On a late spring evening in 1936, the family gathered in the living room. Lying on the couch, Nora inspected Dale's report card. "Can't you do better, Dale? To go to college, you have to get better grades."

"I know." He hung his head. His folks just didn't understand. Consumed by their own problems, they gave him little attention. He silently carried the burdens of his mother's illness, and poverty so severe food seemed their only pleasure. Now in painful adolescence, he had difficulty making friends and was too shy and self-conscious to approach girls.

Looking up, Jenny said, "Dale gets to go to college?"

Clyde said, "He may have to work his way."

"What kind of work can he do?" Jenny asked.

Clyde shook his head. "I'm not sure."

"Oh, dear," Nora said, "I think going to college, studying and working besides, is just too much. He might get sick."

"Now, Nora, don't worry. If I can scrounge up tuition for the University of Colorado, he'll only have to make enough for room and board."

Sitting up, Jenny exclaimed, "He gets to live up in Boulder?"

"Going to Denver University would be more expensive than his going to CU." Clyde rattled his newspaper. "If he gets to go at all, he'll go to Boulder."

"I wish I could go some place. Boys get to do everything."

Frowning, Nora said, "Jenny, I hate to hear you talk that way."

"Well, they do. Dale gets to go dude ranches, and away to school and I have to stay home and do housework."

"Now, Jenny," Clyde chided, "lots of us can't do what we'd like. I'm surprised to hear you grumbling. It's your bedtime, and before you go to sleep, I hope you'll count your blessings."

Jenny rose and ran down the hall, fighting back tears. Life just wasn't fair. Nobody ever paid attention to her. Boys needed an education, but what about what she needed?

Hours later, Nora said softly from her twin bed, "Clyde, are you awake? I can't sleep. I'm worried about Jenny."

He roused. "Jenny? Why?"

"She keeps saying she'd like to be a boy."

"Oh, balderdash."

"Remember that doll we gave her when she was six, the one with the curly reddish-brown hair and blue eyes? I think I liked it better than she did. She never seemed to care much for dolls. It worries me."

He rolled over. "She liked them when she was littler. Remember how she hung onto that baby doll the Christmas she was two? Just adored it, but she's athletic like me. Dale's bookish, like you. That's just their personalities. Don't worry, she's every bit a girl."

Nora became quiet then and Clyde guessed she had drifted off to sleep, but now Clyde lay thinking. When Nora became ill, he told seven-year-old Jenny to take care of her mother and be a big girl. Maybe he shouldn't have told a child to take care of a parent. Maybe that's why she wanted to be independent—like a boy.

Guilt gripped him. Perhaps Jenny wanted to be taken care of herself. He had tried, tried to be everything to everybody. Nora tried, too, tried to be a mother from her bed, but she couldn't go to school events, take Jenny shopping to choose the right clothes, or teach her how to entertain.

His mind went off on another tangent. Nora had been bedridden five interminable years. When would she be well? Jenny's childhood was gone. She was thirteen now, and Dale, seventeen. Nora's last bout of illness had sent the doctor bills mounting again. He needed the solace of sleep, but his mind churned on.

Last week he'd again stopped at the YMCA looking for work. He thought wistfully of the sixteen years he'd been a physical education instructor. How he missed it!

Business wasn't going well. Maybe he wasn't cut out to be a salesman. He believed in insurance and knew it helped people, but with everyone so poor, few could buy. He felt ashamed to provide so little money, to constantly borrow from the company.

Discussing work problems with Nora upset her too much. He had to be the strong one, stay positive for everybody's sake. Now, he needed money for Dale to go to college next year. Fretfully, he punched up his pillow.

Last week he'd met a dirty, grease-encrusted fellow at the gas station who had turned out to be a wealthy genius who'd invented a wheel balancer. His name was Pete. Maybe somehow, through Pete, he could meet some rich men who might need insurance. But how? He didn't move in those circles, but maybe he'd come up with some idea. Right now he needed sleep.


Saturday, after Clyde had gone to the grocery, Nora walked slowly into the kitchen. "Pull out that chair for me, Jenny."

"Mother, what are you doing up?"

"I've decided it's time you learned to bake. Men like good cooks and it would save us buying pastries at the store. Bring me the *Homemaker's Best*

164

*Cookbook*. You get to make your first cake today, sweetheart. The secret is to level all the ingredients as you measure them. Sift the flour and don't press it down in the measuring cup. Cream the oleo till soft, and add the sugar gradually, beating all the time. Your arm will get tired, but beating hard makes a cake light."

"Can I make the gold cake?"

Nora's face fell. "The gold cake calls for five egg yolks—I'd thought the two-egg cake." At the disappointment on Jenny's face, she relented, "All right, go ahead. We'll use the whites for meringues or cornflake macaroons. I'm going back to bed now. Follow the cookbook directions and if you have any questions, come ask me. Better light the oven."

When the cake was baked to golden perfection, Jenny iced it with brown sugar seafoam frosting. Her cake was light, tender, and wonderfully delicious.

After that, Jenny baked continuously. She made burnt-sugar cake with burnt-sugar icing, devil's food cake with gleaming white, seven-minute frosting; angel cake, Lazy Daisy cake with broiled brown sugar-nut topping; economical one-egg cake. The family raved. Jenny glowed. Nora felt relieved, thinking Jenny was on the way to femininity.

Clyde liked pie, so Jenny learned to make flaky crusts and baked apple, mince, pumpkin, lemon meringue, cherry, peach, rhubarb, butterscotch and chocolate pies.

She learned the secret to keeping the crust crisp in a pie with filling was to place several tablespoons of sugar and flour on the bottom of the crust before pouring in the filling.

When summer came, Nora enjoyed lying in the back of the car as they drove to the farms north of Denver where they purchased bushels of peaches, cherries, tomatoes and apples. Then Jenny and Clyde would can fruit and make applesauce and catsup. Jenny loved the smell of bubbling red chili sauce the best. She liked pitting cherries with a hairpin, but hated it when the juice ran from her hands to her elbows.

That summer, for the first time, Daddy decided to make root beer. A few weeks later, someone would sit up and say, "Listen. I hear a pop."

Clyde would burst out of his chair yelling, "The root beer!" and pound down the back stairs into the basement to try to stop other bottles from blowing their corks. He'd come upstairs holding a foaming bottle and grinning. "We're going to have to drink this one." And it tasted good!

Home baked pastries were inexpensive and filling, making up for the lack of meat, so Jenny made cookies, too—sugar cookies, gingersnaps, oatmeal, and butterscotch. At Christmas, Nora asked for the old German cookies her mother had made—springerle, pfeffernusse, cinnamon stars, and sand tarts. They gave Mrs. Wheatley, and the Vandermeers next door, cookies as gifts.

Nora thought they were finally making a real girl out of their daughter until one Saturday.

That day Jenny was in the basement washing. When it was first manufactured, Clyde had bought a Lazy washing machine which had a spinner basket to save labor. Nora insisted the clothes go through three rinses so Jenny spun out the soapy water, then lifted the clothes out of the Lazy and through three rinses in two laundry tubs and a galvanized wash tub on the floor. Finally, she put the wet clothes back into the washer basket to spin dry. At least she didn't have to scrub them on a board or put them through a wringer.

When the spinner stopped, she carried the laundry through the basement, up the steps and hung it in the backyard. If the weather was bad, she hung the clothes in the cellar. Jenny sometimes wondered why Mother never considered washing as working too hard.

Tall and athletic, Jenny didn't mind the heavy lifting. She liked being alone in the basement away from the demands of her mother's ever-clanging bell.

That day she got the clothes into the washer and watched the three, round, silver cups plunge up and down. The swish, swish, swish lulled her into daydreams.

*What will I be when I grow up? A movie star?* She sighed. *Fat chance!* She didn't mind sick people, so had talked of being a nurse, but Mother strongly objected.

"I'd love for you to be a nurse, but nurses lift people, do heavy work, and even scrub floors. No, Jenny, you might get sick because the work's too hard."

*How can I not work too hard?* Jenny wondered. Grinning, she remembered when she was six, Dale had said, "Hey, the newspaper is having an art contest. Why don't you draw a picture, Jenny? I'm sure you'll win."

She knew he was teasing, so to show him, she drew a picture of a tree, making big billowing rounds for the branches of leaves and then outlining the edges with a second line. Daddy sent her sketch to the contest.

She won! With hardly any effort at all, she'd won a crisp, one dollar bill.

Now she sat thinking. *There must be some other easy way to make money.* She still drew like a six year old, so being an artist was out. *There has to be some way.*

As she wandered into the storage room, she caught sight of an old birdcage. Lifting it down, she remembered the basement in Ferguson, where Daddy raised canaries. Lost in nostalgia, she saw the hopping birds, heard their cheerful warbling.

When she set down the cage, a long box way back on the shelf caught her eye. Curious, she pulled it out, removed the cardboard lid, and unfolded yellowed tissue paper revealing two tarnished silver fencing foils. Having seen pictures in her father's photo album of his YMCA days, she recognized what they were.

Taking out a long slender sword, she ran back into the laundry room and leaped on a chair shouting, "Beware there! This is Drayton Castle and you shall not enter!"

Jumping down, she swished the blade back and forth, smiling at the whistling as it sliced through the air. "I'll get you, you devil. No one will harm the princess. Away! Back, you scoundrels." Thrusting at an imaginary foe, she shouted, "Take that, you dog. Got him! He's down. Run for the parapets, boys!" She ran in place, panting furiously. "We made it. Drayton Castle will be safe. Now pull up the drawbridge, boys. Hurry!"

A voice called, "Jenny?"

Whirling, she saw her father standing in the doorway. Running toward him, she pointed the foil at his chest. "Another invader. Halt! En garde!"

"Stop it! What are you doing? Stop it!" Red-faced, Clyde lunged forward and grasped the foil blade in his fist. "That's dangerous. Don't you ever do that again. Never point a foil at anybody who isn't masked. You could put out somebody's eye."

She gulped. "I was just playing. I didn't know you were down here."

"Never play with these foils without wearing the masks. Where are they?"

"I don't know." Daddy never got mad. "I got this one out of there." She pointed.

He went into the storage room and she could hear boxes scraping. When he came out, he held the other foil in his hand and two fencing masks pinned under his arm.

"Put this on." He helped her into the round black helmet—and she looked out through wire mesh. Putting on the other mask, he said, "I used to teach fencing. I'll show you how to stand—this way." He turned his feet at right angles. "Curve your other arm over your head like this. You move forward and back, forward and back. It's formal—stylized. And when you lunge, you drop the overhead arm behind you for balance."

He positioned her. "Now advance toward me. Straight little steps. Now retreat."

Inside her mesh globe, Jenny grinned. She had her father's complete attention and he was playing with her. *This is fun!*

"Step like I do. Forward, close, forward, close. Lunge! Back. Lunge! Back. Good, Jenny. That's good. Now face me."

She turned.

"Hold up your foil. When you start a match, you cross swords with your opponent. Like this, with the tips pointing up toward the ceiling." The metal blades clinked as they crossed their foils. "Now, put your point toward the floor." He examined the end of his. "These rubber tips still seem okay, but we can't play any more. We need padded chest protectors. But I tell you what—I'll chalk a heart on the wall and you can practice lunging at that. But remember, no playing with these with anyone else unless you are both wearing body padding and the masks." He put the equipment away. "I just got home from the store and heard you shouting. I must say you surprised me. I need to check on Mother."

When he entered Nora's bedroom, he was grinning. "Guess what Jenny was doing."

"Isn't she washing?"

"Yes, but between loads, she found my old fencing equipment and was dashing around fighting off adversaries at some imaginary castle."

"Oh, dear."

"Now, Nora, I thought it was inventive."

"There she goes again, acting like a boy."

"Yes, acting, using her imagination. The kids don't have many games or toys. We can't afford vacations or excursions, or even movies. What else can they do but pretend—Dale with his writing and Jenny with her castles? I think it's—healthy. What's the harm?"

"The harm is, that even these days, a girl has to find a husband. You know an old maid has a terrible life. Women have to make a good marriage. How is she ever going to get a husband if she acts like a boy?"

"For heaven's sake, Nora, she's only a kid."

"She's turned thirteen. Thirteen already."

"Come on, honey, she has plenty of time. You're worrying over nothing. She doesn't mind women's work like washing or ironing, and she loves to cook. She's a wonderful baker. Those are girl things. She'll get interested in boys. I just hope she doesn't get too interested. That could give us real problems."

# 31. The Secret in the Cellar

"This is the dress I bought with my savings for Jean's birthday party. What do you think, Mom?" Jenny smoothed the flowered, smoky blue fabric and slowly revolved in front of her mother's bed.

"It's lovely, dear. I'm glad you bought a brassiere too. You're already developing. Do you know what we girls did before the brassiere was invented?" She smiled. "We had to tie an inch-wide ribbon around us so we wouldn't jiggle. I wish I weren't so full breasted. You look very nice— just remember—don't let a boy touch you between the neck and the knees."

"What if they play post office?"

"A little kiss on the cheek or the lips might be all right, but no long smooches, now. It's too bad you had to invite your own young man. What do you know about his family?"

Jenny sank down onto her father's bed, "Don's in lots of my classes and he lives on the other side of the block."

"What do you like about him?"

"I don't know. He's tall with brown hair and I think he's handsome, but he always looks sad, so I'd like to make him happy. I heard that his parents are divorced and he lives with his mother. I wish he was picking me up here, instead of meeting me at Jean's. It makes me feel like he didn't really want to go with me."

"He accepted didn't he?"

She nodded.

"Jenny, you don't seem very happy."

"I'm scared. When I asked Don to go, he acted sort of reluctant. I think it's dumb for his mother to take him, and Daddy to take me when we live so close."

"Now, it's all been arranged. Just believe you'll have a good time and you will."

But Jenny didn't have a good time. Don paid no attention to her. The only thing he'd said all afternoon was "Hello." None of the boys talked to her. During most of the party, she sat at the side of the room, wearing a brave smile, pretending she was having a marvelous time. But her face lied, because inside she was in despair. Nobody talked to her or danced with her. Of course most of the boys didn't dance at all. Girls sat awkwardly on one side of the room and the boys on the other. After they ate ice cream and cake, Jean opened her presents.

Everybody giggled when they sat in a circle to play post office. Jenny hoped Don would kiss her. Her heart pounded and her hands felt sweaty, but it was Mary he kissed for a long time and everybody howled. Other girls got kissed and finally, tall blond Sammy spun the bottle, but when it pointed to Jenny he yelled, "Oh, no, not Jenny." And he wouldn't kiss her. The group burst out laughing.

Jenny laughed with everybody else and held her head high even though inside it hurt so much it took her breath away.

When her father drove up to take her home, Jenny jumped in the car and said, "Let's go, Daddy, hurry," as her brave face began to crumple. On the way, she squeezed out a few details of her humiliating afternoon.

Her father made sympathetic noises. "They just don't know what they're missing."

That didn't take the hurt away. She felt as if a mountain had fallen down and crushed her, but she sat up straight in the car, trying to block it all out. Floundering for some comforting thought to hang on to, she pretended she was a queen, a movie star, above such nonsense. *I'll show them*, she thought grimly, *Someday I'll show everybody. I don't know how, but I will!*

After Jenny went to bed, Clyde tiptoed into their bedroom. Nora was still awake and he softly related details Jenny had left out when telling her mother about her unhappy experience.

"Oh, no," Nora cried. "That boy probably wouldn't kiss her because of me, probably afraid he'd catch TB."

"Now Nora, I doubt it was that. The kid was probably embarrassed. I wish we hadn't let her go. She seems awfully young for a boy-girl party. Poor Jenny." He shook his head and then smiled. "One good thing, you don't have to worry about her wanting to be a boy. She really likes boys and wants them to like her, or she wouldn't be so heartbroken. I'd like to knock some sense into that Don."

"His behavior was downright rude. As her guest, he should have paid attention to her. Maybe you need to pay more attention to her, Clyde."

"I thought I did. You know Jenny and I are real close."

"We should spend more time with the children."

Jenny tried to hide her dismay so it wouldn't upset her mother, but the wound throbbed and festered inside. She tried to bury it, but it was still there. Forced by circumstances at home to do things alone, it seemed easier to go places by herself than risk rejection. Inside was still that yearning to be noticed, to be part of the group, to be loved.

Not long after the party, Jenny went downtown to run errands. On the way home, as she boarded the streetcar and sank down next to a smartly dressed woman reading a magazine, she said again to herself. *I don't care if nobody likes me. I don't care! Someday they'll all pay attention to me. They'll see!*

The conductor clanged his bell and the trolley rocked back and forth as the wheels grated down the track.

Glancing at the magazine her seatmate was reading, Jenny saw the bold type of an article headline: *"Your Voice Can Be Your Fortune."* Jenny drew a breath and bent closer.

Just then the woman slapped the magazine shut, reached for the buzzer cord and rose to leave. Jenny leaned from her seat trying to see the cover of the magazine clutched against the woman's black coat. "Excuse me," she called. But the woman hopped off the steps, walked rapidly away, and the streetcar careened on.

Jenny wanted to read that article, but how could she ever find it? She didn't even know the name of the magazine. Frowning, she sat thinking. How could your voice be your fortune? Maybe if she was a singer she could make money without working too hard. That would please Mother. Singing for a living would be such fun. That's what she'd do—use her voice to make money.

That evening at home, Nora felt increasingly uneasy. Something seemed wrong. She sensed the family was drifting apart. With the children off somewhere, the house seemed eerily quiet. She rang her bell. No response. "Clyde?" she called. "Clyde?" *Where is he?*

She listened for water running in the kitchen or bathroom, but heard nothing. "Clyde!" Frightened now, she hit her little Japanese gold bell with the mallet, over and over, faster and faster, beating on it in a frenzy.

Finally, she heard his footsteps on the back stairs hurrying up from the basement. Coming into the room, he looked at her fearfully. "What's wrong, Nora?"

"You didn't come when I rang. Where were you?"

His voice turned sharp. "Don't scare me like that. I was down in the cellar."

"Why?"

He sighed heavily. "It's quiet down there, and I need a little time by myself."

Her white hands drummed on the covers. "But you've disappeared several evenings. What on earth are you doing?"

"Nothing."

She coughed into a tissue. "You can't do nothing down there night after night."

"Now, Nora, please don't scold."

She hung her head. "I don't mean to. You've been wonderful. I'm so glad to have you, Clyde. But I feel lonely in the evening when you're not around. An empty house is bad enough during the day with the children at school. Thank God for the radio and soap operas. At least they keep my mind off things. Evenings I'd like the whole family to spend time together, but you keep disappearing."

"I'm just down in the cellar."

"Doing what? If you don't tell me I'm going to walk down there and find out."

"You know you're not well enough to navigate all those steps. Believe me, I'm not doing anything wrong." He hesitated, face torn as he tried to avoid telling her. "It's a surprise. I'm making something," he swallowed, a large unnatural gulp, "something for us all."

"What?"

He grinned. "A handle for a flour sack."

Surprise crossed her face. Then she laughed. "Clyde, that's a silly old joke. Tell me what you're up to."

"Nora, don't press. I'll finish in a few days. This is important to me. I can see you don't like it, but this is the way it has to be."

She gave up and changed the subject. "Clyde, I want the family together every Saturday night. I feel as if we don't do anything with each other any more. Dale will soon be off to college. Mrs. Wheatley stopped by and brought me three books she thought I'd like to read, and this article she clipped from a magazine about the authors—Nordoff and Hall."

"Yeah, I've heard of them."

"They're novelists and these books are based on a true story. I think the children would be interested, so I want us all to read them together—you know—a family thing. We can take turns reading out loud."

He shrugged. "Might be a little boring, but if that's what you want, okay. What're the books?"

"*Mutiny on the Bounty, Men Against the Sea,* and *Pitcairn Island.*"

"I suppose they'd be decent for children."

"*Mutiny on the Bounty* came out in 1932, and was very popular, but we were busy with our own problems that year. What do you think?" Now she was eager. "Can we read them together?"

"Sure, but I don't know if two teenagers are going to be interested. Don't know if I really am."

"We're going to do it. I want Jenny and Dale involved, and I want you to stay out of the basement."

The first Saturday, Clyde directed the children to sit on pillows on the floor next to the couch where Nora lay. Clyde passed around bowls of popcorn and announced the start of Family Reading Time.

Dale rolled his eyes and Jenny made a face, but with their usual effort to please their parents, they sat, munched their popcorn and prepared to be bored.

Clyde opened *Mutiny on the Bounty* and began reading. Soon the other three were listening intently. Dale eagerly read the second chapter and passed the volume to Jenny to read the third.

By bedtime Jenny begged, "Can we do it again tomorrow?"

Dale jumped up. "Look, if we get our homework done early, we can read every single night. I can't wait to find out what happens."

"Okay," Clyde laughed. "No peeking, now. We all want to read it together at the same time. I'll make penuche for tomorrow night."

"Dad," Dale said, "this book is so good, we don't even need any food."

Nora was pleased at the children's enthusiasm, and relieved that Clyde wasn't running down to the basement every evening, but soon discovered he was down there early Saturday mornings. Once she walked to the head of the basement stairs and listened. She could hear Clyde humming, but it was too great an effort for her to go any farther.

She felt a vague uneasiness, like waiting for something to happen, and her sleep was riddled with frustrating dreams of repeatedly trying to catch a train.

The night they finished *Men against the Sea*, the children were gathered at the foot of the couch. Nora, lay against the pillows, white and breathing heavily. Suddenly, Clyde jumped up.

"Where are you going?" Nora asked.

Without answering, he went out through the kitchen. They could hear him running down the basement steps.

"That was such a good book," Jenny said. "I wondered what happened to Fletcher Christian and his men."

"Gee," Dale said. "I'd like to go to the South Seas sometime."

"Me too," Jenny cried.

"When Daddy gets back, we can start *Pitcairn Island.*" Nora leafed through the pages, smiling.

None of them was conscious of Clyde coming up the basement steps and through the kitchen. When he reached the couch, Nora saw him and her jaw dropped. Jenny and Dale looked up at their father, then frowned in puzzlement. The room fell silent. No one moved. No one spoke.

Clyde looked at Nora and in a quiet voice said, "This is the surprise." In his hands he held an enormous rifle.

# 32. What's the Rifle For?

Nora looked up at her husband, uncertain, frowning. "What are you doing with that rifle?"

"Pete gave it to me. The stock was cracked and I got a new one. I've been attaching it and sanding it down, getting it to fit my shoulder just right. Isn't it beautiful? Look at this wood."

Jenny watched warily and glanced at Dale. Their mother and father never argued in front of them, but Jenny could tell something was wrong. She wished her heart would stop beating so fast. Why did Daddy need a rifle, and why was Mother so upset?

Nora's blue eyes were hard. "What do you need a rifle for?"

"Deer hunting." Clyde went on enthusiastically, "I can hardly wait till the season opens. God, I've missed hunting. Dale, do you remember back in St. Louis, how we used to hunt duck and pheasant and quail?"

"You went." Dale said. "I didn't like it. The only thing I ever shot was a squirrel and when I saw it all lifeless and bloody, I decided I didn't like hunting at all."

"You did go quail hunting with me. I remember that distinctly."

"Just once. But if you remember, I never even shot the gun."

"I'm surprised you don't like hunting. To me, it's sort of a primitive instinct. Man, right out there in the wilds, taking action to provide for his family. Humans have hunted since they were cavemen. It's in our blood. Nothing wrong with it."

For a minute, Jenny wondered what she would do if Daddy took her hunting. Could she shoot an animal? Watch it die?

Nora noticed how Clyde beamed, how his hands rubbed the satiny wood of the stock. "Clyde, it's just that Jenny has only two dresses for the school year."

Jenny felt uneasy. It was true, but she hated for her parents to disagree.

Her mother went on, "And the holes in your shoes have worn holes in your socks too big for me to darn. How could you spend money fixing up a useless gun?"

"Useless?" Clyde said. "This isn't useless. I'm going to get us some meat. No more red rarebit, chipped beef and scrambled eggs for dinner. We'll have steaks and roasts."

Nora frowned. "Wild meat? How will that taste?"

"Hunters consider it delicious. Not everybody can be treated to real venison."

Jenny watched her enthusiastic father and her doubtful mother and felt herself leaning to her mother's side. Deer meat? Ick! How could Daddy kill one of those graceful creatures with the big brown eyes?

"Besides," Nora went on. "Deer hunting isn't safe, and you know it. Every year, you read in the paper about some hunter getting shot."

With a gasp, Jenny closed her eyes.

Dale's heart sank. If his father got shot, the family's welfare would fall on him. "Dad, it is dangerous, isn't it?"

"Look, we're packing in by horseback, way up above Aspen near the Maroon Bells. It's really wild there. No people around. My friends are experienced hunters and we'll all be wearing bright red jackets. Nobody'll get shot. I'm more likely to get hit by a car in downtown Denver. We'll be safe."

"Who's we?" Nora persisted.

"Six of us are going. Friends of Pete's. And we're going to hunt and I'll take the pictures. I'm going to take movies. Just a minute."

*Movies? Moving pictures?* Jenny was confused. *Whatever was he talking about?*

Clyde went to the closet, propped up the rifle, reached up on a shelf and brought back a small box. Opening it, he said, "This is an eight-millimeter movie camera."

"Clyde!" Nora voice was tinged with tears.

"I won it in a raffle," he said defensively.

"What? Whose raffle? How much were the tickets? How much did you spend?"

Jenny wrung her hands. Everything was going wrong. The rifle, and now this. Mother was really upset.

"Now, Nora." Clyde looked down at the floor.

Jenny felt dismayed. *Mother doesn't believe him.* Over the years Jenny had learned that sometimes, to avoid getting scolded, her father told little white lies, some not so little, and others not so white.

Her father's voice sounded soft and miserable. "Don't scold, Nora."

"But to spend money on raffle tickets when we need so many other things! How could you?"

"All right, there wasn't any raffle. I went without lunch for months to buy this camera. Now are you satisfied?"

She lay back speechless.

"Don't you see, Nora?" he pleaded. "Pete's friends are well off. If I hunt with them and take their pictures, maybe they'll buy some insurance. That's why I got the gun and the movie camera. I have to do something to get in with those men. It's business." He looked into her pale, stern face and said, "All right, it's a little pleasure, too. I'll admit it. But business mostly." He hesitated. "I have to have something. I haven't had a vacation for seven years."

From where she sat on the floor, Jenny reached up and squeezed her mother's hand. Since Mother had gotten sick, she hadn't had a vacation either. None of them had.

Exuberant again, Clyde crowed, "Just wait till you taste that venison. We'll have meat, Nora. Meat!"

For a minute everyone was silent. Dale sat next to Jenny on the floor, hands wrapped around *Pitcairn Island,* the next book to read together. Jenny wished Daddy wasn't going hunting and wished Mother wouldn't worry and get upset so often. When they read books together, she felt warm and wonderful and almost as if they themselves, were aboard a ship floating in the South Seas.

Turning a determined face to Jenny, Nora said, "Jenny, bring me the *Homemaker's Best Cookbook*. I want to see how to cook wild meat."

Deer season came and the family waited anxiously for Clyde to return from his five-day trek into the wilderness.

When he walked in the back door and gave Jenny a hug, she made a face. His growth of beard scratched her cheek and he smelled of smoke and sweat.

He wore grimy clothes and a wide grin. "I got one! A big five pointer." His eyes glowed. "We all had success. I took the carcass to the frozen food plant and they'll butcher, package and freeze it. Wow! I'm going to go hunting every year." He walked with a funny gait. "Riding a horse that long can be hard on the bottom, but I loved it!"

Jenny followed him to her mother's side and listened as he regaled them with details about his trip. When at last he paused, Nora asked quietly, "Get any business?"

"I wanted to bring home the liver, but it spoils too fast. When the deer is still warm, we cut out the liver and cook it right away. You never tasted anything so good."

"Clyde, did you sell any policies? Get any business?"

"Business? Not so far. You have to build friendships, Nora. It takes time."

Unfortunately, despite Nora's best efforts, no one except Clyde cared for the venison. It was too tough, too strong. In the end, Clyde gave most of it away.

To show the films, Clyde had to buy a projector and a screen. Jenny woke one night to hear her parents arguing over money again. It made her sad, yet she felt Daddy had to have something. He had no social life, few friends. But neither did Mother.

After the film was developed, the family gathered in the living room to watch the hunting expedition. Six inches of snow covered the ground on a cloudy day. The trees were black skeletons clawing at the gray sky. Men emerged from a dirty white tent, and huddled around a crackling campfire, stamping their feet and blowing on their hands. The wind blew a cascade of snow from a tree branch. A close-up shot showed a hand opening a can of beans.

Jenny watched in dismay. "That looks awful. You all look so cold and miserable. You call that a vacation?"

Over the hum of the projector, Clyde called out with a smile gilding his voice, "It was so much fun. I had a wonderful time. Just wonderful!"

# 33. Daddy's Despair

As the months passed, Clyde realized that for his family things were not at all wonderful. The men from the hunting trips all had insurance and didn't want to change companies. He sold no new policies. Poverty still dogged them.

Fifteen now, Jenny was finishing up her first year in high school. Clyde dropped her off mornings on his way to work. He watched her scurry into East High, smarting with the fact she would walk four miles home because she didn't have a nickel for the trolley.

Dale attended the University of Colorado, thirty miles away at Boulder, working for room and board. To pay his tuition, Clyde again had borrowed from the company against his renewals.

The summer of 1939 came with debt his constant companion.

Worst of all, in July, Dr. Milstein sued him for Nora's long-standing unpaid bills. Clyde went to his office and demand to see the doctor. "What have you ever done for my wife?" He surprised himself with his sudden rage.

The doctor's face turned grim. "I've done all I could."

"It hasn't been enough. Why hasn't she gotten any better? Why?"

Steel blue eyes met his. "Look, man, don't you realize the truth? No matter what I do, or anyone else does, she's not going to improve. Your wife will never be well!"

Staggering from the office, Clyde stumbled down the stairs and walked the streets like a lost man. He'd always thought, hoped, dreamed, that someday Nora would be her old self—the bright, happy, laughing girl he'd fallen in love with in college.

Clyde leaned against a light post and, with a sudden pang, again remembered his stepmother's words so long ago: "Clyde, I'm afraid if you marry Nora, you'll have a very hard life."

He hadn't believed her. He loved Nora—liked taking care of her. But he didn't know the care-taking would become all consuming, didn't dream it would never end.

Now, his vision blurred. The tall office buildings cast long shadows and he felt cold. He stepped down into the street and cars honked. Looking up, he saw the signal light was against him, but somehow he got safely to the other side and trudged on.

A hand grabbed his arm and a stranger said, "Look here, are you all right?"

He mumbled and walked on, block after block, across Broadway and up the hill near the gold-domed capitol. Somehow he knew where he was headed.

At last he pushed open the door to Pete's mechanic shop and sank into a chair.

Startled, Pete looked up. "Clyde, what is it? You look awful. What's wrong?"

"Nora. It's Nora." He dropped his head in his hands and his shoulders shook.

"Is she...? You mean Nora...." Pete swallowed.

"She's never going to get well. It's always going to be like this. I'd always hoped—I'm at the end of my rope. I can't take it any more."

"Here, have a doughnut and some coffee. We always keep the pot on. You go without lunch again? You've got to take care of yourself, for God's sake—for everybody's sake."

Clyde thought he wasn't hungry, but the coffee and doughnut tasted good.

Pete shooed out a mechanic who'd started into the office, then sat beside Clyde. "Look, you need some cash? I've got plenty."

Miserably, Clyde shook his head. "I've borrowed from Nora's mother, from the company, from you, from Dale, even from Jenny's piggy bank.

When is it going to get any better? When? Do you want to know? Well, I'll tell you. Never!"

"Now, don't think like that. Sure, the Depression doesn't seem over, but things don't look good in Europe. If there's a war over there, our economy might improve. Times can't stay bad forever. Look, take this and don't worry about paying it back." He tucked some bills into Clyde's suit coat pocket. "Listen, I have an idea. My wife and I know this woman, Sophie Hines. I want you to go see her. She lives two blocks from here."

"Pete, I don't need a woman. I need Nora to get well."

"Sophie's not just any woman. She's a religious lady, a metaphysician. She's helped me with my back trouble. You've never seen me doubled over, have you?"

"No."

Pete sipped his coffee. "You knew I've had back problems, didn't you?"

"Yeah, but they haven't stopped you. You're always here at your business, and people say you're a mechanical genius."

"It hasn't always been easy for me, Clyde. But Sophie helped me—a lot. I'll call her right now and, if she's available, I'll drive you right over. You need to talk to Sophie."

# 34. The New Woman

When Clyde stepped into Sophie's apartment, he was engulfed by an unexpected rush of nostalgia. The rich blues and maroons of the Oriental rug, the gleaming mahogany tables, and the fringed scarf on the grand piano, reminded him of his childhood home.

Sophie closed the door and rustled past in a long green paisley gown that shimmered in the light. Gray softened her auburn hair caught up in a bun at her neck. "When Pete phoned, he said you hadn't had lunch." She pulled out a dining room chair and faced it toward the kitchen, visible through a wide arch. "Come talk to me while I fix you something."

Her demeanor, her glowing brown eyes, her soft warm voice reminded him of his mother. Without protest, he sat.

As she sliced wheat bread, she said, "Pete has often spoken of you— and always with admiration. Now, what seems to be the trouble? You talk while I cook."

He felt more comfortable unburdening himself while she had her back to him, as she clattered plates and ran water into the teakettle. Still, she listened intently, occasionally stopping, turning her head, or nodding in understanding.

Out it all poured: the discovery of Nora's illness in 1931, the deepening Depression, giving up his beloved career in athletics, and moving cross-country; how he tried to be a good husband, constantly waiting on his wife, worrying about being both father and mother to his children; his despair at his inability make a decent living; and how that had steadily eroded his self-esteem.

He spoke of the never-ending doctor bills. And finally, the terrible indignity of being sued by Nora's physician and the awful shock of being told that she would never recover—would never be well.

Now, here it was 1939. The Depression was still ongoing and Nora was no better after eight years in bed. They had no doctor, no money, no hope. He realized suddenly that he really had had no one to talk to about his troubles. He stopped—silent—shorn of pride—despondent.

Setting a tray before him, Sophie said, "Things always look especially bad when you're suffering from an empty stomach."

"I did have a doughnut."

"That's not enough."

He looked down into a big bowl of steaming vegetable soup. The sandwich was stuffed with thick slices of chicken. A cup of spicy orange tea steamed near a huge slice of apple pie. He ate ravenously. When he finished, she spirited the tray away and led him to a deep chair in the living room.

"Now," she began gently, "you must never lose hope. Are you a believer, a churchgoer?"

"Not lately because I haven't wanted to leave Nora alone on Sundays." He sighed. "To be honest—I wasn't getting anything out of it."

"Where have you been going?"

"We're both Methodists." He felt grateful for the cool shadowy room.

She studied him thoughtfully. "Just as there are advances in science and industry, there are new developments in spiritual thinking. Thoughts are very powerful. When Pete brought you here, he first had to think about it. All life originates in the mind. Even Lincoln said, 'As a man thinks, so is he.'"

Clyde fidgeted. "I don't see what you're getting at."

Leaning forward, she said earnestly, "If you free your mind of negativity and open yourself, you can receive the world's abundance. God created a beautiful world and He expects us to enjoy it."

Shaking his head, Clyde said, "I grew up with the idea that having money was a sin, and sacrifice was the way to sainthood."

"The Christian Scientists would say that is an error in thought. The Bible says—not money—but the love of money—is the root of evil."

"Are you a Christian Scientist? Because I don't believe in faith healing. The tuberculosis has destroyed Nora's lung tissue. You think faith'll grow her new lungs?"

"No, Clyde, this is not Christian Science, though we use many of their ideas. And healing has many aspects—like the healing of the spirit. I imagine both you and Mrs. Pate feel angry with God. But now you must open yourselves to the inflow of goodness. What you think, you tend to materialize."

"It doesn't work." Clyde sprang from the chair and paced the floor. "I keep thinking I'm going to get some big policy and I don't. Why? Why?"

"Never give up hope. You must believe—not that you must sell—but that your product will help people. Every day say, 'I am helping others. I am entitled to God's abundance and I open myself to new ideas.' Constantly repeat those affirmations, and see what happens."

Clyde sank into the chair. "I don't know. I guess I can try."

She fixed her warm brown eyes on him. "I know a talented, inspiring minister who preaches this line of thought, even though he is an Episcopalian priest. Why not give his church a try? It's not too far from where you live. Could you go next Sunday?"

Hesitantly, Clyde murmured, "I guess so."

"Pete told me your wife needs a new doctor. I know a very fine chest specialist—Bernie Zeller." She looked at him carefully. "Would you folks object to a Jewish doctor?"

He shrugged. "Why would we? Jews have done wonderful things in the world."

She rose. "Well, then, while you call Pete to pick you up, I'll write down Dr. Zeller's address and phone number, and the address of the church."

After Clyde phoned Pete, Sophie handed him a piece of paper. "There, now. You've received positive thoughts, a new church, a new doctor—"

"And lunch." He laughed. Taking her hand, Clyde squeezed it. "Thank you, Sophie. I feel much better."

"Remember to think good thoughts, Clyde, and good will come to you."

He wasn't at all sure.

Two weeks later, Nora and Clyde sat waiting in Dr. Zeller's office for his report. He had taken an extended history, examined her thoroughly, reviewed Dr. Milstein's records and carefully studied her new x-rays.

Dr. Zeller maneuvered his stout body into his chair, plopped Nora's chart on his desk, and regarded the couple with intelligent hazel eyes that peered from behind horn-rimmed glasses.

Clyde fingered his trouser leg nervously, wondering if the man charged big fees.

Breathing hard, Nora sagged in her chair, bracing herself. In her experience, doctor visits invariably meant bad news.

Dr. Zeller smiled. "Very interesting case, Mrs. Pate. I have a plan for you."

Relaxing, Clyde thought jubilantly, *He's going to take us.*

Zeller looked at Nora. "What you need, Mrs. Pate, is a good long rest, and relief from your household responsibilities. I'll see you weekly and will consult other doctors to determine your best treatment. There will be no charge, because you'll be in the National Jewish Hospital."

Shocked, Nora cried, "Hospital! I have to go to the hospital? For how long? National Jewish—isn't that a sanitarium?"

"One of the country's best," Zeller replied. "I'd like you staying there long enough to do you some good."

Fear robbed Nora's face of color. She protested. "We've seen it on the hill and heard about it, but they wouldn't take me. I'm not—we're not—Jewish."

Zeller smiled. "You don't have to be. They treat everyone."

Clutching Clyde's hand, Nora cried, "But it's a sanitarium. Clyde, you promised you wouldn't stick me away in some hospital. You promised!"

Uneasily, Clyde raised distressed eyes to the doctor. "She's getting all upset." Turning to Nora, he said, "I didn't know he was planning this."

Dr. Zeller's voice was strong and direct. "Look, Mrs. Pate. You've been sick a long time and have never given hospitalization a chance. This is a fine sanitarium. Good food, excellent professional staff, clean, and all free of charge."

"I don't want charity. I've heard what charity hospitals are like," she fumed.

Calmly, Zeller said, "I can arrange a tour, and you can see for yourself."

Clyde looked down at his shoes—shoes he'd half-soled himself with a kit from the dime store. "I don't like it either, Nora, but maybe they can do something for you. Maybe you'll get well." He thought, *Get well! And no medical bills for a while. What a relief. Maybe I could pay off Milstein and get on my feet.*

Dr. Zeller said, "I think I could get you in by September, maybe sooner. I think you should stay a year."

"A year!" Nora's eyes teared.

"That long!" Clyde exclaimed.

The doctor rose. "This is what I recommend. Think it over and let me know. Now, Mr. Pate, why don't you go get your car, and I'll have my nurse take your wife down on the elevator to meet you."

After Clyde left, Dr. Zeller sat again. "Now, Mrs. Pate, you need a prolonged rest. You're a remarkable woman. Despite the virulence of your disease, you must have a strong constitution and a strong will or you wouldn't have survived this long. I think you would benefit from hospitalization."

She clenched her jaw. "It's out of the question."

"The hospital isn't far from your home and your family can visit frequently."

Numbly she stared out the window, "I've always lived in terror of being stuck away in some horrible place and left to rot. You don't know what it's like!"

Gently he said, "I'm sure I don't. But I've heard from Sophie what kind of man your husband is. I'm convinced he would never leave you. And National Jewish is not a horrible place, but a fine one. And you can't be left there, Mrs. Pate. We take patients for a limited time. Try it for one year." At her expression he added, "Perhaps only nine months—your daughter's school year." He leaned across the desk. "Please let us help you, Mrs. Pate."

189

"I don't want to go!" she burst out. "Leave my children, leave my home, leave everything familiar. I can't! I won't! I simply can't!"

He leaned across his desk, regarding her with soft eyes. "Mrs. Pate, you need to do this for your husband as well as yourself. Sophie called me because she and Pete, are extremely concerned about Mr. Pate."

She gasped. "Clyde? What's wrong with him?"

"Nothing, yet. But he's been suffering great distress. This free care will help your husband enormously, relieve his stress, and give him quite a boost financially. It's imperative he get this relief!"

She sat perfectly still, facing the big man across the paper-littered desk. Outside the window a dove cooed, then flapped its wings and fluttered away. Looking down she saw the carpet beneath her seldom-worn shoes was tighty woven, beige and nubby. Her palms felt sweaty and her heart pounded loudly. She could smell her lilac bath powder, could hear the rumbling in her chest. Her head throbbed.

At last, she looked up with bleak eyes. "I guess I really have no choice, do I? I've got to do it for Clyde." Her body shuddered with an enormous sigh. Straightening, she set her jaw.

"Start your paperwork, Dr. Zeller. I'll go."

# 35. How Much Does Happiness Cost?

Jenny woke into the midnight darkness. She lay still in the warm bed wondering what had awakened her. The summer had gone fast. *Am I worried about school beginning again soon, or is it missing Dale away at college taking summer classes?*

Then her mother's voice came through the hot air register. "You're going to that new church again on Sunday, Clyde?"

"Yes, I need to go, Nora."

"But why can't you go back to the Methodist church with Jenny?"

"Honey, I love the pageantry of the Episcopalian church, and the minister's sermons are—well, there's just no comparison."

"Then Jenny has to go everyplace all by herself. She might as well be an orphan."

Listening tensely, Jenny's eyes filled and she felt a sudden gush of self-pity. A cold tear rolled down her cheek. Sometimes she did feel like an orphan. She longed to crawl into her mother's lap, feel her arms around her, and comforting kisses. How she wished her mother could do for her what other mothers did. But she'd go on trying to make the best of it.

Nora said, "If you insist on going, don't linger afterward. I want us to leave for Boulder as soon as we've eaten lunch."

*Good!* Jenny thought. *We're going up to see Dale.* During the summer he'd worked creating publicity for a writer's conference as well as taking courses. She frowned. Funny they were going this weekend. They usually drove up every two months and August wasn't the right time.

Dread hollowed a pit in Jenny's stomach. Her parents seemed different since Mother'd seen that new doctor. She seemed sadder and Daddy more—energetic.

Sighing, she turned over. The mantel clock chimed. Far-off, she heard the mournful whistle of a train calling, and her heart ached with yearning, a longing to visit new places, see new things, go somewhere—anywhere.

Saturday morning Jenny had just finished ironing her father's white shirts when her mother's bell rang.

Nora lay on the couch, unsmiling, deep circles under her eyes. "That chair shouldn't be there. After you vacuumed, you didn't put it back in the right place."

Jenny turned. The small gold chair had been given them by Mrs. Wheatley. "I thought it would be nice on the other side of the fireplace."

"No. I want it there." Nora waved a hand.

Confused by the indistinct motion, Jenny asked, "Where?"

"There!" The hand waved again.

Still uncertain, Jenny stood waiting for further direction. "Where?"

"What's the matter? Are you stupid or something!"

Shocked, Jenny stared at her. Then, with a little gasp, she wheeled, and ran, ran through the dining room, past her father unloading sacks of groceries. As she rushed by, he looked up and she couldn't hide her anguished face.

Down the back kitchen stairs she went, holding her breath until she got out the back door into the yard. There, she burst into sobs.

She heard the screen door slam and felt her father's hand on her shoulder.

"What happened, sweetheart? Tell me what's wrong."

"Mother called me stupid."

"You must have misunderstood."

"No, I didn't. Sometimes she says mean things and I can't talk back or she might get sicker, and if she gets sicker she might die, so I just bottle up everything inside."

"She doesn't mean it, Jenny. Why would she say such a thing?"

"She waved her hand at me to move the gold chair, and I couldn't tell where she meant, and she called me stupid." Jenny swallowed her sobs. She didn't want to worry Daddy.

He was silent a moment, his face grim, and then he hugged her. "You're not stupid. You're very bright and we all know it. Mother has a hard life, so you have to forgive her. She's just having a bad day. Why don't you run up to Hilda's to play?"

She stood hesitantly, then finally said, "Okay."

"Oh, Jenny, I'd like you to go to church with me tomorrow. I met a nice man there who runs a jewelry store and has a daughter about your age. I think you'd like her and like that church. How does that sound?"

Jenny liked the church and the new girl. After lunch, the Pates drove to Boulder, picked up Dale at the boarding house, and proceeded to the Colonial Dairy for ice cream.

Dale and Jenny helped their mother walk the few steps into the store. "That table in the back corner." Nora pointed. "It's more private."

The chocolate malts that Dale, Jenny and Clyde ordered were so thick they had to eat them with spoons. Not wanting to risk spreading her germs, Nora had Clyde ask the waitress to put her sundae in a paper container and she got out her own spoon.

For a time there was no sound except lips smacking. Groans of pleasure came from the children, but not from their parents. Clyde's face looked strained. "Your mother and I have something to tell you."

Nora sat quietly hunched in the corner. The dairy smelled of vanilla and chocolate. A bell jingled as customers streamed in and out. The sun painted a golden patch on the black and beige checkered floor.

Clyde took a breath. "Mother's doctor is getting her into the National Jewish Sanitarium to stay full time, and she'll be going there pretty soon. We don't know exactly when."

Jenny gasped. "For how long?"

"A while." He went on, "She needs a good rest. The hospital's nationally known and, Jenny, every day after school, you could walk there to visit Mother."

Dale looked worried. "Are they going to operate or something?"

193

"I certainly hope not," Nora said.

"No, no," Clyde said reassuringly, "nothing like that. Dr. Zeller's her new physician and he'll take good care of her."

"How long will she be there?" Jenny asked.

"Long enough to do some good. The time will go fast."

Gloom descended on her, but Jenny bottled up her distress. Dale was gone and now mother would be, too. *I do feel like an orphan*, she thought, *but I can't let it show.*

When Clyde and Dale got up to take their dishes back, Nora put a hand on Jenny's arm and said stiffly, "I'm sorry, Jenny, for what I said yesterday. It isn't true."

"That's okay." *I see now why you were cross.* Jenny wondered if her mother had cried about going to the hospital. She rarely cried.

As Clyde helped Nora into the car, Dale turned to Jenny. "You going to be okay?"

He seemed embarrassed. It was nice of him to ask, but he was gone from home, out of the situation. "Will you be okay?" he repeated.

"Of course I will," she said. There was nothing else to be.

When Jenny returned from the opening day of high school, she dashed in the rear door, up the stairs and through the kitchen, excited to tell Mother about her new classes. She ran into her mother's room. The bed was empty. "Mother?" Turning, she sped down to the bathroom. Nobody there. "Mother?" No answer. The house was eerily silent.

*She's gone! Mother's gone!*

They hadn't told her it would be today. Maybe it was better this way. No awkward, teary goodbyes. Tomorrow after school she'd walk up Colfax to the hospital. But now she wandered aimlessly around the house, trying to get used to the quiet, the emptiness.

Finally she ate an apple and some cookies and spread her homework on the dining room table. She kept listening for her mother's bell. It was sort of nice not to have to jump up and run answer it. There'd be no trays or bedpans to carry, no dishes to boil, no tissues to burn.

Inside, the house was too quiet. From outside came shouts of children playing. She felt lonely. Ever since she could remember, her mother was always home. Maybe she couldn't do much for Jenny, but she had always been there.

Twin beds stood in her mother's room and when she got home from school, Jenny would lie down on Daddy's bed and she and Mother would listen to the soap operas.

Suddenly she missed her mother dreadfully. Loneliness washed over her. Being an orphan was no fun.

Finally, the back door banged. Daddy was home. She ran to him and he gathered her into his arms, and gave her a big hug and a kiss. His ready physical affection almost made up for receiving no touching from her mother.

Jenny said, "Mother's gone."

He looked at her. "We didn't have any notice, so we couldn't warn you ahead."

She wondered if that was another of his little white lies.

Hastily he said, "You're not going to cry, are you? That's my big girl."

Jenny blinked back tears. She would always have to strive to be a "big" girl.

"Mother's all settled. After supper, we'll go see her. And guess what? Friday is bank night at the Bluebird Theatre. They give money away at a drawing, so we'll go every Friday. Maybe we'll win. How was school, today?"

"Fine. I'm taking a drama class."

"That's nice." He unwrapped a package. "Look at this book, Jenny. I've heard of it, so I bought it at Goodwill, *Think and Grow Rich.* They say hidden in this book is the secret of becoming wealthy. When I get wealthy, I'm going to take you all to Yellowstone."

Jenny watched her father thumb through his new book, grinning and spinning dreams again, dreams that never came true.

But now, Daddy promised seeing a movie every week. They had never been able to afford movies! Her cheerfulness bubbled back. Maybe Daddy would win bank night, and she could study the stars' acting, could pretend she was up there on the screen. Was this promise really coming true?

On Friday when Clyde bought their thirty-five cent tickets, Jenny thought that wasn't much to pay for a few hours of happiness.

# 36. Low Days in High School

A few weeks later after school, Jenny walked the mile from East High up busy Colfax Avenue to the hospital. She didn't mind. She thought Denver's Indian summer sky arching overhead looked like blue custard dotted with floating islands of white meringue. The cool breeze hinted of coming winter snows.

She loved to walk, legs stretched, back straight, head high. Gym teachers stressed good posture. Stores lining the street held little interest for Jenny. For as long as she could remember, when she'd asked for a toy or a book, her mother had always said, "Sweetheart, that's probably just a passing fancy. Later, you probably won't want it."

When Jenny persisted, Mother would say, "It's probably just a fad. Wait until tomorrow."

Before long, Jenny realized Mother kept putting her off because there was no money. Even though disappointed, she found her desires gradually became unimportant. She learned to want nothing. Finally, she didn't even ask. Doing without became a point of pride.

Walking rapidly, she glanced at the array of merchandise crammed into the drugstore window. Proudly, she thought, *"Who needs any of that?"*

She frowned. She could do without many things, but a few clothes would be nice. Yesterday in glee club a girl asked, "Why do you always wear that same old blue skirt?"

Jenny shrugged. "Because it's the only one I've got."

Then there were saddle shoes which everybody wore, but Jenny's instep was so high she couldn't lace them up. Her brown moccasins weren't in style at all. Her shoes, her height, and her sick mother all made her feel different from everyone else.

Someday it would be nice to have lots of money and be somebody. If she could only figure out how. She remembered the headline of that magazine article, "Your Voice Can Be Your Fortune." But it wasn't coming true. She hadn't even been chosen for a cappella choir.

At Smiley Junior High she'd been one of 600 students. At East High she was one of 3,000. The wealthy kids were easy to spot—boys driving flashy convertibles and girls wearing fluffy angora sweaters. Even if those sweaters were a fad, she wished she could have one. They made you look soft, and the girls who wore them always had boys hanging around and carrying their books.

Now Jenny climbed the long flight of steps to the red brick hospital on the hill. She took the elevator and walked down the white hallway. When she reached her mother's large room, Nora looked up from her bed, "Hello, dear, how's everything going? Can you crank me up?"

Grabbing the bed handle, Jenny turned it until her mother was nearly upright.

"That's fine."

Jenny sat in a bedside chair and noticed the other bed in the room was rumpled, but empty. "Do you have a roommate now?"

"She's down at x-ray. Her name is Clara and she's from New Jersey and talks with a funny accent. She didn't even finish high school."

These days her mother always had her hair combed, wore a little makeup, and didn't scold like she used to at home. She seemed to try hard to be pretty and nice. Jenny asked, "Are you glad to have a roommate?"

"In a way. I've never been around anyone else who's been sick like me, but aside from that, I don't think Clara and I have much in common. Would you believe it, Jenny? She worked in a bakery, icing cakes, and all the time she had TB. I can't believe they didn't x-ray those workers. Imagine her handling food."

"That's awful," Jenny agreed.

"She doesn't know about nutrition. She told me she'd diet and then get hungry and eat sweets. That's unhealthy. I've taught you better than that, haven't I?"

"Yes." Mother was finally in a situation where she could feel proud of herself.

"Now, tell me about school."

Jenny scuffed a foot on the linoleum floor.

"What's wrong?"

"I wanted so much to sing in a cappella choir. You have to try out and I didn't make it. My pitch wasn't true or something. Mrs. Bond told me to sing in the glee club."

"Isn't that just as good?"

"It's girls' glee club. The a cappella choir has boys and the popular kids." She paused. "I wish I was popular, was somebody. I wish...." She looked at her mother with pleading eyes. "How do you make a boy like you? What are feminine wiles?"

With a sigh, her mother said, "Oh, Jenny, I wish I knew what to tell you. I honestly don't know. You have plenty of time for dates. I never went out with anyone but your father, and that wasn't until college. And I got a wonderful man. Some boy will like you someday."

"I keep waiting all my life for someday!"

The two sat in silence. Outside a siren shrieked. Nora looked up at her daughter. "Sweetheart, you didn't expect to have an easy life, did you?"

Tears suddenly smarted Jenny's eyes. How could she complain about so little, when her mother never complained about so much, like being sentenced to lie in bed for years, never knowing the satisfaction of a day's work, never even allowed to embrace her family? No wonder she often fussed and scolded. "Easy? I never thought about my life being hard or easy, it's just I've always wanted to affect people, to—I don't know— change them, be important."

"You're important to me, Jenny."

The girl stared at her bedridden mother and couldn't help wondering if she was important for the care she provided. Taking care of Mother always made her feel good, feel needed, feel virtuous. But would she someday have to choose between duty to her parents and her own desires? She felt a sudden stab of anxiety.

Abruptly, she said, "I had to spend $10 for a student ticket that gives me a yearbook, and tickets to all the football games." She brightened. "Did you know last year East won championships in every sport—football, basketball—well, all of them—even the minor ones like tennis? Oh, and we have these two football players that are fabulous. They call them the touchdown twins." Her face clouded. "I want to go to the games, but I don't know who to go with. All my friends are in White Jackets."

"What's that?"

"The drill team. They practice at seven, before school. I wanted to be one, but you have to buy a red skirt and white jacket."

Nora looked out the window. "Those items must be pretty expensive."

"I know, and they have to wear saddle shoes, and those don't fit me."

"Maybe it's just as well. I don't want you catching cold in the early morning air."

"I thought you'd say that." She sighed. *Wanting to be a White Jacket is probably just another fad and I'll get over it.*

Noticing a book on her mother's hospital table, she asked, "What are you reading?"

"*Gone with the Wind.* The nurses bring around a cart of library books every day. This one is historical, interesting and touching."

"The movie is coming out soon. I hope Daddy and I can see it." She leaned closer and said quietly, "Did you know that if a movie is too sad, Daddy gets up and goes to the bathroom, or the lobby, or someplace for a while? I guess he doesn't want to cry, but sometimes it makes me feel good to cry in the show."

Nora looked toward the doorway and her face brightened. "Oh, here comes Daddy now."

After greeting each other, Nora and Clyde held hands. "Clyde, I need to talk to you. The doctors want to do a thoracoplasty on me. I'm afraid."

He hesitated. "I think you should trust the doctors."

"You don't understand." Her eyes widened. "That's a horrible operation. They slice you open and remove some of your ribs. It leaves you horribly deformed and it's permanent. I don't want to be left looking like a freak. Please don't let them do it!"

He patted her shoulder. "All right, honey, calm down. We'll just tell them you refuse. I'll call Dr. Zeller about it tomorrow."

Jenny frowned. "What's that operation for?"

"To collapse the lungs, so they don't work so hard and can heal. But they could collapse them another way by pinching the nerves to the diaphragm. That wouldn't be so bad. I'd let them do that."

"When they collapse your lungs, how do you breathe?" Jenny asked.

"They do only one side at a time. You can breathe with only one lung."

Clyde said, "The second procedure is what we'll ask for. Well, now, here's some good news. Dale's coming home next week."

"That's nice. I miss him."

"He can help me move the furniture to the basement and refinish the hardwood floors. They're bad. With us doing the work, it won't cost much."

Nora looked at him. "That house needs so much more than just the floors redone."

"I've been thinking, Nora," he said, "after finishing the floors, we could rent the upstairs, and Jenny and I can live in the cellar."

"It's only a half-basement and there's no bathroom," she protested.

"We'll share the bathroom with the renters. People are doing all kinds of things to get along in the Depression. Harry and Rose are renting to a couple. Think of the extra money."

"No, Clyde. I don't want you two living below ground. It's not healthy."

"Honey, the furnace keeps it nice and warm, and Jenny's in school most of the day. We could get ahead for once." Looking away, he muttered, "I can't borrow any more from the company."

Silence encompassed the room. Down the hall, someone dropped a tin pan.

Jenny felt bewildered. Her father stood at the end of the bed looking miserable. Her mother hunched over into a coughing spell and then drank a glass of water.

Looking up, Nora regarded her husband with troubled eyes. "Clyde, if you rent out the house, I feel as if I'll never come home."

Fear knotted Jenny's stomach. If Mother didn't come home, would

Daddy stay? Was he thinking of leaving them? What if he did? Then she'd be left to care for her mother all alone. He wouldn't! Bottling up her fears, she put on a brave face.

Clyde held up his hands. "Okay, Nora, we won't do it. I've been reading this book, *Think and Grow Rich*. It suggests thinking in creative new ways. I just thought renting would be one. Maybe I'll get a better idea."

Nora said faintly, "I hope so."

"Don't worry." Clyde squeezed her hand. "Oh, here comes your dinner, so we'll run along." He chuckled. "It's bank night at the movie. Maybe we'll be lucky."

"Maybe. What about your dinner?"

Laughing heartily, Clyde said, "Oh, we'll pick up a little something and eat it in the show. See you tomorrow, honey."

It took only five minutes to drive down Colfax to the Bluebird Theatre. After they parked, Clyde led the way into the doughnut shop next to the theatre. "Listen, Jenny," he said impishly, "we'll buy a dozen glazed doughnuts. That's a quick, easy, cheap dinner. Now, don't tell Mother. That's seven for me, and five for you."

Jenny's mouth watered, and then her heart burst with relief. Of course Daddy would never leave them. He'd promised going to the movies and they were actually going! They'd see a movie and savor all those delicious doughnuts!

At that moment, life seemed pretty good after all. Jenny's spirits lifted. Maybe some of Daddy's other promises would come true, too!

# 37. Trapped Between Duty and Desire

The football stadium stood beneath a cloudless blue sky that seemed to reach up forever. Afternoon shadows spilled across the field and a brisk breeze rattled red and white pom-poms shaken by shiny-faced fans. But Jenny and her father didn't buy any.

On the green field below, bright white paint marked off the yardage. Referees in black and white uniforms consulted each other. In the stands, the crowd in colorful garb milled about, calling, finding seats, waving to friends.

Jenny and Clyde climbed up the stadium stairs. "Let's sit above the fifty-yard line," Clyde said. "That's right in the middle."

"I'm so glad you came with me, Daddy."

"It's crowded. We'd better sit here on the forty. Since this is your first game I'll teach you all about football, Jenny. If you understand the rules and signals, you'll love the game just like I do. Who's East High playing today?"

"Manual High—the ones in the royal blue and gold jerseys."

A shout went up from the spectators. Jenny leaped up, "Here comes our team!"

The squad in red-and-white uniforms trotted onto the field. Six cheerleaders in red sweaters and pleated white skirts shook pompoms and led a cheer, "Red and white, fight, fight. Red and white, fight, fight."

"After the teams warm up," Clyde said, "the captain who wins the toss will elect whether to kick off or receive."

They sat again and Jenny thrust her hand under her father's arm and cuddled close. She was so happy and proud. For once she had her father's complete attention and it filled a deep yearning inside her.

He explained, "East is receiving and there's the kick! Your man caught it on the eighteen yard line and there he goes, running it back. Wow! Look at that kid go!"

Jenny pointed. "That's Skip."

"He's fast and had great blocking. He got up to the forty-five. Now they have four chances, called downs, to make ten yards. If they don't, the ball goes to the other team."

"He has his picture in the school newspaper all the time."

Clyde took in Jenny's flushed face, the soft expression, the admiration in her eyes. *Oh, oh,* he thought, *she's got a crush on Skip.* Clyde kept up a running commentary, explaining the fine points, even describing the penalties before they were announced over the loudspeaker.

A girl in the row ahead of them turned around. "Gee, mister, you sure know a lot. Are you a coach or something?"

"No, I used to play myself. Later, I was even a referee."

"Swell," she said. "I've learned a lot listening to you."

Clyde laughed and watched East High emerge from their huddle. "Watch the guy in the backfield, Jenny. See, they faked a pass, and they're running it instead."

Jumping up, Jenny screamed, "Go, Skip, go!" But Skip was thrown for a loss.

For an instant Clyde felt he was down there himself again, clutching the ball under his arm, legs pumping, chest bursting, dashing down the field. He once again was jolted by the thump of a tackle, felt bodies heavy atop him. Then he scrambled up and glanced toward the stands. He couldn't spot her, but he knew shy, sweet Nora was sitting up there, watching him. He swaggered back to the huddle.

A whistle brought him back to the present. The voice on the loudspeaker boomed, "Fourth down, six to go."

He turned to Jenny, "Manual's line is tight, East will probably kick."

East kicked, just as he'd said. "Now Manual will try to advance the ball ten yards for their first down. Whoops, look at that, Jenny. Your man intercepted their pass."

"Hooray for Skip," Jenny squealed.

Clyde jumped to his feet, yelling with the rest of the East High supporters. "Look at him go! He's going to make a touchdown!"

Skip dashed into the end zone, and the referee's arms went up.

Jenny and her dad hugged each other. Eyes sparkling Jenny cried, "Oh, Daddy, isn't he wonderful?"

He grinned. "Yep, almost as good as I was."

East won the game 21 to 6.

As they filed from the stadium with the noisy crowd, Jenny's heart was bursting. She knew all about football now, thanks to her father, and she'd feasted her eyes on Skip. Skip with the broad shoulders and the quiet smile. Of course he was in the grade ahead and she never saw him at school, but she could still dream about him. And Daddy had been hers for the entire afternoon. Maybe he'd come to all the games with her.

On the way home, they stopped at the hospital. As Jenny walked down that long white hall, all the joy of the bright blue day evaporated. She almost felt guilty for having so much fun when her mother had so little.

When they stepped into Nora's room, the other bed was empty and her mother was lying nearly flat with her bedside lamp off. Eyes closed, she looked so white, Jenny's heart pounded.

"Nora?" Clyde said softly.

She opened her eyes.

He squeezed her limp hand. "How are you feeling?"

"Funny," she said quietly. "They collapsed my left lung. I feel like it's harder to breathe, but they said I'd feel better soon."

"Well, sure. They're going to make you well."

"Oh, Mom, I'm sorry you don't feel so good."

"It's all right, Jenny. Don't worry. You went to the football game?"

"Yes, and we won, and Daddy taught me all about it."

"Good," Nora said with effort. Turning her head away, she said, "Sorry, dear, I don't feel like talking. Don't stay."

Patting her shoulder, Clyde said, "Of course not. You need to rest and get well. We love you, honey."

"We love you, Mother."

Nora said weakly. "Love you, too."

On the way out, Clyde stopped at the nurse's station. "How's is Nora Pate doing?"

The nurse's voice was a crisp as her uniform. "It's too soon to tell. She needs complete rest for a time. For the next few days, don't stay very long when you visit."

On the way home from the hospital, Jenny suddenly said, "I've always been afraid of coming home from school and finding Mother dead."

"Oh, Jenny, don't think like that. Mother's getting good care now, and she's going to get well. You have to have hope, to believe.

"Sometimes it's hard."

"I know."

Finally, Jenny asked, "Are you going to the game with me next week?"

He frowned. "We have to refinish the floors, and then you and Dale need to help me polish them. Then I've got to attend to my business."

Jenny looked out the window, feeling as if she were a rag doll and all her stuffing was running out. The world seemed filled with nothing but work and poverty and sickness. To keep hoping was hard. She sat up straighter. She'd try, but happiness never lasted.

Saturday, Dale and her father moved the furniture, swept the floors, then sanded and applied shellac. They didn't talk, concentrating on their work instead.

After dinner, Dale went off to study and Jenny tried to talk to her father about football, but he said, "Honey, I have to know what's going on in the world for my business." He turned on the radio to the commentary of H. V. Kaltenborn. Midway through the broadcast Clyde muttered, "Things look worse in Europe. I hope we don't get pulled into war over there"

The following weekend Dale came down again. Clyde stood with the two children in the empty rooms and handed Dale a can of paste wax. "I need you two to wax the floors and then polish them. "Here are some rags—old sheets—to use. Rub hard until the floor shines. I expect a good job."

Taking the can, Dale asked, "You going to rent the upstairs like you talked about?"

Jenny froze, frightened.

"I thought it was a good idea, but Mother doesn't, so that's it."

Relieved, Jenny let out her breath.

Clyde turned, "I have to go to the grocery store. You guys get busy."

For a while the two worked with fierce young energy, waxing a yard square area and then rubbing with the rags. Finally, Dale straightened. "Look, Jenny, I've got an idea. Let's wax a big long area and then you sit on this piece of sheet and I'll pull you across to wax it."

She brightened. "That sounds like fun, like a ride."

After they'd waxed a long portion, Dale said, "Now, sit on the sheet and I'll pull you." After she sat down, he tugged, and soon was pulling her faster and faster.

"Whee! This is fun!"

Back and forth they went, waxing, pulling, polishing. He spun her around and she tumbled off, giggling. "This is as good as a ride at Lakeside."

Dale was breathing hard. "And it's free! Okay, now it's my turn. You pull me."

"I can't. You're too big."

"Just try it."

"All right." She grunted and groaned and pulled.

"See, Jenny, I'm sliding."

"That's because we hit a spot we already polished. You pull me again. Get off."

He got up. "You get all the breaks because you're the baby. You're the lucky one."

Jenny had plopped down on the sheet and glared up at him. "Lucky? I am not. You get to go off to college, and to the dude ranch. You got to go canoeing with Daddy. Me? I have to wash and iron and cook and clean—"

"Oh, come on, all girls do that."

"—and take care of Mother."

"And I had to give Dad my earnings from the paper route, and my money from the ranch for college."

They worked in silence. Then she said, "What are you going to do when you get out of CU?

"I don't know. I wanted to be a writer—so they make you take English Literature. But who wants to write like that? I want to be another Jack London or Richard Halliburton. Or else they say to take journalism. I don't want to be a newspaperman. Dad says I should be a teacher, but I don't want to teach. What are you going to be?"

"I don't know either." She couldn't confess that she desperately wanted to be a star, a somebody.

"Mom said you'd make a good nurse."

"Yes, but then, right away, she said nurses have to work too hard—scrub floors and lift patients, and I might get sick. Besides, I'd have to get a good grade in chemistry."

"So? You're smart."

Clasping her hands, she said, "Not about chemistry I'm not. I don't understand it, and you know what? The kids all say to get a good grade from Mr. Teel you have to be small, blonde and pretty—and I'm none of those."

"Rotten guy. Let's rest." They scooted over and leaned against the wall.

They sat quietly. Suddenly Jenny blurted, "They want me to stay home and take care of Mother. Oh, nobody says it out loud, but I can tell. Like, Mother doesn't think a girl should leave home unless she's going to get married." Her face turned wistful. "I'd love an apartment of my own, to be my own boss, and not have to take orders from anybody else. I hate reporting everyplace I go and when I'll be back."

"When you go out, they're just worried about you."

"They don't worry about you. You're free. I don't have a boyfriend. I'm afraid I'll never marry. I'll be an old maid stuck at home with Mother!"

He laughed. "You'd probably be a good old maid. You're good at everything else."

After a minute her eyes twinkled and she started singing, "*Nobody loves me, everybody hates me.*"

He joined in, *"Think I'll go out and eat worms."*

They both doubled over with laughter.

Jenny sobered. "But seriously, I don't want to be an old maid school teacher. You know what I do want? I want to go dancing. They taught us how in gym class and I'm good at it, but nobody's ever asked me to a prom." She giggled. *"I'm going to eat worms."*

Dale sighed. "I'm not so hot in the love department myself. There's this girl at school—she's the only one I really like, but she's already got a boyfriend."

"That's what they ought to teach in school—how to make somebody love you."

Both sat thinking. Dale said, "Tell you what, Jenny. You are going to go dancing—next summer. I'll take you to Lakeside. It's a date."

"Oh, Dale, you're such a good brother."

"Hey, listen," he said, "you'll find the right person someday."

"So will you!"

The school year wound on. Jenny went faithfully to all the football games, often alone. She went even when it was snowing. She clipped pictures of Skip from the school paper and kept them in her dresser drawer.

Although her other grades were A's and B's she only managed to scrape through chemistry class with a C. She hated chemistry. *So much for a career in nursing.*

Second semester she loved the drama class and was getting A's, but the teacher seemed to give special attention to the rich girls in angora sweaters and boys in athletic sweaters.

One night Jenny dreamed about that magazine title she'd seen, "Your Voice can be Your Fortune," and awakened exhausted and frustrated. In the dream she tried to run after the woman with the article about your voice—tried and tried—but her legs wouldn't move.

At the hospital one afternoon she asked her parents, "Do you suppose I could have a career in music?"

"What kind of music?" her father asked.

"Singing in operas, or in operettas like Jeanette MacDonald."

"You have a beautiful voice, Jenny." Her mother frowned. "But music training takes money—money we don't have. And making a living that way is extremely hard. Maybe you could teach music."

"I'm sorry, sweetheart," her father said.

The dream faded, like a singer disappearing when the curtain falls. *So much for my voice becoming my fortune.*

Finally in the spring her father said gaily, "Guess what Jenny? We've got to spruce up the house. Mother told Dr. Zeller she couldn't stand being in the hospital any longer, so they're letting her come home."

"For Easter?"

"Yes, and to stay. Isn't that wonderful? Mother's coming home for good."

Jenny's heart surged with happiness. "Then she's well. Mother's well!"

Her father didn't answer.

When the day came, Jenny held her mother's arm as they walked slowly from the garage to the house. Disturbed, Jenny thought Mother looked as pasty and sad-eyed as ever.

In all those months Nora had been in the hospital, her only treatment seemed to be the collapse of her lungs, one in the fall and the other later on. After a time, the lungs completely expanded again. That treatment was supposed to help the tuberculosis heal, but as Jenny walked beside her mother she could hear the familiar whistling and gurgling in her mother's chest.

Jenny's eyes met her father's as he walked on the other side of Nora. All those months, all that hope, and nothing had changed. They helped Mother to bed.

Lying back against the pillows, Nora smiled and gasped for breath. "It's so good to be home. I couldn't stand it there any longer, away from you, away from everything I love. I never want to see a hospital again."

"It's great to have you home, dear." Clyde sounded as optimistic as ever.

*How can he keep on?* Jenny thought. *How can Mother? How can I?*

Deep inside, Jenny came to a sudden bitter conclusion. Nothing would ever change. Her mother would never get well, never hug her, never come to a school event. Mother had been bedridden since Jenny was seven, and she always would be!

In her white face, Nora's eyes looked large and dark. She looked up at her husband and her daughter, standing beside the bed. "I'm sorry. Every little thing they said to do, I did. I followed all the instructions to the letter. I tried so hard." Her voice caught.

Nora took Jenny's hand. "I need to tell you something and want you to always remember it. At the hospital, I did learn something—one big thing." Her eyes glowed. "The chief of staff," she said proudly, "told me." She paused and the labored breathing went on. "Dr. Oswald said that when something is too terrible to bear, you have to wall it off—shut it out. You just don't let yourself think about it any more."

Stunned, Jenny wondered, *How can I?* As she stood, holding her mother's hand, she could see the years stretch out ahead of her, see herself washing, cleaning, carrying bedpans and bed trays—lugging Mother's pillows into the yard, jumping up to answer her ever-clanging bell.

The bedroom walls seemed to close in like a trap, holding them all there—Daddy, Mother, and she herself. She—who so wanted to be independent, make her own decisions, and go adventuring. She—who so longed to sing and dance and be somebody. Instead, she was trapped—trapped in four suffocating walls—and she was never going to get out.

Her mother's voice came from far away, "When something is too terrible to bear, just don't think about it any more!"

# 38. What Will Become of Jenny?

By fall, when school started again, Jenny was astonished to find her mother seemed somewhat better. Being back at the house on Holly Street seemed to have lifted her spirits.

That October morning of 1940, her mother's blue eyes shone with life. Smiling she said, "I was lying here listening to the sounds of home. At the hospital I heard sirens screaming, feet tapping down the hallways, and at night—muffled crying."

"Oh, Mom, I don't think we realized how hard it was for you."

"It's all right, dear. No one can really enter into another person's experience, and I'm glad for that. Jenny, listening makes you feel so alive. Stop, and really listen."

A lawnmower whirred, birds warbled, and far off an airplane droned.

Looking up, Mother said, "How I'd like to be up there going somewhere."

A car roared past, a door slammed and a voice called, "Don't forget your lunch."

"Take time to listen to life, Jenny. Soak it all up."

"Mom, you sound like a poet."

"I thank God every day to be with my family again. How you children are growing! I can't believe Dale's a senior at college, and you're a senior at high school. How's this year going?"

Jenny hesitated, weighing her words, not wanting to spoil her mother's happy mood. She wanted to burst out with her complaints—that she wasn't pretty, didn't have nice clothes, or a boyfriend. So far high school hadn't been much fun, except for going to the football games.

She wanted to sing solos at school or church, but no one ever asked her. She might as well forget about being a singing star, forget new clothes, too. They had so little money.

Babysitting had paid her quite a lot this summer, but family birthdays and Christmas were coming.

Just then Clyde came into the house with his usual buoyant step, grinning, but saved his news until dinner. Mother was able to eat at the table and, after they finished dessert, he said, "I told you things were going to get better. Everybody says we're nearly out of the Depression and it's certainly time." His eyes twinkled and he paused dramatically. "I just landed a mighty big policy."

Jenny looked up eagerly. "I can get a new skirt and an angora sweater!"

Her mother said, "We can spruce up the house!"

Clyde's face fell. "Look, we'll have to postpone those things until later."

Dismay and suspicion changed Nora's face, "You just said you've finally made some money. Surely our bills won't take all of it."

"No." He said slowly. "We will have a new bill, but now I can manage that. I've made a pretty good down payment."

"Down payment on what? Clyde, what have you bought?"

"A new car," he blurted and grinned.

Nora's face darkened. "A new car!"

"Isn't that great? A brand new one."

"All through our marriage," Nora said dully, "it seemed every time we got a little ahead, you had to have a car."

"I didn't want to worry you, but I've been having trouble with our old one, and you know I have to have a car for my business. Besides, Hitler's invaded Poland. All businessmen think war is coming, so cars are going to be expensive—and scarce. I know I've done the right thing. It's a Ford, a nice green color. You'll like it. The next time we drive up to Boulder, won't Dale be surprised!"

Nora's lips were thin. "What about money for his last year at school?"

"Now, Mother, it's good for him to work."

"Clyde, his grades are down and he doesn't seem very happy. Working plus studying is too much." She cocked her head. "So while Dale works himself to death, you go buy a car."

Jenny cringed. She had to agree with her mother. What was Daddy thinking? She wished she knew how to make a fortune.

But a bright spot suddenly lit up Jenny's senior year. She won the part of the mother in *Young April,* the Senior Class Play. Being on stage, making people laugh, and hearing all the applause transported her into another world, a wonderful world. And everybody declared that she was very good.

But the senior year passed rapidly. Fear gnawed at her. When high school ended, what would become of her?

# 39. They Forgot to Make Plans for Jenny

One day in May of 1941, Jenny sank down at the table in the lunchroom and opened her brown paper sack.

Across from her, Thelma brushed back blonde hair from her freckled face and said, "Jenny, I'm going to the University of Colorado. My dad finally came through with the money. I don't think my stepmother liked it, but who cares?"

Jenny looked down at her tuna sandwich. "CU is where Dale goes." Thelma had confided long ago how much it hurt that her parents had divorced. Like Jenny, Thelma had troubles, too, but at least her family had money.

Just then Libby rushed up and threw her arms around Thelma. "I get to go to CU too. Maybe we can room together and join the same sorority. It'll be such fun." She sat next to Thelma.

As they laughed and chatted, Jenny slowly munched her sandwich, feeling excluded. Head down, she hoped nobody would say anything to her, but then it came—the dreaded question.

"Where are you going next year, Jenny?"

Her stomach clenched. "We haven't decided yet." She was lying, and they probably knew it, because they turned away, ignoring her again, chattering on about clothes, boys and sororities.

Loneliness welled up in her. At home, nothing had been said about college, or a job, or Jenny's future. It was already May, and the class of '41 would graduate in June, and her parents had made no plans for her.

Jenny had never brought it up. Knowing her family had so many problems, she tried not to add to them—always keeping her burdens inside.

But it wasn't fair. Seized by anger, she bit down hard on her apple. Dale got to go to college. Mother and Daddy both went to college. Even her grandmother had a higher education. Jenny had always assumed she would too.

She ate three sugar cookies she'd baked last Saturday. Dread gnawed at her and the old suspicion surged into consciousness. *They want me to stay home and take care of Mother.*

"See you around, Jenny." Thelma and Libby rose, gathered their books and left. Jenny gave a half-hearted wave and then noticed Hattie Flint hurrying up.

Hattie sank down opposite Jenny and said breathlessly, "I've got to rush through my lunch. I just got back. Hope I finish before the bell rings." Unwrapping a sandwich, she glanced at the clock. "I didn't know I'd be gone so long."

Jenny roused from her black mood. Hattie, like Jenny, was plain and poor. She wore her brown hair pulled back from her round pink face, and her green eyes squinted from behind thick glasses. She wore the same cheap clothes repeatedly, just like Jenny. They were kindred spirits, but not good friends.

Jenny had few close friends among the 800 seniors, and she suspected that some people were afraid of her because they found out that her mother had TB.

Hattie seemed in very good spirits. Jenny asked, "Where have you been and what are you smiling about?"

"I'm going to college in the fall."

"Seems like everybody is." Jenny was surprised because the Flint family didn't seem to have much money either, except enough for Hattie's violin lessons.

"Where are you going?" Jenny asked, even though it hurt to hear about it.

"Colorado Woman's College."

"Oh." Jenny was vaguely aware of the small college on the east side of Denver not far from home. She wouldn't want to go to a girl's school where there wouldn't be any boys. Jenny had never had a date, and she was sure Hattie hadn't either, but she seemed pleased to be going there.

Mouth full, Hattie mumbled, "I have a scholarship."

"You do?" She knew Hattie wasn't an A student. "How did you get a scholarship?"

"It's a music scholarship. I played my violin."

"How exciting! How did you manage to do that?"

"It was easy," Hattie explained in her high nasal voice. "I called up the school and asked for an audition, and after I played, they gave me a scholarship for next fall."

"Congratulations!" Jenny studied the homely face across the table, glad for her and sad for herself. *Even Hattie Flint*, she thought dully.

"Thanks." Hattie wadded up her lunch bag. "See you."

The bell rang. Jenny stood, staring after Hattie. *She'd always known her own grades weren't good enough for a scholarship, but Hattie's scholarship seemed a different kind.* Suddenly, determination flooded her. *If she can do it, I can too.*

*I'd go to Colorado Woman's College, even if they don't have any boys. But what can I do? I don't play the piano, or even the triangle but, by gum, I'm going to do something!*

Walking the four miles home, she thought about it all the way. Since her parents hadn't provided for her, she'd have to provide for herself. But where should she start?

At home, Jenny put away her books, greeted her mother, and fixed them both a snack. She sat on the bed across from her mother and ate silently.

Nora said, "Honey, what's wrong?"

Jenny gulped a swallow of milk. "Hattie Flint got a scholarship to CWC and I figure if she can, I can."

Smoothing the sheet, Nora frowned. "Really! How did she get this scholarship?"

"Played her violin." She hesitated. "I've decided to sing."

For a minute the only sound was the crunching of their sugar cookies.

Finally Mother said, "That might work out. You could still live at home, so there wouldn't be room and board to pay."

Surprised at her mother's approval, Jenny said, "The school's only a mile or so away." Her stomach churned. She really wanted to go away and live in a dorm, but any college sounded pretty good. If she couldn't go to college, what would she do with herself?

"So!" Her mother thought for a minute. "What are you going to sing? And how can you practice without a piano?"

"I don't know."

"We'll just have to think about it. Oh dear, look at the time. You'd better put the potatoes in to bake. We're having leftover roast for supper. Divide it in half. We need to stretch it for two meals. And make a carrot-pineapple-gelatin salad so it's ready for tomorrow night. How was school, today?"

Jenny collected their dishes. "Okay. How were your soap operas?"

Her mother laughed. "Fine. Remember, Lux Radio Theatre is on tonight. Try to get your homework done. I like for us to listen together. You could even make popcorn."

"I wish I could go to CU."

"I wish you could too, but I don't see how. And I don't want you working. I worry about your health all the time."

"It's still not fair."

"What's not fair?"

"Everything! The Depression, and Daddy having to give up his Y work, and your being sick. Life's just not fair." The minute she said the words she knew how selfish they sounded.

From the prone figure in the bed came the labored breathing, then a big sigh. "You're right, Jenny. We all have to learn that life's not fair, and there's nothing we can do about it." Turning her face to the wall, she said, "Just try to make the best of whatever you're handed and don't think about it. Now, you'd better start supper."

When Clyde bounded into the kitchen from work, Jenny told him about Hattie and that maybe she could sing for a scholarship. His smile faded. Hanging his head, he rubbed his hands on his worn trousers. "I wish I could send you away to school, Jenny, but I can't. It would be great if you could get a scholarship. But how could you make a living in music? We've discussed this before. If you get to go, prepare to teach."

Jenny stared at him. She didn't want to teach. "Daddy, there was this article in a magazine—"Your Voice—" But Nora's bell interrupted.

"I'll go," he said, hurrying away. Watching his retreating figure, she realized she'd never mentioned that article title that promised, "Your Voice Can Be Your Fortune." A tingle ran up her spine. *Could it come true some day?*

First, she had to audition at the college. She needed an accompanist, a number to sing, and a piano to practice on. She didn't have any of them. With a sigh she began to serve dinner.

That evening Mrs. Wheatley stopped by with a bunch of fragrant lilacs for her mother. Hearing the story about the scholarship, she said, "Sue next door has a piano. I'm sure she'd let you practice on it. We'll go over right now and ask."

The idea embarrassed Jenny a little because they had never neighbored with Sue. Almost too dazed to be excited, she got her sweater.

Mrs. Wheatley was still talking to her mother. "Nora, did I tell you Larry did go ahead and enlist in the army? He's in the Philippines, seeing the world."

Nora's eyes shone. "How exciting! Oh, I wish I could travel."

"I'm glad he's not in Europe with Hitler taking over countries and all." Turning to Jenny, she said, "If you're ready, Jenny, let's go."

Sue readily agreed to let Jenny use her piano and added, "I have a friend named Laura who's a pianist. I'm sure she'd be willing to accompany you, Jenny."

At Sue's a few days later, Jenny met a small, dark-haired, vibrant woman. After the introductions, Laura handed Jenny some sheet music. "Sue said you're a mezzo soprano and I brought some music, 'Trees,' and 'Ave Maria.' They're beautiful, but the range might be too high for you." She sat down at the keyboard, "'Alice Blue Gown' would be good." She spread the music on the piano rack.

"Oh, yes, let's do 'Alice Blue Gown.'"

Laura's fingers rippled up and down the keyboard and then played the introduction.

Following the music, Jenny sang the verse. Caught up in the story, her nervousness slipped away. It came naturally to act out the song.

When she finished, Sue clapped and Laura exclaimed, "Very nice! You have a lovely voice, and won't need much more rehearsal."

Jenny glowed. *Maybe my voice will be my fortune!*

Laura said, "Let's practice next Saturday. Go ahead and make an appointment for your audition for the following week, any time. Oh, and remember to smile at your audience. You will be giving them a wonderful gift."

On the appointed day, Jenny and Laura entered Treat Hall at Colorado Woman's College. A student at the reception desk hopped up. "They're waiting for you in the music studio. Come, this way."

Jenny felt terribly nervous as she followed Laura into a large room containing a piano. Across from it, a man and woman rose from their chairs. The plump, pretty woman introduced herself. "I'm Mrs. Willis, the music professor." She turned to the tall, gray-haired man next to her. "And this is Dean Archer." He nodded and they both sat down again.

Laura arranged the music on the piano. In her blue dress, Jenny stood in the curve of the mahogany grand piano, straightened and smiled, but her heart pounded. Her entire future rested on the next few minutes. Could she win the scholarship? She just had to!

Tense and frightened, she took a deep breath, listened to Laura's introductory phrases, and bravely made eye contact with her two judges. Swallowing, she wondered if any sound would come out, and if it did, whether her voice would shake as much as she was shaking inside. Laura played the introduction and gave her a firm nod. Jenny opened her mouth—and sang. She became the girl in the song—proud and shy—the girl wearing the Alice Blue Gown, and her voice rang out sweet and true.

When the song ended, she remained still, waiting breathlessly. In three minutes of music her chance had come—and gone.

No one clapped. She hadn't been sure they would. Mrs. Willis and the Dean had their heads together, talking. Then both smiled as they rose.

Laura gathered the music from the piano and stood next to Jenny, a questioning look on her face. Mrs. Willis whispered to the Dean again. In a moment she straightened, frowning. "We want you to be aware that we may have exhausted our scholarships for this year, but we'll tell our Board of Trustees about you. Thank you for coming in. We'll let you know."

Jenny's heart plummeted. The scholarships must be gone. Hopelessly, she thought, *I'll never get to go to college. I'll be stuck at home with Mother—forever.*

Outside, Laura exclaimed, "Jenny, you were wonderful!"

"But they gave my friend a scholarship on the spot. I must not have been good enough."

"Don't worry. You were in good voice, and just charming."

Laura had driven them to CWC in her own car. On the way back home they rode in silence. When they arrived, Jenny leaned over and hugged Laura. "It's been so nice of you to help me. Please come in, I have a little something to thank you."

In the house, Jenny presented Laura with a large box, prettily wrapped, and tied with a pink ribbon that didn't show it had been used before. "It's just some home-made Snickerdoodles."

Taking the gift, Laura smiled. "My favorites! How sweet of you. Thank you!"

From her bedroom, Nora called, "How did it go?"

Laura went to her doorway. "Just fine. Jenny was perfect. She'll probably get good news in a few days. I think she's a wonderful young lady."

Nora nodded. "Jenny's a great help to me. I don't know what I'd do without her."

"Mom," Jenny said glumly, "the music professor said they might be out of scholarships. They'll let us know, but it doesn't look good."

"I think they were impressed," Laura said. As they walked to the front door, she patted Jenny's arm, "Keep up your spirits." Laura's eyes danced, "Just you wait. You might be surprised."

With every passing day, Jenny felt terrible. After two weeks crawled by, Jenny gave up. Then one day when she got home from school, her mother called, "Jenny, you received two letters from Colorado Woman's College."

Jenny rushed into the bedroom, took the letters and felt blood rush to her face. Suddenly she couldn't breathe, couldn't think. She didn't want to open them, didn't want to know, didn't want to face the awful truth.

Gently, her mother said, "Here's the letter opener."

Jenny hefted the envelopes. "They're postmarked the same day." She shrugged. "Well, here goes nothing." The sound of the paper slitting made her want to jump out of her skin. Slowly, she unfolded the sheet. Tears welled into her eyes and the printing danced. She blinked, trying to focus through the blur.

"Well, what does it say?"

Her voice shook. "It says, 'We are pleased to notify you that you have been awarded a two-year scholarship of $200 for each year at CWC based upon your musical ability. A brochure about the school, a catalog, and further registration information will be mailed soon.'"

Twirling, she waved the letter over her head. She felt like sunlight had suddenly engulfed her in warmth. Grinning she cried, "Hooray, I got it! I get to go! I'm going!"

"Jenny, I'm so glad. That's wonderful!" Taking the letter, she read it. "My, it's a two-year school, and you have a scholarship for both years. You certainly deserve it." Smiling, she thought a moment. "After you graduate from CWC, maybe you could go to on to the University of Colorado. I'd love for you to have that experience. By then, perhaps Daddy's business will be better. Open the other envelope. Maybe it's the brochure they mentioned."

Tapping the second envelope on her hand, Jenny frowned. "They look exactly alike." Worried, she looked at her mother. "Oh, dear—maybe this one says they've made a mistake and they take it all back." She sank down onto her father's bed.

Nora leaned back against her pillows, hand at her breast. "Surely not, Jenny. That would be terrible. Go on, let's see what it says."

After extracting the letter and unfolding it, Jenny studied the paper, mystified.

Nora leaned forward, "What's the matter?"

The paper crackled as Jenny waved it. "I don't understand. It says, 'You have been awarded a two-year scholarship of $200 for each year, courtesy of Mrs. Hubert M. Garner.'" She looked at her mother and frowned. "Do they mean she's the one who gave me the other scholarship? Is this just a duplicate letter because they forgot to mention her in the other one? And who's this Mrs. Garner?"

"I've never heard of her. Let me see both letters."

Nervously, Jenny waited while her mother examined each sheet. Nora looked up. "One letter says your scholarship is based on your musical ability. The other is from Mrs. Garner." She broke into a broad smile. "Jenny, you must have two scholarships."

Leaping up, Jenny cried, "Two?" For a moment she stood stunned and then she realized she had been awarded $400 a year. "Oh, Mom, I can't believe it!" She wanted to throw her arms around her mother, but she couldn't. Dancing around the room, she chanted. "Mrs. Garner, who is she? What a delectable mys-ter-y. Mrs. Garner, please come out. Tell me what you're all about. Mrs. Garner gives me glee. Who's this lovely mys-ter-y? Mrs. Garner, hooray for you. What a terrific thing to do!" She twirled faster.

Nora laughed. "Jenny, you're a poet. Did you know it? You've said a verse, but what is worse, we're in a tiz' 'cause we don't know who in the world this Mrs. Garner is."

They both laughed so hard they cried.

For the next few days, they asked everyone they could think of about the mysterious woman responsible for the second scholarship. No one had heard of her.

They debated about phoning the college, but Mother thought that would be too embarrassing and nosy and, besides, they weren't sure who to ask. They still worried that it all might turn out to be a mistake.

They asked people at church, Jenny's school friends, her glee club teacher, and even the neighbors. Sue shook her head. She didn't know the woman either.

Jenny said, "I've been trying to reach Laura to tell her, but she's not home."

"She's been substituting for an organist," Sue said, "up at Estes Park."

When Laura finally answered the phone and heard about the music scholarship, she exclaimed, "That's wonderful, Jenny. I knew it! You sang so well. Congratulations!"

"There's another scholarship from a Mrs. Garner. We're trying to find out who she is." There was a silence on the other end of the phone. "Laura?"

"I'm still here." She paused. "Jenny, I know Mrs. Garner."

"You do?" Jenny nearly burst with curiosity. "Who is she? I'm dying to know."

"Mrs. Garner is a friend I've known for many years. I happened to mention you to her. You see, when her husband died, he left a substantial sum to Colorado Woman's College. In gratitude, the college allows Mrs. Garner to give an annual scholarship to a deserving young woman of her choice. For the next two years, you are that deserving young woman. She chose you."

"Can I meet her to thank her, or write her, or do something for her?"

"No, no. She's very private, and prefers no contact. I'll let her how happy you are."

"Would you tell her I read someplace that my voice might be my fortune? If it is, it'll be thanks to her."

Laura said, "She'll be pleased."

When the college catalog and brochure arrived, Jenny sat down to study them. Right off, she noticed a photo of students putting on a play. Her mind raced forward to the fun she'd have, the college activities, and best of all—there were boys in the picture and a footnote said male students from nearby schools often took part in the CWC productions. What a surprise! She'd meet boys! Her heart rose. She'd major in drama as well as music. Maybe a girl's school wouldn't be so bad after all. It was time to prepare dinner, so she couldn't read more.

After supper she handed the material to her father. A few minutes later he looked up and pronounced abruptly, "The tuition is $700 a year!" He let out a gigantic sigh. "We need $300!"

They all sat in stunned silence.

Jenny said fiercely, "I'll babysit all summer."

"Oh, Jenny," Mother protested, "you can't make $300 that way. And I don't want you staying up late all the time. You need your rest."

"Vallorie's clerking at Sears. Why can't I work there?"

Nora scowled. "I think that would be too tiring. I won't have you risk getting sick like me." She sighed heavily. "Oh, I wish things were different." She suddenly bent over, convulsed with a coughing spell.

Running from the room, tears brimming, Jenny wanted to scream, "Life's not fair," but she knew that life hadn't been fair to any of them.

# 40. Is It Too Late for Jenny?

Even before graduating in June, Jenny took every baby-sitting job she could find. She posted notices at school, on the bulletin board at the library, and at the little corner store. She especially liked sitting when the children were already in bed and she could eat a snack and read the family's magazines.

But sometimes she'd hear an automobile pass outside trailing strains of music from its radio along with bursts of laughter. Looking up from her magazine, she'd sit wishing could be dating and having fun, but she had to work if she wanted to go to college. Most people paid her only 15 or 25 cents an hour. Uncle Harry gave her 50 cents for an evening.

With mid-June, graduation gifts arrived. Along with the bath powder, necklaces and notepaper came a few dollars tucked into almost every package. Word must have gotten out that Jenny needed money for school. Mother's four siblings and Grandma sent cash, as did Daddy's three half-brothers.

Daddy always gave her a big hug when he came home from work, and then they'd prepare dinner together. When they could afford meat, he liked to cook it, and she'd fix the rest of the meal. If she had a babysitting job, he'd say, "You go on. I'll do the dishes," and that would make her eyes fill. He was such a good dad.

After supper, he usually sat in his worn green chair reading, first the newspaper, and then his tattered best-seller—*Think and Grow Rich*.

One night Jenny asked him, "How does that book say to get rich?"

He looked up. "Well, it doesn't tell you exactly how."

"Then why are you reading it?"

"I'm getting a lot out of it, Jenny. For example, the author—Napoleon Hill—talks about making your own breaks."

Jenny nodded, "Like I did getting the scholarship."

He looked away. "I'm working on getting the rest of your tuition, Jenny." He rested the book on his lap, lost in thought, then roused. "Another thing he talks about is the power of positive emotions—like faith, enthusiasm and hope."

"Yeah," said Jenny dully, afraid to release the sigh of disappointment that welled up in her chest. She was always hoping, but she was rapidly losing faith. Glancing at her father, she noticed how his face glowed as he said, "I believe in this book. You have to believe that good will come, and it will!"

Jenny studied his smiling face. *What would we all do without his enthusiasm and cheerfulness and hope? It would be easy for him to go around sad and worried, but instead, he's always optimistic.* Her heart burst with love.

Returning to the book, he said, "Hill says to have imagination, Jenny. Someday I'll sell a lot of policies, you'll go to college and—tell you what— we'll go to Yellowstone." His gray eyes sparkled. "Yes sir!"

"That'll be nice," Jenny said half-heartedly. She'd heard the empty promises before. Daddy was a wonderful man. To help you out, he'd give you the shirt off his back. The trouble was—Daddy never had a spare shirt to give.

One of the best things about summer was that Dale was home from the University of Colorado to stay. Though only a few classes short of his Bachelor of Arts degree, he had run out of steam as well as money. Besides, Mother worried about his heavy burden of work and school. Her family's health was a constant concern.

A few days later Clyde asked, "Son, have you looked for a teaching job yet?"

Dale frowned. "I want to write, not teach, Dad. Maybe that's why I had trouble controlling the kids." He hesitated. "I tried, Dad, I really tried, but I couldn't do it."

"I'm disappointed. Teaching gives you security. They always need teachers."

Behind his glasses Dale's blue eyes were intense. "In student teaching, I worked up these good lessons about Shakespeare and other writers—and I don't know—the kids were terrible—wouldn't behave for me. I just don't have a way with kids."

Nora looked up from the couch. "But maybe you could learn."

Grimly, Dale said, "The whole class started clicking their tongues, laughing, throwing spit wads. I can't teach," he said miserably. "I don't want to!"

Jenny thought of when she'd tried to darn her father's socks. Her handiwork never looked like her mother's beautiful weaving. She knew how Dale felt—sometimes something just wasn't what you were cut out for. She noticed Daddy was unusually quiet.

"Son," he said, "you need to start looking for a job."

"I know. I've been reading the ads."

"That's not enough. You've got to pound the pavements like I do, and knock on doors. And when you get one no, you've got to keep on going. Do you understand?"

"All right, all right. I'll try harder."

A few weeks later, Dale started working as a copywriter at the Layton Rubber Company in south Denver an hour away, so he was often late getting home.

One night as Dale morosely ate a warmed-up dinner, Clyde tried to cheer him up about his new position. "Lots of folks are still out of work, Dale. Just be mighty glad you were able to get that job."

"The pay's nothing, Dad." He looked up with a worried face. "And I can't seem to please my boss. This kind of writing isn't what I want to do with my life."

Clyde went to him and patted him on the back, "Be proud. You got yourself work and they're paying you to write. Writing is what you wanted to do."

"Yeah, but instead of stories and novels, I'm stuck trying to say something fantastic about ugly automobile tires. Big thrill!"

Jenny smiled at him sympathetically, but he didn't notice. No wonder he was down in the dumps. A job he didn't like, and last week he'd told her that the special girl at college was marrying somebody else.

Jenny felt sad. *Neither of us seems any good in the love department.*

Dale roused and turned to her, "Hey, Jen, that's great about your scholarships. Keep working, you'll make it!"

But Jenny wondered.

Depriving herself of even the smallest purchase, she watched her savings account grow, but by mid-July, including the gift money, she had only $80 which she deposited at the college to hold her spot. She was afraid to ask if her scholarships would still be good a year later, and if she could get her deposit back if she didn't have the entire amount by fall.

After dinner she went next door to babysit for Dora Vandermeer. Mrs. Vandermeer said, "Jenny, I'll give you extra for doing the dishes and, after the girls are in bed will you wash the bathroom bowl, put out some guest towels and dust the living room? The girls' scout troop is meeting here tomorrow afternoon."

After Jenny got the girls to bed and settled, she started thinking as she cleaned. Scouts earned merit badges for various skills. What did she know something about? She remembered her high school drama class and some of the acting exercises.

When the couple got home, Jenny said, "Mrs. Vandermeer, I was wondering if I if I couldn't teach your scout troop dramatics—for a small sum for each girl."

Mrs. Vandermeer clapped her hands. "Jenny, what a great idea! I was undecided about which program to do with the girls meeting here this summer. You've saved my life. Let's do a four-week class in drama toward their Junior Theatre Badge. I think about an hour for your activity would be fine. There are 10 in the troop and I think we could charge $3."

"Three dollars a class?"

"No, $3 for each girl for each class. That's $12 a girl and we'll get the money up front."

"You're talking about $120!"

"Can you start tomorrow afternoon?"

"Of course I can."

Jenny worked all morning drawing up plans for the lessons, so when afternoon came she was ready. But when she faced the group of jabbering scouts, her heart thundered.

Mrs. Vandermeer helped hand out name tags so Jenny would know who they were, and then sat in the corner.

Jenny stood before them, scared. "Hi, I'm Jenny. I studied drama in high school and was in the senior class play, so I'm going to teach you acting. Today we're going to start with pantomiming. That's acting without using any words. Your body and your facial expression tell the story. We'll start by pretending to put on hats."

All the faces were eager but one. "This is dumb!" said the tall girl in the middle.

Panic washed over Jenny. This girl could turn the whole group against her. Thinking quickly, Jenny said, reading her name tag. "Oh, Carla, that was really good. Your facial expression and what you did with your shoulders. You and Mary hop up here and, Mary, you gesture at the pretend store window here, and point at the imaginary hats. Carla, you act out thinking that's dumb. And then you both go into the store and Mary tries on a big hat and a small hat, and one with a veil and, Carla, you stand beside her and gesture how wrong all the hats are. Okay?"

Jenny swallowed and looked directly into Carla's eyes. The room was silent, waiting for the troublemaker's response.

After a moment, Carla rose and followed Mary to the front of the room.

With a sigh of relief, Jenny felt she had crossed the rickety bridge of her first challenge. As they performed, she smiled and whispered, "That's good, girls, keep it up. Excellent, Carla."

When the two had finished, the other girls clapped and clamored to be next. As the afternoon went on, Jenny noticed a skinny little girl at the back of the group. She sat shoulders hunched, head down, watching furtively out of the corners of her eyes. Her name was Blanche.

When all the others had had a turn, Jenny turned to her. "Blanche? Would you like to try?"

A quick shake of the head was the only response.

"She's scared. She's scared of everything," Carla sneered.

Jenny nodded. "Everybody's scared. I've been scared. But you know what? Scared is another word for being excited. Being scared and excited gives you energy to be really good at whatever you do. You don't have to do anything, Blanche, but I wonder which hat you'd choose—a big picture hat with ribbons down the back and a rose to smell on the brim, or a snood that you smooth over your hair in back, or a little pillbox with a veil you'd pull down to your chin? I wonder."

Blanche studied her a moment. Jenny's heart went out to her. Her head was capped by an explosion of black bushy hair, her white skin was blemished by too many freckles, her mouth too thin, her eyebrows too thick. When he'd reached Blanche, God must have been fresh out of his supply of beauty.

The other girls turned in their chairs, staring at her, but to Jenny's surprise Blanche stood up and, right where she was, pantomimed each one of the imaginary hats Jenny had suggested, then plopped back into her seat and hung her head.

"That was delightful, Blanche! I'm so proud of you. I'm proud of all of you. Oh, look at the clock. Time's up. I'll see you all next week."

Mrs. Vandermeer stood up and joined her. "Don't forget your money next week, girls. Give your parents this little note I've written about the classes." After the girls were picked up by their parents, she hugged Jenny. "It went wonderfully. How good you were with the girls. They all liked it and liked you! I can hardly wait until next week myself."

By mid-August, Jenny still didn't have enough money. She knew she wouldn't make it to college this fall.

At the last class she gave a recital and invited the parents to attend. The girls did pantomimes, monologues, speeches, and acted out scenes from plays. Carla was actually cooperative and noticeably enjoyed herself, while Blanche had lost her shyness, gained confidence and shown real emotional depth.

The parents applauded loud and long, and the girls took repeated bows. Mrs. Vandermeer served lemonade and cookies, and Jenny heaved a sigh of relief.

A tall woman with deep brown eyes, a flawless pink complexion and a mound of glossy chestnut hair cornered Jenny. "I need to speak to you." Her voice was rich and low. Jenny almost gasped when the woman said, "I'm Blanche Stoltz's mother."

*Poor Blanche,* Jenny thought, *to have a mother that's such a ravishing beauty.*

Jenny braced herself. Mrs. Stoltz in her expensive suit obviously had something on her mind. "Yes?"

"When I received the note about these classes, I wasn't enthusiastic. I thought the worst thing for Blanche would be to be paraded before prett—before other girls." She smiled. "But I can't thank you enough for what you've done for my daughter. She's a different person! We're so sorry the classes are over."

"Blanche has been a real delight, and has just blossomed!"

"We've noticed. I was wondering if you could give her more lessons, privately, say three times a week?"

Jenny hesitated.

"I'll pay double. Shall we say $6 a lesson for the next two weeks?"

"Why, I'd love to." Jenny's heart had always gone out to little Blanche who somehow reminded her of herself.

She enjoyed the private lessons with Blanche, and the little girl's continued growth and affection for her. And the money helped.

So by September first, Jenny had $177. That plus her $80 deposit was $257. It had been a wonderful summer, but CWC started in a few days. She was so close to going to college—and yet so far. *Believe,* she thought. *Believe!*

On Labor Day the family went on a mountain picnic. Jenny tried not to think of two weeks away when all her friends would be leaving for college. Listening to the rushing mountain stream, she watched a bluebird bobbing in a nearby pine. After they all ate lunch, Dale said, "Jenny, I owed some rent and other stuff from being at CU, but I managed to save $17 for your school fund." He handed her some bills.

Mother said, "I shaved $14 off the groceries. Here, sweetheart."

A chill ran up Jenny's spine. It was almost enough, but not quite.

Then her father put an envelope in her hand, "I went without a few lunches, and I sold a couple of auto policies. Besides your tuition, you'll have school fees and books and, of course you'd like a new dress, maybe even two. With what you've earned, this envelope should cover it. We love you, honey."

Jenny sighed in relief and then leaped to her feet. "Oh, thank you, thank you! How I love you all!" Her next thought was *I haven't paid all the tuition yet. Is it too late? Can I still get in?*

# 41. Where Is Love?

Jenny did get in. In September 1941, Jenny Pate began attending Colorado Woman's College. Treat Hall, a red brick building where the classes met, stood in the center of the campus. On either side rose dormitories in English Tudor style, their beige stone walls covered with ivy, their diamond-paned windows shimmering in the light. Jenny loved the story-book appearance of Foote and Porter Halls, wistfully wishing she lived in one of them.

A large dining room filled a wing of Foote Hall—and tuition included noon meals for Denver day students. Jenny loved eating there with the entire student body. Each table seated eight, and the students rotated, so each experienced acting as the hostess.

They all stood for the Pledge of Allegiance, bowed their heads for the invocation, and sat down again. Jenny liked the emphasis on gracious manners; and eating with others made her feel she belonged. Soon Jenny knew most of the 300 students, a welcome change from the 3,000 at East High.

This year, maybe she would meet a special boy—somebody to love—somebody who'd love her—somebody who'd put her first.

Often she became lost in misty daydreams of walking down the aisle in a fluffy white wedding gown, then being carried over the threshold of her own home. She yearned to have a place of her own, to shed all responsibility, to feel free!

The future looked so bright—she was actually going to college and could possibly meet that special someone—but at a girl's school? When would that boy come to be in one of the plays?

Jenny majored in Liberal Arts and minored in drama. Each week she had a singing lesson, and two private sessions in dramatics.

Although she longed to be the school's best singer and star in the solos, Jenny soon discovered that Gina Bonnelli's glorious voice was far better than her own. Gina was always chosen to sing at chapel and at other special programs. Listening to Gina's "Habenera" from Carmen, a difficult mezzo soprano piece which showcased her rich, resonant voice, Jenny realized that although her own voice was pleasant, it was "thin." Gina had been born with a gift. Jenny had not.

With a jolt, Jenny recognized her voice would never be her fortune.

Recovering from her dismay, she threw herself into the drama lessons which she found great fun. She enjoyed using her emotions—emotions she had had to submerge for so many years.

Looking forward to having boys in the plays, Jenny discovered that the first play, *Danger—Girls Working,* had an all female cast. Ruefully, she ended up in the role of the maid, a part that for her, required no acting— she, who so longed to be the ingenue, the star.

Her drama teacher, Mrs. Roscoe, was a roly-poly, baby-cheeked, gray-haired woman with dancing blue eyes. Although married only five years before her husband died, and with only one daughter, still, Mrs. Roscoe was rumored to have vast knowledge of men and dating. She was the school counselor and a confidante to any girl needing advice.

One day at the lunch table, Jenny heard whispers. Finally, Hattie said, "They're having an assembly in early December about men and," she snickered and lowered her voice, "sex."

Jenny swallowed. She'd lived a protected, isolated life. Her folks had no friends and Jenny felt self-conscious, awkward, and tongue-tied around boys. Even thinking about sex made her uneasy.

"If you have any questions," Hattie said, "Mrs. Roscoe is going to answer them."

"I wouldn't want to display my ignorance," Jenny said.

"You don't have to ask them out loud." Hattie bridled. "You write them down and put them in Mrs. Roscoe's box and then in November, we're all going to have sex education. It'll be a big assembly in the auditorium." She laughed. "Sex assembly."

Jenny wasn't sure anyone could answer questions she was too timid to ask.

Sex! Sitting there, she blushed—remembering. She was four years old and Mother had caught her and the neighbor boy playing doctor. Mother cried and said, "I'm a failure as a mother." Then she spanked Jenny—the only time she was ever spanked.

Now she sat at the table with Hattie, lost in thought, as the girls filed out to their afternoon classes.

Much later her mother had gently told her things she needed to know. Other girls groaned and called their monthlies "the curse," but Mother had said it was natural, and necessary in order to have a baby. Someday Jenny wanted to be married and have babies.

Her parents had done a good job about another thing, too. Earlier that summer, a startling movie had come out called, *Birth of a Baby,* showing a baby actually being born. The movie horrified some people and created a lot of controversy, but her folks thought it would be wonderfully educational and sent her and Dale together to see it. Jenny thought it was a beautiful movie, and felt grateful that her folks had such intelligence and good values about topics that mattered.

Sex! The college fall prom had come and gone and Jenny didn't get to go. Not even Dale took her. He was too busy trying to learn to write advertising to suit his boss.

It had hurt Jenny so much to miss all the school dances at high school and now here at college too. She felt utterly despondent. What was wrong with her? At seventeen, she had never had a date. Instead of dating on Friday or Saturday, she babysat, using the money for much-needed clothes.

In mid-October when the Nordahls had asked her to babysit, she'd worn a new beige dress with a square neckline and a gathered skirt with embroidery around the hem. Lars Nordahl had been in her class at East, but she'd never cared for him. He seemed arrogant, cold, and unfriendly—always treating her as if she were lower class. But she liked his mother and father and the other four children. It was the two smallest girls, six and eight, she sat for.

From life experience Jenny had learned there were two classes of people in the world—the rich, like the Nordahls; and the poor, like the Pates. At East, the rich kids always hung out together and Lars was one of them. She had never fit in.

Still, working for the Nordahls was pleasant. The little girls behaved well, and loved the stories she read in her best dramatic voices. Futhermore, Mrs. Nordahl always left her a big snack.

Besides, after she put the girls to bed, she could spend the evening reading magazines, and the Nordahls took them all—*Life, Colliers, Liberty, Saturday Evening Post, Woman's Home Companion* and more.

On this Friday night, Jenny had been reading in the living room when she saw Lars come in the front door with a tall, slender young man. Lars went upstairs, and his companion walked to the doorway and looked in at Jenny. She glanced up and found the tall redhead staring at her. She smiled in acknowledgment, and went back to her reading.

Lars came downstairs, and then the two went into the kitchen. From all the clattering, she knew they were getting something to eat and drink. Though Lars was home, Jenny couldn't leave until Mr. and Mrs. Nordahl returned because Lars might go out again.

A few minutes later, turning a page, she suddenly felt as if someone was watching her, and looked up to find the same man staring at her again. She wondered why, and then went on reading.

"Come on, Vic, you laggard," she heard Lars say. Vic said something she couldn't hear, and the two laughed as they went out the front door.

Saturday morning the phone had rung. "Jenny, this is Vic Swenson. I saw you last night at the Nordahls. I thought maybe we could catch a movie tonight. What do you say?"

Astonished, joyful, Jenny gulped a surprised breath, "Just a minute, please."

Quickly, she asked her mother if she could go. She wanted to go. A date! Her first one! Somebody liked her!

Her mother hesitated. "Oh my, I don't know. He's a perfect stranger."

She frowned and thought a minute. "I suppose, since he's a friend of the Nordahls, he's all right. I guess you can go."

"I'd love to," Jenny said into the phone.

"All right!" He sounded jubilant. "Give me your address."

After she told him, he said, "I'll pick you up at eight."

After hanging up, Jenny danced around the room. "My very first date! And I get to go a show besides. I've got a date!"

Nora frowned. "I wonder if I should call Mrs. Nordahl and ask what kind of a boy he is."

"Oh, Mother! Mrs. Nordahl told me the son of a well-known architect was visiting Lars. I guess that's Vic. That should be recommendation enough."

Nora thought a minute. "Movies are such a treat and you seldom get to go. That seems respectable and safe. Which film are you seeing?"

"He didn't say, but you know me. I love anything. Should I put my hair up on rollers, or do you think it looks curly enough?"

"It looks fine to me. What are you going to wear?"

"My blue dress with the little flowers."

With a nod, Nora said, "That sounds just right."

Jenny drew a breath. "Oh Mom, I won't know what to say to him."

"You'll think of something. Besides, you'll be watching the movie."

"We'll probably go out for something to eat afterward, don't you think?"

"Probably. Just don't stay out too late."

Pressing her hand to her heart, Jenny said, "What if he tries to kiss me?"

"On the first date?" Nora's brows went up.

"What shall I do if he does?"

"Now, Jenny, do you think it's a good idea to let a boy kiss you on the first date?"

"No. Especially when I don't know him."

Her mother looked at her sharply. "A nice girl doesn't let any boy kiss her on a first date. Remember, men only marry nice girls, they don't marry loose women."

"Oh, Mom, a little goodnight kiss wouldn't make me a loose woman."

Her mother laughed. "Of course not, but we mothers have to protect our daughters. Seriously, don't let a boy touch you between the neck and the knees."

"Mo-ther! You told me that years ago."

"I'm glad you get to go, but mothers can't help worrying a little."

When Vic had arrived, he spoke briefly with her folks, then looked Jenny up and down and, though he didn't comment out loud, she thought he appreciated how nice she looked and her good figure.

She liked his being so tall. He had a serious expression, curly auburn hair, and lots of freckles. He didn't linger long over the introductions to her parents and Dale. In no time, he glanced at his watch. "We'd better get going."

"Yes," Jenny said, "we don't want to be late to the show." He helped her with her coat. Eyes dancing, she waved goodbye, and they went out.

Vic opened the door of his small gray coupe. Delighted, and thrilled with excitement, she settled into the seat. When he drove down the block and turned left, she wondered why. She couldn't remember any theatre to the east.

"Where are we going?" she asked.

"Just relax. You'll see."

She frowned. If he got lost, he probably wouldn't like it if she said anything. Boys didn't like girls telling them what to do. She felt she should make some brilliant conversation, but what should she say? "Have you known the Nordahls very long?"

"Yeah, my folks and the Nordahls have been friends for years."

"I understand your father is an architect."

"Yeah."

She wondering again where they were going. "Are you going to be an architect too?"

"Nope. I'm taking engineering."

Looking into the dark, she said, "Is there a theatre out here? We're near the airport."

"Right. I thought we'd sit out here a while."

"Oh, yes, that's fun. Our family loves to come out to Stapleton Airport and watch the planes come and go. It's one of our chief recreations. Cheap too." Inwardly she groaned. *What a dumb thing to say! He'll think I'm saying he's cheap.*

He drove to the top of a small rise, stopped the car, and turned off the engine.

She said, "You'll have to watch the time, or we'll be late to the movie, won't we?"

He rolled down the window. "Are you a little worry-wart or what?"

Rubbing her hands nervously on her thighs, she laughed. "I just thought…"

He turned, facing her. "Don't think so much. Come here."

She stared at him in the dim light. "But—but—" This wasn't what she expected.

"Come on, let's have a little kiss."

She swallowed, and shifted against the door, pulling up her knees as a barrier between them. "I thought we were going to the movies."

"Maybe later." He reached out and rubbed her shoulder. "Come on, give a little."

"But I don't really know you."

"In a while, you'll know me very well."

Cringing against the door, she said, "This is awfully sudden."

"Look, let's not play games. Do you believe in free love?"

Eyes wide, she thought she knew what he meant. Looking around, she saw she was in a lonely car on an isolated hilltop overlooking a noisy airport. If she got out, there was no way to get home.

He leaned closer. "You know what free love is, don't you?"

"Isn't that love without marriage?"

Laughing, he said, "It's love without any attachments. Just plain love that's free. What does a piece of paper mean, anyway? Life's for living, having pleasure, experiencing. Don't be coy. Come over here."

"I'd have to think about it a while. Why don't we just go to the movies?"

It went on and on. His constant talking about free love and her fumbling attempts to cope with his arguments. He kept looking at her, making half-hearted attempts from time to time to kiss her. She kept pushing him away.

Her heart was breaking. This was her first date and all he wanted was sex. Sex for himself. He didn't like her. He didn't care anything about her!

Finally, he got out of the car without explaining. He walked a few steps away and she wondered if he was going to the bathroom. In a minute he got back in the car and turned on the ignition. "Listen, kid," he said, "I'm taking you home. I have to go to the hospital first thing in the morning."

She stared out the windshield. If that was true, why had he asked her out at all?

"I have to have my appendix out, so I need a good night's sleep"

She sat silently in the corner, not believing a word he'd said. He drove like he was mad. In a few minutes the car squealed to a stop in front of her house. Hesitating only a moment, she quickly understood that he wasn't going to open the car door for her, or walk her to her front door like a gentleman. But then, he hadn't been a gentleman at all!

Without a word or a backward glance, she got out of the car. Drawing herself to her full height, she raised her head proudly and moved gracefully up the walk. Before she could get the front door open, she heard his engine roar away.

Her father and mother were waiting up for her in the living room, questions on their faces. "You're home awfully early," her father said.

"We didn't go to the show," she said numbly. "He parked out by the airport and asked me if I believed in free love. When I said no and wouldn't let him kiss me, he got disgusted. He wanted more than a kiss, he wanted sex." It hurt too much to cry.

"I shouldn't have let you go." Pain showed on her mother's face. "We didn't know that boy. I should have called Mrs. Nordahl!"

"It's not your fault."

"We love you, Jenny," Clyde said. "I'd like to punch that stupid kid in the nose."

Nora said, "Honey, I think you handled the situation very well. I'm proud of you."

Jenny said, "Yes, but will anybody ever like me?"

Her father had patted her shoulder. "You bet your life they will."

Now, Jenny sat in the assembly hall at Colorado Woman's College, waiting for Mrs. Roscoe to read the first question and give the girls their education about sex.

*Sex education,* she thought bitterly. *I've already had mine. It's not what they tell you in classes—real sex education is the men you meet and how they treat you.*

"Now for the first question." Mrs. Roscoe read from a paper, "What do you think about a French kiss?" The pink-cheeked counselor looked over her wire-rimmed glasses at her audience of fresh-faced girls and said emphatically, "A French kiss is always an insult! Always!"

Jenny whispered to Hattie, "What's a French kiss?"

# 42. The Starring Role Jenny Didn't Want

After that dreadful date, Jenny vacillated between depression, and trying to reshape her feelings of worthlessness into courage and self-esteem. Maybe she should get down the worn copy of *Pollyanna* Grandma had given her so long ago. It helped her be cheerful, which sometimes was mighty hard.

She felt humiliated and disappointed that Vic hadn't liked her for herself—even disappointed that she didn't get to see a movie, which for her was such a treat.

The following Saturday, Jenny stood on the floor register, trying to warm her soul as well as her body. Outside, the sky was gray, the leafless trees naked and lifeless—a day as bleak as she felt.

From the kitchen her father called, "I'm making waffles for breakfast."

Jenny's eyes misted. She loved waffles. He was trying to make her feel better.

"Wonderful!" As she turned to go to the kitchen, Dale came down the hall. He smiled and patted her on the shoulder. "I'll help you with the dishes after breakfast."

Her chest felt tight. Everybody kept on being so nice.

When breakfast was ready, Jenny carried her mother's tray to her room and put it on her bedside table, and fluffed the pillows behind her. With a recent setback her mother had been taking her meals in bed.

"I do hope I'll get better soon, so I can eat at the table with you."

"I hope so too," Jenny said. Guiltily, she felt she shouldn't feel sorry for herself for her little problems when her mother had such big problems.

As they ate, Dale seemed nervous. First he hunched down over his plate, and then shifted in his seat. "I have something to tell everybody."

Clyde stared at him apprehensively. "What's the matter, Dale?"

"Nothing's the matter, Dad. It's actually good news. I've quit Layton Rubber."

His father paled. "You what?"

"I'm not out of a job, Dad. I'm going to work for the May Company."

Clyde put down his fork. "Well, this is a surprise. Doing what?"

"Writing advertising, just like I did at Layton, but I really couldn't get very enthusiastic about automobile tires. At the May Company, I can write about all different kinds of merchandise. I'll be a real salesman, just like you, Dad, only on paper."

Jenny was surprised at the gloomy expression on her father's face. He was usually so easy-going about everything.

"I don't know, son. Layton is a good outfit. You weren't there long, and I hate to see you be a job hopper. In my day, you got a job and stuck with it. Companies prize loyalty."

"I didn't like it there, and they didn't like me."

Jenny wondered if he quit so he wouldn't get fired.

Mother spoke up. "The important thing is for you to be happy."

Dale gulped some milk. "The pay's about the same, but I'll save carfare and all that time on the bus, since I'll be able to ride downtown both ways with you, Dad. I can walk the couple of blocks from your office to the store. Okay?"

Clyde sighed. "Sure. Sure."

"That's good," his mother said. "You won't have to get up so early."

"I start Monday. It's a good move."

Noticing her father's disapproval, Jenny said brightly, "Congratulations, Dale."

Dale's blue eyes grew intense, "Something else—Colorado University has evening extension classes downtown. I've registered for one for the term coming up—in radio."

Clyde frowned. "Radio? What good is that going to do you?"

"Well, they have classes in radio advertising, production and radio writing. I plan to take them all. Maybe someday I could work in the radio business. The course will count toward getting my diploma. I'm only short a few credits. He raised his head defiantly. "And the classes should be fun, too, for a change."

Nora said, "If they help you get your diploma, you certainly should go."

Pursing his lips, Clyde said, "Getting a better job and sticking with it— that's what you really need." He shook his head. "I always thought an English Literature major wasn't best."

"Dad, if you wanted to write, it was that or journalism, and I'm not cut out to be a pushy reporter."

"For a writer, I don't see you working on any stories."

"Well, I have been, and I keep a journal of ideas, and I'm not going to send out junk. I have to polish my work. It takes time."

"We all know Dale's a perfectionist," Jenny commented.

Nora said, "Clyde, it's good to have standards."

"Just the same, he's got to make a living. I thought you were going to teach. Well, maybe if you get your diploma, you still can."

Jenny noticed Dale didn't answer. How could her father disregard Dale's devastating student teaching experience when the kids were so mean?

Clyde said, "Don't let that radio class interfere with your new job."

"Don't worry. I won't."

Taking a sip of coffee, Clyde looked at the others over his cup. "Well, now, I have my own announcement to make." His face lit up." I know you all think I've been wasting my time studying *Think and Grow Rich*." He set his cup down on the table. "But that book has guided me to a new decision."

"You're not quitting your job!" Nora cried.

"No, no, no. I have a wonderful opportunity at the company. It's too complicated to explain, but the government has changed the tax laws, and a business gets a tax break if they buy a pension plan for their employees. I'm studying how to sell pension plans."

"Pension plans?" Nora said. "I don't understand."

Face glowing, Clyde said, "Don't you see? Instead of selling individual policies, if a company has ten employees and buys a plan, I'll have sold ten policies at once."

"Wow," exclaimed Jenny. "That sounds good."

Clyde said, "These new rules will take a lot of study, but if it works the way I think it does, by golly, we're going to be on Easy Street."

"Yeah," Dale said indifferently. "It'll be real nice to finally be on Easy Street."

Silence. Nora finally said flatly, "Sounds good, Clyde."

*How can he not notice that nobody else is getting excited?* Jenny wondered. *We've all heard his promises about Easy Street and Yellowstone so many times before.* She got up and started to clear the table.

"Hey, Jenny." Balancing a pile of plates, Dale followed her into the kitchen and whispered, "Forget the somedays. Forget Easy Street. Want to go to the show tonight?"

He was still trying to make up for that disastrous date she'd had. "Oh, Dale, I'd love to." Dale was such a good big brother.

"How about seeing *Citizen Kane?*"

They went back into the dining room for more dishes. "Yes! Orson Welles is great—and his deep voice gives me chills."

"The critics say the picture is really good." Dale picked up cups and saucers. "I've checked the paper. Be ready to go at 7:00."

"Wonderful," Jenny said. "That'll give me time to work on my recital. I have to cut a book down to an hour and then play all the characters myself."

"That sounds like a lot of work," Nora said. "What book are you doing?"

"*Pride and Prejudice.* I love Elizabeth, and I'll play her mother like Billie Burke. You know, all twittery."

Clyde looked up from the morning paper and shook his head. "All that work for drama seems foolish to me. I hope you plan to teach, Jenny."

As she carried the syrup pitcher and oleo to the kitchen, Jenny frowned. *I don't want to be an old maid school teacher.* Oh well, a career was far away. Tonight in the theatre she'd forget everything but the world on the screen. She'd escape into fantasy.

For a moment she realized everyone in the family was trying to escape. Her father fantasized about Easy Street. Her mother forgot her troubles by listening to soap operas. She and Dale daydreamed of the future and, on rare occasions, even blotted out their difficulties at the movies.

*Citizen Kane* was great and they came home thoroughly satisfied.

But the next day, there was no escaping reality. On Sunday, December 7, 1941, the family sat huddled around the radio, shocked. The Japanese had bombed Pearl Harbor!

The following day President Roosevelt asked Congress to declare war against the Japan. On December 11, Germany and Italy declared war on the United States and Congress then declared war on Germany and Italy.

At the news Nora gasped and went white, "They might send Dale!"

"Don't worry, Nora," Clyde assured her. "They'll never take Dale into the service. Without his glasses, he's absolutely blind."

Grimly, Nora shook her head. "He's healthy. He's twenty-one. With a war, you never know. Mrs. Wheatley last heard from her son from somewhere in the Philippines!"

All around them the world rapidly changed. First, Jenny heard that Thelma and Libby had left Colorado University and gotten jobs. Next, the newspaper ran columns of enlistees, and she saw name after name of boys she'd known at East High. Mrs. Wheatley still hadn't heard from Larry. Soon Nora was coping with ration coupons as she made menus. Soldiers were seen all over downtown.

Then, Jenny's best friend, Vallorie, left for a job in Miami. Having studied Spanish through junior high and high school, she was hired to censor incoming Spanish mail.

After a few months, bombers roared above the street at the end of the block every ten minutes on their way east to landing exercises at Stapleton Field.

Looking up at plane after plane, Jenny wished she could be a pilot, or a war correspondent, or help the war effort in some way, but she was too frightened to leave the security of home, and the slightest wistful wish she expressed threw her mother into turmoil. Jenny realized she was needed at home, and told herself that that was a service too.

Dale plugged away at the May Company and took the radio advertising class. Jenny performed *Pride and Prejudice* to applause, praise, and Mrs. Roscoe's adulation, and received an A in drama for her efforts.

In February, at her private drama lesson, Mrs. Roscoe's blue eyes twinkled. "I have exciting news for you, Jenny. The college authorities have encouraged me to present a special Easter play for the student body. There's a marvelous character—in fact it's the leading role—and I'm not bothering with auditions. I've selected you."

Jenny glowed like a candle. "You want me?"

"It's a wonderful story. I know that you can give this part exactly what it needs."

Breathless, Jenny could hardly contain her pleasure. "Thank you. I'll do my best."

Mrs. Roscoe picked up a paperback play from her end table. "This is about the Peter in the Bible who denied Christ three times. You know the story. It's a wonderful play about the transformation of Peter the Betrayer, into Peter the Rock of the Church." Mrs. Roscoe sat in her easy chair beaming.

*Oh,* Jenny thought with a thrill, *I'll get to act with a boy. I wonder where she's going to get the fellow to play Peter in these war times?*

Mrs. Roscoe took off her glasses and polished them with her white hankie. "Jenny, I am so impressed with you. You were outstanding in your recital. I don't know if you realize the depth of your talent."

"Thank you!" Jenny basked in the compliments. "In this production, who do I play?"

Mrs. Roscoe stared at her. "Why, I thought I'd made myself clear." She smiled again. "My dear, you will be Peter."

"Peter?" The flame inside her suddenly went out.

"You'll make a convincing Peter. You have the voice, the stage presence, the emotional range."

"Peter!" Her heart plummeted. "But that's a man!"

"In *Pride and Prejudice* you were excellent as the male characters."

246

Weakly, Jenny said, "But…"

Holding up the play, Mrs. Roscoe said, "I want you to take this home and start memorizing your lines." She got up and handed Jenny the script. "The remaining drama students will play the other parts. This will count as a third of your spring grade."

Jenny sat numbly, hands clutching the play. She didn't want to be a man, even if it was the lead. Although she loved to act, loved to change into another character, she always yearned to be the beautiful heroine.

Mrs. Roscoe's voice came from far away, "Jenny, you'll be the STAR."

Her mind went back to when she was in kindergarten and teacher said, "Jenny, you get to sing a solo. You'll be the STAR." But the other little girls played beautiful parasols, while she was an ugly black umbrella. She had wanted to be one of the pretty ones.

Now—she stared hopelessly at Mrs. Roscoe At seventeen she'd had only one disastrous date. She yearned to HAVE a man—not BE a man.

So far the men pictured in the college brochure had not materialized, and now the war was taking them all away.

When she got home, she complained to her parents about being cast as Peter. But they said you had to do what you were assigned, especially when it counted toward so much of her grade, and that it was a compliment that Mrs. Roscoe believed in her. She should be happy she had the leading role.

So she swallowed her feelings and got down to work. Soon she began to appreciate the emotional story and the powerful part. Finally, much as she hated playing a man, she felt confident—ready to deliver the performance of her life.

On the fateful day, the audience clapped when the curtain opened on the sets the art department had painted suggesting sand and sea. All the characters were costumed in the flowing garments and sandals of Biblical times. Jenny wore a robe of brilliant blue.

Then the applause died away and a hush fell over the audience. Before her lay the empty stage, a space she always longed to fill. Her fright evaporated and she strode out with long masculine strides. Her lines came out clearly in a voice as deep as she could muster.

Since it was an afternoon performance, no one in her family could attend. The men had to work and her mother was too frail, but she didn't mind. She actually felt more comfortable when they weren't watching.

The performance was going well. She remembered every line, her blocking, her gestures, her props, gave the audience the gift of her emotions.

In the climactic scene, at the play's highest point, as she poured out all of Peter's feelings, she heard a twittering in the audience and tiny suggestions of laughter. Stunned, she delivered her next speech. The lines weren't funny. They were laughing at her! Her heart broke, but somehow she carried on, staying in character to the very end. She held her pose, kneeling at the papier-mache' rocks as the curtain closed.

For a moment there was no sound, and then the audience applauded. The laughter was gone now, but the memory hurt like a stab wound.

The curtain opened and Jenny bowed. But even as she took a second curtain call, and a third, she was miserable. Unable to hold it in any longer, she rushed into the wings, tears streaming down her face—straight into Mrs. Roscoe's arms.

The drama teacher hugged her. "Jenny you were absolutely wonderful! I'm so proud." Then she saw Jenny's face. "My dear, whatever is wrong?"

Jenny felt alone and ugly, just like the umbrella left on the mat. Trembling, she blurted, "They laughed at me!"

Face white, Mrs. Roscoe said, "Oh, my dear, no. You misinterpreted. It was—just—they knew it was you. They were surprised and delighted you were such a wonderful man—such a wonderful Peter. Listen, they're still clapping. Take another curtain call. Go on."

Wiping her wet face on the sleeve of her robe, Jenny took a breath. She would not let the audience see her distress. *I'm an actress*, she told herself, *so act*. Going onstage with the rest of the cast, she smiled and bowed. But when the curtain closed, she dashed into the wings and struggled against crying.

Mrs. Roscoe patted her arm. "There, there, dear."

Holding back tears, Jenny said, "I never want to play a man again!"

"Oh, my dear, I didn't realize you felt that way, but you were wonderful!" She paused and then said emphatically, "Someday, Jenny, you'll find having played Peter with that deep voice will help you immeasurably."

Jenny gave her a long look of disbelief. "I don't see how."

# 43. Will Jenny Get a Chance?

One Monday evening while Jenny caught up on ironing, Dale, just home from work, trudged up the back steps.

"Boy, I'm tired. It's good to be home. Where is everybody?"

"Daddy's out on an appointment, and Mother's napping. "I've kept your dinner warm. I'll serve it up."

"Great." He took off his coat. "I'll go put on my slippers." He returned carrying a yellow notepad which he dropped on the table. "Supper looks good." He appreciatively eyed chili, garlic bread, pineapple gelatin salad, and a slice of chocolate cake.

"How are things at work?" Jenny hooked a finished shirt on the door hinge.

"Rough. They're whipping us like we were horses. Next they'll want us to pull wagons. We're advertising big post-Easter sales."

"At least you're writing, and getting paid." Jenny unrolled another dampened shirt. Steam hissed as she pressed down the iron. "I'm stuck behind this iron. Housework—blah! When it comes to laundry, I'm all washed up, and ironing is a pretty pressing business. All housework is nothing more than rearranging dirt."

Dale laughed. "You're funny."

She grinned. "I'd like to be funny on the stage. Gee, I'd love to leave home and go places and do things and be somebody, but how can I when the folks need me? Dale, where does duty end and desire begin?"

"Gosh, Jen, I don't know. You have a right to your own life."

"But I'd feel guilty to leave Mother."

"I don't know what to say." When he finished eating, Dale sat back and the fatigue drifted from his face. "Thanks for supper. You're a good cook." He put his dishes in the sink, sat again and picked up the yellow pad. "Now, I've got to get busy."

"What are you doing?"

"I'm finishing a radio play for Todd Ramsey's class in radio production." He flipped through handwritten pages in his pad.

Interested, Jenny said, "I didn't know you could write a radio play. Will you let me read it some time?"

"Sure. I'm hoping that Todd'll produce it in class. But with my schedule I don't know if I'll get it typed before the term's over."

"I'll type it, Dale. I don't have much homework, so I could do it right away."

Beaming, he said, "Hey, that would be nifty. I'm just touching up the last scene now. I should be done in a few minutes."

As he wrote, Jenny finished the shirts, tiptoed into her parents' closet, then returned with her portable typewriter and paper.

Dale had brought a script from his bedroom and placed it on the table. "Jenny, you can use this radio script for a model. Todd gave it to me."

Eyes wide, Jenny leafed through the pages.

Dale pointed. "The characters' names go on the left side in caps, followed by a colon, and their speeches go on the right. Stage directions are in caps, too. See?"

"Yes." Reading, Jenny asked, "What does segue mean?"

"It means to go to the next thing, sort of like a bridge. See the FADE OUT and FADE IN? Those indicate scene changes."

"I see." Reading the first page of Dale's handwritten story she said, "Wow, this looks so interesting. I love the Arabian Nights setting. How many copies do you want?"

"Original and two carbons. Todd can make more copies at the Radio League. This is swell of you, Jenny."

"No problem." She smiled, then put her fingers on the keys.

"Hey, I've got a great idea," he said. "Why don't you come to class with me Thursday and see how it's produced?"

A flush of excitement reddened her face. "Are visitors allowed?"

"I don't think Todd would throw you out. Just sit there and watch."

She clapped her hands. "I'd love to go!"

"Listen, if you have time, get *Writing Radio Dramas,* from the library. It's got the neatest radio plays." Sitting on the edge of the table, Dale's eyes danced. "Great dramas!"

Beaming, Jenny cried, "I love radio." Her face turned wistful. "How I long to have a little drama in my own life!"

"Don't we all? Say, what story are you using for your spring recital?"

"I had to cut a three-act play down to an hour, and then I play all the parts. I'm doing Edith Wharton's, *The Old Maid.*"

"Then in that one you'll have to be a man."

"Several men."

"I thought you were never going to play a male again."

Jenny made a face. "I have to, for my recital. But it's not so bad, because I also get to be the leading ladies too." Face intense, she said, "In regular plays I want to play the ingénues, but they always cast you for what you look like, and I always end up a character woman. Besides not being pretty enough for the love interest, I'm too tall. In high heels I'm six feet, and tower over all the men."

"What men? They're all in the service. I would be, too, except for my eyes."

"I'm so glad you're not going into the army. Well, I'd better get to typing."

Dale patted her shoulder. "Listen Jenny, you're good at acting. Your teacher, and the reviews in the school paper both say so. I wish your recitals weren't in the daytime, so we could all come see you."

"That would be nice."

"Can you finish my script by Thursday night? It's a half-hour show, so after time for lead-ins and lead-outs and commercials, it's only about twenty minutes playing time."

Jenny started to type. "Don't worry, I'll have it done."

"Great," He lowered his voice in a Charles Boyer imitation. "Then you can come weeth me to the Kasbah—thee Western Radeeo League."

Thursday as Dale parked the car near 18th and Broadway in

downtown Denver, Jenny asked, "Exactly what is the Western Radio League?"

He turned off the ignition. "Colleges in Colorado, Wyoming and Nebraska, contribute money to the League which records radio shows and then mails them to stations in surrounding states. The airwaves belong to all of us, so stations are supposed to give time for non-commercial shows like these—as a public service."

"Oh." They got out and walked down the hill. A cool breeze freshened the evening, and yellow street lights blinked in the purple dusk.

They passed four houses when Dale gestured. "This is it."

Following, Jenny said, "It looks like an old house."

"It is—or was, but the Radio League took it over and remodeled it."

They opened the glass door and walked back through two rooms furnished with worn sofas and chairs. As they passed through a third room, Dale said, "This is Todd's office. The control room is there to the right, and the studio is just ahead. I'll get the door. It's real heavy, for sound-proofing. Go down three steps into the studio. Don't fall."

As they entered the studio, Jenny grimaced. "It smells musty."

"It's the sound-proofing," Dale said.

White acoustical tile lined all the walls. In one corner stood a wooden door in a frame, and a large black cabinet on wheels.

"Come over here." Dale led her to the cabinet and pointed to two turntables on top. "This is the soundman's 'truck.' In the cabinet below, is a library of sound recordings he plays on the turntables and then cues into a show at the right time."

Pivoting, he motioned to a large drum. "That's the wind machine. When I turn this handle," he demonstrated, "it sounds like wind blowing."

Appreciatively, Jenny's eyes glowed. "What a gale. Wow!"

Picking up two coconut shells from the sound truck, Dale said, "I'll make a horse galloping." He clapped the shells together.

Laughing, Jenny said, "I can almost see that horse, Dale. So that's how they do it." She turned as other students filed in.

The class sat in a circle of folding chairs and Dale introduced Jenny.

Pointing to a big glass window, Dale explained, "Behind the window is the control booth where the director and the engineer work. Norman, there, is the engineer and he controls the sound level."

Heart flipping, Jenny thought, "*Oh, he's so tall, dark and handsome.*" He studied his equipment and failed to notice her.

"When we record," Dale said, "that red bulb above the window lights up and everybody has to be quiet. Microphones pick up the slightest sound."

"I'll be quiet." She kept watching Norman, but couldn't catch his eye. Jenny noticed two standing silver microphones in the center of the room.

The big clock on the wall above the glass window read 7:25 when the door opened and a man carrying a stack of papers bounced into the room oozing energy. "Good evening, folks." Curly black hair tumbled over his forehead, his smile flashed white teeth, and he looked around at his class with enormous brown eyes.

*Any woman would kill to have eyelashes like those,* Jenny thought.

"Todd," Dale rose, "I brought my sister Jenny."

The instructor gave her a brief glance and a dismissive nod. "Hi."

Dale got up and handed Todd the scripts that Jenny had so carefully typed. "Uh, Todd, I wrote this radio play, and I hoped we could put it on tonight."

The instructor flipped through the pages. "What's your story about?"

Embarrassed, Dale shifted his weight. "Well, it's set in ancient Arabia, and it should have Oriental music, and it's all about why men have beards and women don't."

With a quick laugh, Todd laid the scripts on a nearby table. "Sounds interesting. We'll see, Dale. Maybe we can do it sometime, but I have other plans for tonight."

Dale sank into his chair, and Jenny could see his disappointment.

"Tonight," Jack said, "we're having acting exercises." He moved around the circle distributing a paper to everyone, including Jenny. "On this sheet is the word, 'John,' followed by the emotion you're to express as you say the name. Number one is anxious, two—horrified; three— pleased, and so on." He pulled up a tall wooden stool and sat down. "You start, Tony, and then right around the circle."

"John," "John," "John," different people said. Dale said his "John."

The room fell silent. "Well?" Todd said sharply to Jenny, "It's your turn, young lady."

Taken by surprise, her stomach lurched, but she reached into her emotions, drew a deep breath and said a pained, "Joh-nn?"

They worked through the fifteen emotions all around the class, with Jenny participating, hoping to see the teacher approved, but he gave her no sign. Then Todd pointed a finger at one person and shouted an emotion. He jumped around the circle. His finger pointed at Jenny. "Sexy."

Her eyelids lowered, lips parted, voice turned husky, "Joh-nn." Eagerly she looked for a smile or praise, but got none. She ached with disappointment.

Todd drilled the class, frequently returning to Jenny and she wondered why he kept picking on her.

Then he handed out scripts and they did cold readings. After she finished her lines, she found his eyes on her, and he shook his head. He seemed to disapprove of her work. Her stomach knotted. She had thought she was a pretty good actress.

At their break Gale, Todd's wife, was introduced. She was tiny, pale, red-haired—very delicate. *Jack must like small women. That counts me out*, Jenny thought.

Norman entered and Dale said, "Norman, meet my sister."

She smiled up at him, heart thudding, immediately liking his dark hair, tan skin and gentle smile. His handshake felt warm and strong. When she saw no wedding ring, her heart sang. "Nice to meet you," he said in a resonant voice, but then nodded and left.

"Is he married?" she whispered, and when Dale shook his head, she tumbled into love on the spot.

The class resumed reading scripts aloud, and at 9:30 Todd said, "Okay, folks, that's all for tonight. See you next week." The students handed him their scripts as they filed out. When Jenny passed, he took her arm, "Wait. I'd like to talk to you a minute."

*Is he going to reprimand me for coming?* After all, she hadn't enrolled, nor paid any fee. She glanced at Dale, who shrugged and sat down again.

Todd said, "Stay right here, Jenny. I'm going into the control room."

In a moment he appeared behind the glass, standing next to Norman. Todd's voice boomed over the loudspeaker, "Ever done any microphone work before, Jenny?"

Heart thumping, she fought for breath. What came out was a small, "No."

"I can't hear you. Stand about three inches from the mike and speak directly into it. Do you have any mike experience?"

Jenny eyed the silver microphone with all the little black holes, positioned herself, and said, "No, but I'm a fast learner."

"I want to hear how you sound. Say something."

Frightened, she finally ventured, "Should I say some Johns?"

He frowned. "I think we've had enough Johns for tonight."

Dale nodded, looking bored.

The voice boomed again. "Do you have a Southern accent, Jenny?"

Uneasily, she said, "Yes, I think so."

Norman stood beside Todd, face immobile. Todd said, "Okay. Go ahead."

Nervously, she wiped her sweaty hands on her skirt. *Why doesn't he give me a script?* "What do you want me to say?"

"I don't care." He sounded irritated. "Just say anything—with a Southern accent."

Jenny raised her head, gripped her shoes with her toes—a trick she had learned to assuage stage fright—and thought frantically. *This must be an audition.* But without a script she would fail miserably. She wanted to please him, make him smile, make Norman like her. She opened her mouth, but couldn't think of any lines. Then suddenly, in her head, she heard the girl from Georgia who had visited Essie once. She remembered the drawl, but what words could she say?

Todd said, "I'm waiting."

Perspiration ran down the backs of her thighs. A lump blocked her throat. She fought for breath. And then she imagined a soft, pretty woman standing in a field with a plantation in the distance so she drawled, "Hey, yah-all. Duh yuh see tha-ut purdy purple cawh in th-ut field ova the-ah. Ah tole ma mama ah aways wan-tuhd a purdy purple cawh." She stopped, devoid of any further ideas.

The room fell silent. Time seemed to spin out forever. No comment came from the control room. Dale slumped in his chair. Jenny studied the beige linoleum floor.

The speaker came on. Both men were laughing.

Oh, no, they were laughing at her! Humiliation washed over her.

"Okay, Jenny," came the voice.

She held her breath.

Then Todd said, "I think I can use you. Stay right there."

Use her? She couldn't believe it. He was smiling. Norman was smiling. They liked her after all! When she glanced at Dale, he shrugged.

The door opened and Todd hurried down the steps. "I like your Southern accent, but you could tone it down a little. It's a bit too broad." His eyes were shining. "I have a few lines for you on a show next week on Friday evening. I'll take a chance on you on our *Tall Tales* radio show. Can you make it?"

"Oh, yes." She wanted throw her arms around him. He thought she was good, after all. She'd even get to see Norman again. "Yes," she cried, "I'd love to."

"Be here at 7:30 sharp. We'll rehearse twice or so, and then record. We should be done by 9:30. *Tall Tales from the New World* is a series of folk tales. This is the next to last one. No pay because this is public radio, but you'll be getting experience."

Stunned and grinning, Jenny said, "Fine. Thank you. See you Friday."

Todd nodded. "I was impressed with your renderings of John." He turned to Dale. "Thanks for bringing her."

Rising, Dale muttered, "Yeah, sure."

"Oh, and your play—I'll try to read it pretty soon, but we don't have any call for originals, so I don't know if we'll be able to do anything with it."

Jenny could tell Dale was upset.

As they walked to the car, Dale said, "I can't believe it. I take the class, and you end up being on a radio show."

Jenny sneaked a glance at him. "You aren't jealous are you?"

"No. It's just that everything I do, you do better."

"That's not true at all. I've always admired you and tried to be like you.

I've never told, but I've tried to write a few stories. I can't write like you do."

"Someday you will, and better than I do too."

Her happiness rapidly dimmed. "Oh, Dale, I'm so sorry Todd didn't do your script tonight. Surely he'll do it in class sometime."

"Yeah, maybe. I'm going to go out and eat worms." He unlocked the car door and they got in. "You know what got you the job, don't you?"

"No? What?"

"The way you said John in that sexy voice."

"Really? I had a sexy voice? Me?" They both laughed. "Dale, when will they put my *Tall Tales* show on the air?"

"Like I said, the Radio League productions aren't broadcast in Denver. They're sent to the small stations in surrounding states." He started the engine.

"Then Mother and Daddy won't be able to hear me?"

"That's right." He smiled. "You can come out and eat worms with me 'cause you won't be heard in Denver."

Jenny thought the idea left him feeling rather pleased.

# 44. Don't Build Dreams

When Jenny and Dale got home from the class, Nora called from her bed, "Dad and I are still awake. Come in and tell us all about it."

Jenny related the evening's events. When she said she was to be on a radio show, she braced herself for the usual objections from her mother. To her surprise, Nora smiled. "How exciting, Jenny. It'll be something you'll always remember."

Clyde gave her a long look. "I know it sounds like fun, but you have to think about getting your degree and making a living. Don't build dreams on one radio show."

Jenny said, "I won't."

But during the next week, Jenny couldn't suppress the excitement that bubbled inside her. She was going to be on the radio, and she was sure she could milk every bit of emotion from her part. *Her part!* The thought made her tingle all over. The more she dreamed, the larger her role grew.

The week dragged. Nothing else seemed important. She pictured herself at the mike and Todd and Norman in the control room, laughing and smiling at her, and afterward someone handing her a bouquet of red roses, they way they did at the theatre. She'd be a star, just like she'd yearned to be since kindergarten.

Finally, Friday evening came. Daddy had taken the car for an insurance appointment so she allowed plenty of time for her three-block walk to catch the trolley at the end of the line. Hurrying down the back steps, she saw the sun was just setting and scarves of pink and purple were flung across the sky. As she turned into the alley, she heard a growl. A black Doberman Pincer flashed out of nowhere and as she stepped, she heard a rip of her new red coat right at her calf. If she hadn't stepped just then she would have lost a chunk of flesh. The dog bounded around in front of her. He reared up on his hind legs, brown eyes gleaming. Fear drenched her. She couldn't move. Her hand shot to her throat. "Nice doggie." Time seemed to stand still.

The dog landed on his paws in front of her, stared at her a moment, then bounded away. Frightened, she stumbled forward, turned an ankle, and fell. Heart pounding, she glanced down the alley. Thank God the dog was gone.

Gingerly she got up and retrieved her purse. Her knees were scraped and bloody, her hose were full of holes and runs. *The show! I'll be late.*

Dashing back into the house, she frantically dabbed her bloody knees with alcohol and changed her stockings. She asked Dale to call the Radio League. As she ran out, he called after her, "Their line's busy."

The streetcar was late, running behind schedule. The conductor repeatedly clanged his bell and the car rocked back and forth on its rails as he tried to make up time. Jenny's knees hurt and the palms of her hands were painfully scraped. She had had no time to do anything about the three-inch tear in the kick pleat of her coat.

Clambering off the trolley, she ran the long block down Broadway to the Radio League. A glance at her watch made her wonder if she could make it. As she burst into the studio, she was struck by the muffled silence. Around the standing microphone was a circle of five chairs.

There, three men and a woman sat reading their scripts. The raven-haired woman looked up and said, "You're late."

Glancing at the clock, Jenny saw it was 7:41. "I had an accident. I'm sorry."

The woman smoothed her blue suit, "A professional is always on time and doesn't make excuses."

Angrily, Jenny opened her mouth to explain, but then simply said, "My name is Jenny Pate."

"I'm Carol Chesterfield."

In a deep bass voice a swarthy young man said, "Hi. Alex Garcia."

"I'm Tony," said the dark-haired man. "Jimmy Sanders here does voices, and he's our soundman."

After nodding, Jenny sank into the empty chair, grimacing at her sore knees.

"Pate?" Carol's voice was as smooth as chocolate milk. "You might consider changing your last name."

Looking up, Tony said, "Come on, Carol, just because you had to leave your Hollywood jobs, you don't have to tell the rest of us what to do."

Carol raised her chin. "I was only trying to be helpful. Well, Miss Jenny, go get a script."

Like her dad, Jenny had always liked everyone, but she didn't know about this woman! Jenny looked around.

"On that table." Alex pointed.

Retrieving a copy, Jenny scanned the pages, wondering which part was hers. Her heart pounded in excitement. She had to do a good job, she just had to.

Suddenly Todd's voice boomed from the control room into the studio. "Evening, folks. We'll do a couple of run-throughs. Then we'll record. Alex—you're the announcer, Tony—John Henry, Carol—John Henry's mother, Jenny—Southern Woman, and Jimmy—Remus and sound effects. Everybody—crowd scenes on pages six and ten. Standby."

Alex sprang to the microphone and Todd threw him a cue. With a voice as deep as the announcer on the Movietone News, Alex declared, "The Western Radio League presents Tall Tales from the New World. Tonight's folktale is from the South, the legend of John Henry!"

On the script, Jenny read, SEGUE INTO MUSICAL BRIDGE. Dimly she could hear music. Tony pointed. The sound of music came dimly from the control booth.

Jenny read FADE OUT TO BABY CRY.

When Todd threw the cue, Jimmy played a recording of a baby crying.

Next Carol spoke into the mike. "At his birth, my baby, John Henry, weighed not six pounds, not seven, not eight, or nine, not even ten. My John Henry weighed, and don't you dare disbelieve me, John Henry weighed thirty-three pounds! And look at him now. At five years old,

John Henry is the strongest little boy in the whole world. He can do anything. Just you wait till he's a grown man!"

Waiting for her cue, Jenny was beside herself with anticipation.

When they reached page six, where they had a crowd scene, Jenny noticed the director pointed at the cast, and then wiggled his fingers as if playing the piano. Eyes wide, she joined in talking with the other actors, making up lines that would be appropriate about John Henry's skills with a hammer, and his drilling with rock tunnel gangs. In the control room Todd's fingers moved more slowly—then his index finger sliced his throat. At his "cut" sign, the actors fell silent.

Fascinated with the story, Jenny read along. Suddenly she realized they were on the bottom of page eleven and her line was at the top of twelve. Leaping to her feet, she jumped to the microphone and flipped her page over. She had just opened her mouth, when Todd's voice boomed, "Paper crackle! Jenny, for Pete's sake unstaple your script. You have to s-l-i-d-e your pages—silently."

Alex moved to her side and handed her a staple remover. Face crimson, Jenny struggled to remove the staple, but her fumbling fingers slipped. The script flew from her grasp and pages scattered all over the floor. She wanted to hide under them.

Todd's annoyed voice boomed, "That's it. Take five."

Gathering up the pages, Jenny said, "I'm sorry. This is my first show."

"And probably your last," Carol quipped.

Todd came into the studio. "Why didn't somebody tell her? Okay, Jenny, did you underline your lines?"

"Yes, every one. I do that for the plays I'm in too. See, I marked my two speeches. I'll write 'warn' on the bottom of page eleven. I didn't realize...."

"After the break, when I go back to the control room," Todd told her, "I'll raise my hand and when I point at you, that's your cue. We'll pick up with your first speech. Understand?"

"Yes, sir." Jenny's shoulders sagged, her face smarted. He sounded irritated.

Five minutes later, at her cue, Jenny threw herself into her lines. "Have y'all heard? John Henry's gonna compete with thuh steam drill of thuh

Chesapeake an' Ohio Railroad in Weyust Virginiyah. We yall ah goin' theyre for thuh big contest, thuh most excitin' event of 1870."

Looking up a Todd, she was discouraged to see his face immobile.

She read her second line, left the microphone and sat down. As the script played out, she couldn't tell whether Todd was pleased or not. Her eyes went to Norman, and suddenly a surge of longing went through her. He stood half a head taller than she, and had black hair and clear hazel eyes. She thought he always looked sad. She wished so much she could make him happy. Norman's eyes often rested on her. He must like her.

Swallowing, she thought she was already in love with him. It was spring, and she wanted to be in love with somebody. Both Todd and Tony wore wedding bands. Alex had said he was in high school, and she wasn't at all attracted to Jimmy.

They'd reached the second crowd scene where New York City was going mad over the success of John Henry's drilling. As the actors started talking, Jenny had an idea. In her head, she heard the bellboy who cried, "Call for Philip Mor-rees." Taking a breath, she cried, "Extra, extra, read al-l a-bout it."

"Cut," boomed Todd's voice. "Who did that?"

The cast was silent.

"Who was the newsboy? Alex? Tony? Jimmy?"

They all shook their heads.

Jenny huddled lower in her chair. She'd done it again. She'd made trouble. Shrinking into herself, she found the entire cast's eyes on her. Timidly she raised a hand.

"Jenny—that was you?"

"Yes, sir. I'm sorry. I won't do it again."

"No, do do it again. You were just too far off mike. Let's do the crowd scene again, folks, on cue."

As the cast muttered, Jenny stood, edged two inches from her place, and repeated her newsboy extra.

"Cut. Jenny, move in more, about three more inches. Okay, everybody. Again. Wait for the cue. Now."

Murmurs. "Extry, extry. Read all a-bout John Hen-ry."

Todd nodded, but didn't smile. *Is he pleased or not?*

When they reached the end of the script, Todd said. "Take five."

Tony smiled at Jenny. "Neat kid's voice. That's called doubling."

Jenny glowed. "Thanks." Noticing Carol scowling, she tried to be friendly. "I hear you worked in Hollywood."

"Yes, I've been on Bob Hope's show and Saturday's Child and many others. I'm a professional. I'm only working here as a favor to Todd. I look at it as a contribution, since there's no pay. My husband's stationed at Fort Carson, and it's something to do."

Impressed, Jenny said, "How wonderful to be on those big shows!"

"Yes, and they pay very well." Carol snorted. "It's a shame Denver's such a tinhorn town."

"Oh, but I love Denver," Jenny exclaimed.

"But there's no work here. To be in radio, you have to go to in New York, Chicago, or Hollywood where the big shows originate. Didn't you know that?"

"No, I didn't."

Carol's voice was as smooth as her makeup. "The only live shows around here that pay are a couple over at KLZ and I'm doing those. The pay is paltry, but it is a CBS station. Excuse me, I need a drink of water."

Watching her go, Jenny envied all her experience in the big time, her self-assurance and her expensive blue suit. But Carol seemed…arrogant. Jenny thought, *If I'm ever successful, I won't be like that!*

After the break, they all took their seats and Todd came into the studio. Jimmy ran to get the director's high stool and placed it on the outskirts of the circle of chairs. When Todd perched on it, he said to the actors, "We're three minutes long. We'll make the following cuts."

To her dismay, he cut out Jenny's entire second speech. Her mouth dropped. What if they were still long after the second run-through? Would he cut out her remaining speech too? Oh, no! Maybe she wouldn't be on the show at all!

When the director told Carol to cut her second line, she said. "But Todd that would take out all the sense of my speech and my ability to build to a climax. You surely don't want to do that, do you?"

Todd calmly said, "Sorry," but his face was stern. Jenny thought, *It must be hard to have a prima donna like Carol around. I don't think complaining is professional.*

When the second rehearsal came out on time, Jenny breathed a sigh of relief. She still had her one speech.

The cast took another break and then, from the control room, Todd said. "Okay, folks. We're recording this one. Watch your pacing, keep the crowd scenes going. Be sure to watch me for speeding up," his finger wound in a circle, "or stretching it." His hands resembled pulling taffy. "Stand by."

The studio turned as silent as a cemetery. No one moved. No one rattled a paper. All seemed to hold their breath. Jenny's heart pounded so loudly she thought the microphone would surely pick up the sound and she'd be cast from the room in disgrace.

Suddenly, the light above the control room window glowed red. Alex stood at the mike and Todd's finger threw the cue. In that deep glorious voice, Alex boomed, "The Western Radio League presents…"

Jenny felt as if every muscle was vibrating. Her heart sang. She breathed deeply. This was it. They were recording—recording the show that would be broadcast to hundreds of people across several states.

It seemed in no time they were on the eleventh page. Looking down at her large printed "WARN," she stood and stepped to the microphone, slid her page, sneaked a breath. Eyes wide, she wondered—when her mouth opened, would any sound come out? Would her tongue twist, her accent disappear, her voice crack? Would she—could she deliver?

Her turn came. It was time—her very first time. She breathed, opened her mouth. The words did come out, and they came out just right! She could see this character in her head. Her lines lilted forth with a charming Southern drawl.

Returning to her seat, she glanced into the control room for praise or acknowledgment. Neither man looked at her.

Even when she did her newsboy line in the crowd scene, she saw no smiles from them.

Finally, Alex read the last line. "Listen next week, same time, same station, to Tall Tales from the New World. This is Alex Garcia for Director Todd Ramsey and the Western Radio Players."

The red light went off.

Carol grumbled, "They don't even give us name credits."

Todd came into the studio. "We'll take five and then listen to the playback to see if there are any glitches. If not, Norman will mail off the show tomorrow."

After their break they all sat again, most studying the floor, listening to the show. At the end, Todd nodded, and gave them the "Okay" signal. "Good job. It's a take."

Jenny thought she sounded strange on the recording, but Tony told her that was because when you speak you hear a lot of inner resonance from your own head, resonance that isn't heard by others. Tony repeated that she'd done a fine job. She liked him. Too bad he was so short—and married.

As she was going out, she looked up into Norman's eyes. He smiled and nodded. Still, she was disappointed to get no praise from Todd. But as she started for the door, he called, "Jenny, wait a minute."

He caught up with her. "You surprised me with that newsboy voice. Nice going. Say hello to Dale."

Jenny's heart lifted. *He does think I'm good! I've been on the radio. No matter whatever else goes wrong in my life, I'll always have this night to treasure forever.*

# 45. Why Does the Doctor Pay a Call?

A few weeks later at the doctor's office, Nora waited for her test results.

Dr. Zeller strode into the room, sat down behind his desk, and nodded. "Well, Nora, you've come back nicely from your last setback. Your sputum is negative!"

"Wonderful! It's such a relief when I know I'm not contagious. What about the x-rays?"

"I don't see much change, so I'm encouraged."

Nora leaned forward. "So now how much I can do around the house."

He hesitated. "That's hard to say."

"But when I'm better, I start doing more and more and, before I know it, I've had another breakdown."

"Nora, your virulent strain of TB constantly battles with your strong constitution, so I'm afraid you're going to have ups and downs."

"But I want to know how much I can safely do!"

Dr. Zeller swiveled his chair. "Tell me what constitutes a normal day for you."

"Well, I get up when Clyde does, do my morning grooming and, sometimes clean the bowl and the toilet—if nobody's looking. I eat breakfast and tell the family goodbye. Then I read the Bible for a half hour or so, plan menus and grocery lists and things like fall cleaning or spring cleaning."

He nodded. "Then what?"

"In the morning I read the newspaper and the mail and write letters. After lunch I rest, maybe even nap, and then listen to the radio. I crochet, and maybe dust my bedroom and pick up around the house. But always, after a bit I can't breathe and have to lie down."

"Lying down when you get tired is just what you should do."

"When Jenny gets home, I give her the dinner menu and instructions. Occasionally, when I test negative, I sit on a stool in the kitchen and shell peas, or string the beans. I wish I could work more. Can't you give me specifics on how much I can do?"

"I really can't tell you, Nora. The disease has destroyed a lot of your lung tissue. That's why you get tired and your breathing is still noisy. All I can suggest is to be cautious. Work until you start to feel a bit fatigued and then stop."

"But when I work around the house, it's like eating peanuts. I can't quit." A despondent expression crossed her face. "Do you know what it's like to feel useless, to never accomplish anything?"

He frowned. "What would you like to accomplish?"

"I'm not sure, but something worthwhile, something really important!"

The following week at home Nora could see Dr. Zeller from her bed come up onto the porch and ring the doorbell. She called "Dr. Zeller! Come in. The door's open." When he appeared in her room, she asked. "Why are you making a house call? Is something wrong with me?"

"Not at all, and this isn't a house call, a social call. I just happened to be in the neighborhood."

"Please sit down." Putting aside her crocheting, she motioned to a chair.

Dr. Zeller cocked his head. "What is that you're making?"

"This? Oh, I'm crocheting a bedspread. First I make these octagonal squares, and now I've been sewing them together."

He rose, stepped to the bed, and fingered a completed square. "When you put the pieces together it makes a star pattern. It's beautiful."

"And cheap." She laughed "It's made out of ordinary string. One day my brother Harry was here and said we should compute the number of squares I make. Then he laughed and said, "No, Nora, count the popcorns on each square." Then he grinned. "I wonder how many stitches you make with that hook." We were all laughing when he said, "Nope, what really counts is how many jabs of the needle it takes you to make that spread. It must be millions!" It was hilarious. I think he makes a point of being funny when he comes to visit me."

"That's good." He sat down again. "How long have you been working on this project?"

She shrugged. "I don't know, four or five years. I hope to complete two twin-size bedspreads, and I've crocheted a quarter of a tablecloth in the Cathedral Window pattern. It's of string, too, but a finer gauge than this."

"Those are going to be accomplishments to be proud of."

She looked up, face serious. "Dr. Zeller, I've been thinking. You said the TB had destroyed a lot of my lung tissue." She drew a breath and looked at him intently. "Tell me the truth. I'm never going to be really well, am I?"

He hesitated. "No, Nora, you're not."

"It seems strange that I wouldn't admit that fact into consciousness until just recently. All these years I've kept fighting, hoping." Her eyes seemed to see into the distance. "I recently read a quote in a magazine that seemed to have been written just for me." She paused. "The line was, 'Bear lightly what must be.'"

"Atta girl!" They were both silent. The doctor rearranged his legs. "Nora, I stopped by to tell you what happened today. I've just come from a medical conference over at Fitzsimons Hospital, and one thing we discussed was tuberculosis. With the war, we are vulnerable to increased cases, so there's quite a debate over institutionalizing patients, which is particularly sad for homecoming soldiers who are infected."

"Yes, it would be."

"In the middle of a raging debate over how to control such a contagious disease, I introduced your case."

"My case?"

"Yes. I didn't reveal your name. What I did do, was tell the group that you have been bedridden for eleven years and during that time have been hospitalized only nine months. I displayed your x-rays and pointed out the extent of your infection. Then I explained the precautions you have taken all these years, years that you have lived at home with family. I emphasized that, due to your diligence, no one in your family has ever contracted the disease. 'This,' I said, 'is what can be done!'"

Nora's eyes glistened. "You said that?"

"Yes, indeed." He smiled. "I wish you could have heard the applause."

"Oh, my."

He rose and took her hand. "Nora, making your bedspreads and tablecloth are outstanding accomplishments, but keeping your family safe—now that is something that is most important and what you can be the very proudest of. That is simply marvelous! All those doctors were so impressed, just as I have always been.

"I came here today to tell you that you have done something that is utterly remarkable!"

# 46. A Fortune?

Remembering her radio experience, for days Jenny floated on clouds, but then tumbled back to earth with a thud. She couldn't live at that altitude forever—and Norman hadn't called. Nobody had. In the newspaper she read of two classmates killed in the war—Hank, the champion runner, and Dwight, the basketball star. Her heart jolted in pain. The war kept coming closer, but so far Dale was deferred.

Jenny's life continued as usual: waiting on her mother, doing housework, going to college. Then Dale came home from his radio class, in a buoyant mood. "They performed my play, 'Why Men have Beards and Women Don't.' Everybody thought it was great, Jenny. You're not the only one to impress Todd!"

"I didn't impress him very much. My one show certainly isn't a career." Her voice turned wistful. "I wish something wonderful would happen."

On Monday, Todd called. "Jenny, do you happen to have a South American accent?"

Startled, she gulped. "A South American accent? Why, yes." Right now she didn't have one, but she'd get one—somehow. Her head throbbed with uncertainty and excitement.

"Great! Rehearsal this Friday at 7:30, same place. I need you." He hung up.

He needed her! She tingled all over. Another radio show! Fantastic! She wanted to jump up and down and dance and sing. But then, dismay engulfed her. *How in the world am I ever going to learn a South American accent?*

After puzzling a few minutes, uncertain what to do, she suddenly realized that two students at CWC were from Costa Rica. Maybe they would help her. She hurried out to the campus.

It didn't take much persuasion. After Jenny explained, the Costa Rican sisters loved talking for her. They spent hours together. Imitating her friends' exaggerated articulation left Jenny's lips actually hurting, but she'd gotten the lilt, the intonations, the South American accent.

This time her part was quite large and, after rehearsal, Todd grinned and gave her that prized okay signal. She tried to start a conversation with Norman, but he seemed preoccupied.

Two weeks after that, Todd cast her as a French woman on his new "Civilians at War" show. A gray-haired man named Brant had replaced Norman. After the show, Gale patted her on the arm, "Norman and Tony have left for the service. They'd like mail, so watch the bulletin board for their addresses."

Jenny's heart throbbed. She'd write them both, especially Norman.

With the "Civilians at War" show, Jenny was constantly in demand at the Radio League. She did English, Cockney and Norwegian accents, did German and even Russian. With a good ear and talent for mimicry, she listened carefully to the radio, and even found a library book with phonetic instructions on dialects. Jenny developed a repertoire of foreign accents.

One night Todd discovered he had failed to cast an old man. Jenny cried, "I can do it!"

At first he looked doubtful, but after her performance he shook his head in disbelief. "Great! Where did you get that deep voice?"

Jenny laughed. "At college I had a role playing a man called Peter."

As the days wound on, Norman's letters were infrequent and impersonal. Maybe he wasn't the one, but somewhere there had to be a man for her.

Her friend Juanita called and said the USO wanted girls to square dance with the soldiers out at Lowry Field. A bus would pick them up at the Shirley Savoy Hotel on Saturday nights. Jenny had a marvelous time dancing and soon she was having those longed-for dates.

When Carol announced her husband had been transferred and she was leaving Denver, Jenny scurried over to KLZ on a Friday and auditioned. The director said, "Can you start Monday doing early morning dialog commercials with the announcer three times a week? It pays $2 a show." Of course she said yes.

Daddy dropped her off at the station on his way to the office. Her work was fun and easy.

Thrilled with her first $12 check she decided to do something memorable with it, so half went for a beautiful white plastic compact decorated with pastel pansies and forget-me-nots—a tangible memory of her success. The other half she delivered to their old housekeeper, saying it was from her father. For the past five years, Nora had fretted that they still owed Mrs. Balor $30. When Clyde learned what Jenny had done, he managed to pay the rest.

Soon Jenny appeared on two, weekly half-hour evening shows at KLZ, one a collection of state editorials where she played a woman editor. The other program dramatized the news where she made good use of her accents. Each show paid $5. That made her a professional!

One day, Jenny ran into Libby in downtown Denver. "I heard you left CU," Jenny said.

"Yes, when the war started, I quit college. I'm working as a secretary. Kind of boring. Is that you on the radio? At first I thought maybe it was somebody with the same name."

"No, that's me."

"Wow, I'm impressed! How about that! Guess you showed us. Of all us high school kids, you've turned out to be the one that's famous."

"Maybe just a little." Jenny grinned. "Anyway it's lots of fun." The little exchange left Jenny feeling very good.

As time went on, Jenny was delighted that her picture and name appeared frequently in *The Denver Post's* radio column. Her reviews were excellent. Looking up from the paper one morning, she told her mother, "I always wanted to be somebody. Now maybe I sort of am."

"Of course you are," her mother said.

Jenny sat thinking. *Being somebody! I've always wanted to be somebody, but what does that really mean?* Libby's adulation, and the praise of her acting in the paper's reviews were nice, but suddenly she realized *even if I were to be really famous, being somebody is what a you are inside, how good a person you are, how compassionate. It's not what the world thinks or says about you, but what you do with your life, what actions you take, the love you express.* She glanced over at her mother and smiled, enveloped with great affection.

The terrible yearning that had been inside for years seemed to have vanished. Instead, now she felt filled with contentment. *I think maybe all along I've always been somebody!*

*Why, Mother, Daddy, and Dale—they've always been somebody too!*

One night standing before the microphone, Jenny felt a thrill pass through her whole body. Right now she was essentially the KLZ staff actress—the only woman on the shows—changing her voice, playing myriad roles, having the most wonderful time—having such fun! Occasionally, she even worked for advertising agencies making $15 or $25 per job. Once she even did a squirrel voice on a film for children about dental care.

Even Daddy approved her radio work. One day he hugged her and laughed. "Imagine a woman getting paid for talking!"

Tonight was her crowning achievement, her heart's desire—playing the ingénue, the beautiful married woman whose husband was off at war—a lovely woman explaining life to her little boy. With joy, Jenny realized, *on radio my height and looks don't matter! I can be the leading lady!*

She stood before the mike and acted out her lines. "Son, Daddy is fighting to make our lives better. Even though far away, he is taking care of us. And we who stay behind have a purpose too. We have to be strong and brave, no matter what challenges the world presents to us. We can do anything if we only pull together for each other, for the world, for the greatest good. For good will triumph in the end!"

Jenny thought of her family, huddled around the radio at home, listening to those words. She knew that they all had been brave, they all had pulled together. The little Pate family had stood fast and met the challenges of poverty and never-ending illness with perpetual courage and the greatest love. Her heart nearly burst. She felt so grateful for them all!

At last things were going well for each of them. Daddy was proudly selling pension plans and, instead of talking of going to Yellowstone, actually gave Mother money to decorate the house. Mother seemed happier than she'd been for years. Dale liked his job and had a girlfriend, and Jenny was dating a tall handsome soldier from Iowa. Since the radio shows were at night or on weekends, she could still care for her mother and attend college. Her career was booming and she had attained her life-long dream of becoming an actress and—perhaps in her own little orbit—a star!

The Pates no longer lived on Someday Street. They had actually climbed back up to Happiness Heights.

*Never give up hope*, she thought happily. *Dreams can come true!* She remembered that promise: "Your Voice Can Be Your Fortune." Perhaps her voice wasn't bringing her a fortune in money, but money wasn't the only fortune. She was having fun, and she had a fabulous family!

*Who needs a fortune when you have everything else?*

# The End

*The author having a fortune in fun.*

# An Interview with the Author

**Q.** What started you on the road to becoming a writer?
**A.** I was seven years old when my mother became ill. Her mantra was, "Don't work too hard or you might get sick." I thought writing wouldn't be working hard physically. Additionally, we lived in the shadow of death, and writing seemed a way to leave something to mark the spot, a way to be immortal.

**Q.** When did you start writing?
**A.** I imagined stories starting when I was about nine. Then in college I took a feature writing course and sold a humorous piece about my first attempt to ski. I've published 28 feature articles, a column, and have won article, short story and poetry prizes. I've also written 40 songs, plays and two novels. In the fall of 2008, I'm beginning my seventeenth year of teaching creative writing for the North Orange County Community College District. In 2003 I was given a "Teacher of the Year" award. Teaching is a highlight of my life. My students' stories are enrapturing, and I enjoy passing along tips from my library of 45 books on writing and 7 grammar books. I think knowing good English is great fun.

**Q.** Did your attitudes about your childhood change from writing this book?
**A.** Definitely. For a long time I could remember only the difficult times.

Writing was healing. I now regard those years with the greatest nostalgia and affection.

**Q**. Was writing the book hard for you emotionally?
**A**. Yes, I did cry a lot, but I found it cathartic.

**Q**. Would you recommend that others write their life story if it's disturbing?
**A**. If it's too upsetting, one might instead seek professional help. However, some find re-living traumatic times through writing is therapeutic. Some memoir writing books address ways to handle this.

**Q**. Did you resent having to care for your mother?
**A:** I identified very closely with my mother and loved her very much. I enjoyed being helpful and was praised for caring for her. Then, when I was about sixteen, my feelings changed.

**Q**. Why? What happened?
**A**. Like all teenagers, I longed to be independent, but still felt obligated to my family, worried what they would do without me. I experienced a tug of war between duty and my own desires.

**Q:** What preparation did you have to become an actress?
**A**. I took classes in high school and college. I also had private lessons. Listening to the radio and watching movies helped. I think I was gifted with the ability to mimic, along with having vivid emotional memory.

**Q:** Tuberculosis doesn't seem much of a threat today. Why write about now?
**A:** TB was once the second greatest killer in the world, and recently we've seen the emergence of new drug-resistant strains. With the conditions in many third-world countries and global travel, TB may resurge again. Besides, there are many incapacitating illnesses and this story addresses problems common to patient and caregiver both.

**Q.** I've wondered about the ongoing lives of the characters. I kept wishing the story wouldn't end.

**A.** I'm busy writing a sequel!

# Discussion Questions
# for Book Groups

1. How did you, your relatives, or your friends cope when going through difficult times?

2. What makes a person feel secure? What makes the Pate characters feel secure or not?

3. How did the Pates save money? What tips do you have for economizing?

4. What problems did the father face throughout the book? How did he cope?

5. What problems did the mother face? How did she cope?

6. What problems did the children face? How did they cope?

7. What strengths and weaknesses did each character exhibit?

8. Describe the family if Nora had been hospitalized for 11 years. Describe Nora's life.

9. The Pates were often given things. Discuss receiving gifts. Did the Pates give back?

10. What simple activities did they enjoy? What possessions were important to them?

11. How and when does each character change? What is the meaning of Jenny's dreams of her teeth falling out?

12. What philosophy, religion, or values did the family exhibit?

13. Jenny says, "Life's not fair." In what ways can life be unfair?

14. Describe your actions if caught in an economic depression, war, or severe illness.

15. What diseases or disabilities exist today which require care giving?

16. What are the problems of the caregiver? Of the patient?

17. Tell how you would validate your life if you were confined to bed, blind or disabled.

18. Discuss being dutiful, as opposed to satisfying your own individual desires.

19. What organizations or government help are available today that weren't then?

20. How do you react to words like invalid, disabled, retarded, handicapped, or blind?

21. Explain your overall reaction to this book. What do you find valuable?

Breinigsville, PA USA
04 December 2010
250652BV00002B/12/P